Early acclaim for
Auriela McCarthy's
THE POWER OF THE POSSIBLE

"I want this book at my fingertips, to read over and over. Every time I read it I am lifted and there is more space for love. One afternoon I read a chapter that in a magical moment opened my heart to see what I had missed in all my relationships. That moment changed me forever."

— ALICIA FORESTER, LANDSCAPE ARCHITECT

"Auriela McCarthy's writing had reached into my very soul to extract the damage and beliefs that held me back from everything I had been claiming I wanted but was unable to create. Her wisdom cuts to the core of every issue and it isn't just in the words, it is 'in between' the words. This is an inspired work that will change your life."

— JACKIE SALVITTI, RADIO TALK SHOW HOST

"I was in an emotionally abusive relationship over which I felt powerless. This book made me feel loved regardless of my choices. I could feel the possibilities, a different future. Depression lifted. My life is now on God's path."

— LEE MYERS, GRAPHIC DESIGNER AND SPIRITUAL SEEKER

"If I were to recommend one book to someone about living their best life, this would be it. It never ceases to inspire and expand the mind to all the joy and wonder of what it would be like to live a life truly worth living."

— HALLA AYLA, ARTIST

The Power of the Possible

The Power
of the
Possible

A Book of Hope and Inspiration

Auriela McCarthy

BEAUFORT
BOOKS

NEW YORK

Library of Congress Cataloging-in-Publication Data

McCarthy, Auriela.
  The power of the possible : a book of hope and inspiration / Auriela
McCarthy.
     p. cm.
  ISBN 978-0-8253-0576-4 (alk. paper)
  1. Self-help techniques. I. Title.

  BF632.M355 2007
  158 — dc22

                          2007027479

DISCLAIMER

Some of the names and identifying details have been changed to protect
the privacy of the people whose stories have been included in this book.

Published in the United States by Beaufort Books, New York
www.beaufortbooks.com
Distributed by Midpoint Trade Books, New York
www.midpointtrade.com

10 9 8 7 6 5 4 3 2 1

PRINTED IN CANADA

I dedicate this book to Lazaris, whose love is behind everything I am and every word I write.

Contents

Acknowledgments

No writer writes alone. A book is always a co-creation, even if the task of writing is a solitary one. I have written this book surrounded in a cocoon of love. I cannot begin to name all those who through their energy and inspiration made the entire process such bliss. I have felt your love. I am so grateful.

Many people have touched my life in powerful ways, both light and dark, and in doing so became incredible teachers. I could not have written this book had our paths not crossed. Thank you for your love, and thank you, also, for your "incomprehensible stubbornness" in refusing to change no matter how hard I tried to change you. I am forever in your debt.

Dear Lazaris, without you, this book would never be what it is. Nor would I. It's been now so many years since you first told me that I mattered...a revelation that led to a profound shift. To you, I owe everything. How can I ever express the depth of my love and my gratitude for the part you play in my life? This book is for you. It is also because of you.

I feel deep gratitude for my friend Jackie Salvitti and for her team, the first to suggest that I write this book. Your inspiration and support were the wind behind my sails. I could feel them always. Thank you.

My deep appreciation and gratitude goes to David Nelson of Beaufort Books, who believed in this book from its very conception. Thank you, David, for your endless support and encouragement. I also thank the wonderful team at Beaufort, and especially Margot Atwell, the managing editor, for her attention to detail and for everything she did to bring the manuscript to its completion.

Barbara McNichol's editorial help at the early stages of the manuscript was invaluable. Thank you, Barbara, for your professionalism, warmth and support. You made such a difference.

Barbara Pritchard, my assistant and friend, was the first to hear each chapter. No writer could wish for a more enthusiastic and supportive listener. Thank you for believing in this work and for letting it touch you.

My heartfelt gratitude goes to my editor, Leslie Kirk Campbell, whose amazing editorial gifts have done so much for the readability and flow of the material. Leslie, your commitment to excellence and your profound emotional response to the stories and the teachings have been such a gift.

My work with Dr. Joanna Corti led to profound insights. Thank you, Joanna, for your love, your friendship and your amazing gift of healing.

I would like to express my appreciation to David Berenson, the first to give me the insight into the power of powerlessness. David, your impact on me has been life changing. I hope you know this.

Arthur, my beloved son, you taught me more about love than any other living being. As a child, you stole my heart and changed my life forever. Raising you and then setting you free has been one of the most powerful experiences in my life. I love you more than I can ever say.

And finally, Mykaell, my love and my life. Writing this book would not have been possible had we not lived and breathed every experience, every thought, concept, insight, and idea together.

You are my home, the place where my soul rests. The two of us — our own planet. Marrying you was the best thing that could have happened. You bring such lightness into my life. This book is a tribute to our love.

The Power of the Possible

Introduction

When we fall utterly, something gathers us up. But our falling must be without reservation, without expectation, without hope, though not hopeless. You can't plan that kind of falling. When you abandon yourself utterly to life, the river will flow, and the log jam will free. Impossible is another word for grace. Who would have thought it, life takes another turn, and you are gathered up into a whole different way of seeing and being.

—ROGER HOUSDEN, author of
Ten Poems to Change Your Life

I AM NOT MOVED TO TELL YOU MUCH of my past, simply because I lost my emotional attachment to it a long time ago. It wasn't always so, of course. Like so many others, I, too, used to live in the past continuously, reliving my experiences, carrying on endless dialogues with people I haven't seen in years, regurgitating the old pain without any idea of how to end it. I functioned in the present only to the extent that it was absolutely necessary. Still, I graduated from University, immigrated from one country to another and succeeded in creating a successful art gallery. I had a family, a full personal life, albeit a very difficult one . . . yet I was living surrounded by the fog of pain. This fog was all pervasive. And because it permeated everything in my life for such a long time, I wasn't even aware of it.

I could have written a heartfelt saga based on my life story, complete with the Russian winters, the Soviet regime and its all-seeing eye of surveillance, my grandparents' hiding from the KGB in an obscure Moscow suburb, my mother's five marriages, my father's Machiavellian gifts of emotional torture, and my eventual escape from it all—alas, into a different kind of prison—and finally, coming to this county, the first home I ever had. It would have made for rich reading, even a movie, or a TV series…except that I have lost my emotional attachment to it. It has become *someone else's* story.

Many in our culture share a predominant belief that the destructive things that happened to them in the past have scarred them forever. Not everyone is of this belief of course, but the majority still are. People become invested in their past, using it as a club to beat themselves up with, or to excuse their often reprehensible behavior, or simply because *they don't believe they can ever be emotionally free from the pain that their past has caused them.*

Rather than writing a metaphysical theses on why this is not so (and it is not), I have decided to tell you a few stories instead, including snippets from my life—moments essential to my own personal journey—that have brought me to who I am today. They are true stories, stories of healing and transcendence.

To transcend is to be lifted out of your current level of life, so as to be gifted with a shift in the very core of your being. After the experience of transcendence, something inside us is not just changed, but *gone*, like it never was there in the first place. At times like this, it is as if a hand reaches down, lifting us "out" and washing us in light. There are no words for this love. Once you are so touched, all you can do is weep.

Transcendent moments can be moments of ecstatic joy or moments of incandescent peace…or—just as powerfully—moments of profound sorrow.

They can be the "aha" moments of lightning bolt-like realizations when the veil to *the truth* is suddenly and irrevocably removed and we see the world with new eyes.

The stories of transcendence I want to tell you happened to ordinary people who found themselves in extreme circumstances. I
have changed their names, of course, to protect their privacy.
Some of these people I counseled, some were friends. Of others I
was told and their stories moved me profoundly.

I want to share these stories with you because — among other
things — that is what I do. I have been telling stories of healing all
of my life.

I don't know when it began, but as long as I can remember,
friends and people I've known have turned to me for advice about
their personal lives. Instead of giving them advice, I would tell
them a story. And only after the story was told, would we talk
about other things. I noticed that by the time they left, their eyes
were different — they were leaving with more hope, seeing new
possibilities.

A friend told me once of a tribe in Africa with an oral tradition
of telling stories over and over again. If they wanted, for example,
to bring about a healing of someone's broken heart, they would
tell that person a story. Often it was the same story (or stories) that
they told endlessly. Until the person was healed, for, after all, they
were the stories that heal the heart.

I have an even more ambitious hope. My hope is that as you
read the stories in this book, something extraordinary will happen. Without you even knowing that it is happening — your *Soul*
will begin healing. If your heart heals on the way — grand, but it is
your soul I will be speaking to. So much in this book is not in its
words, but *between* the words, *behind* the words, in what's left unsaid. You will be reading this book on different levels: first, for the
story itself, second, for the thoughts and ideas woven into each
story, and third, for the energy that has imbued the words and that
has brought you to this book in the first place.

Whichever way you have come upon it, if you are holding it in
your hands and have begun to read it — then this book is for you.

*   *   *

UNTIL THE YEAR 1987 I lived in alternating states of determined hope and overwhelming despair. My personal life was falling apart. Trying to ignore this fact brought about physical illness and more pain. I was stuck. I hated the only answer that I knew was the right one, and so I did nothing. Yet hope never left me either. Perhaps because it had always been my natural state, and I simply didn't know how not to feel it, regardless of the circumstances.

For most of my conscious life, I have been a seeker. A seeker of truth, a seeker of love, a seeker of Something More. I've traveled down many paths, most of them blind alleys leading to dead ends. Then a miracle happened. A treasured friend entered my life, not to lead me, but — walking beside me — to illuminate and point the way. *My cup runneth over.*

I began to wake up. Starved for truth, I couldn't have enough of it.

All paths lead to truth. You just have to start walking. Even if a path turns out to be a blind alley, it too has a purpose. We human beings are a stubborn lot. One doesn't need to hit rock bottom in order to discover the truth that has been sitting in plain sight all along, yet a number of people do.

Surrender is a difficult concept for most Westerners. Many are uncomfortable with the very idea of surrender, misunderstanding it, considering it to be a sign of weakness. We like to be in charge, to be in control of our lives, and so the enormous *power* inherent to any *true surrender* remains elusive and is often missed.

I was no exception to this. Grabbing hold of the profound metaphysical truth, *we create our own reality,* I dove into the journey of creating and manifesting the reality I wanted — head first. I was no longer lost. I learned techniques of manifestation, how to change my belief system, how to reprogram my subconscious mind. Over the years, I became very good at these things. My meditations were incredible journeys into the mystery where much was being revealed. I was changing in profound ways. I experienced deep emotional healings and as a result—a more fulfilling life.

But it was not enough.

With time the techniques didn't work as well. Gently and not so gently, I was being pushed to go deeper.

How do you bring together the powerful concept of being *the author of your reality* and another, no less powerful one, *I am not in charge?* Seemingly contradictory, the two go hand in hand. Both are true and one does not negate the other. Understanding this, and eventually beginning to *live* this understanding was a turning point in my life. Until that moment I was accumulating awareness. After that, I stepped onto a whole different platform of being.

To quote Dorothy from the Wizard of Oz:

Toto, I don't think we are in Kansas anymore.

One can devote a lifetime to unraveling this mystery and it would be a richly lived life, with more gifts to discover the deeper you go. For *mystery*, by definition, cannot ever be unraveled fully. Spiritual journey is a journey without an end. You get on the bus, and the bus takes off. No one ever *arrives.* The road goes on forever, but you get to stop at various points and absorb the beauty of this road. The questions, "Are we done? Are we there yet?" do not apply here. Because once we get on *this* bus, everything changes. We are not in Kansas anymore.

*   *   *

THE STORIES IN THIS book are the stories of healing and transcendence.

A terminally ill patient wakes up early one morning and sees the sun rising outside his window. Motionless, struck by the mesmerizing beauty, the man stares at the sky. It isn't sky anymore...

it's an ocean of swirling colors, the fiery red flooding into magenta, the glorious orange mixing with deep violet and pink...all of it—moving, changing, rearranging itself to its own design... the entire sky—an artist's palette, exuberant, overwhelming... The man touches his heart, holding to the window sill with his other hand. Such beauty, such magnificence, such...peace? Peace, the ultimate longing, the endless unrequited desire...suddenly satisfied, his, to touch, to experience, to hold in the palm of his hand, to inhale deeply, filling his body full, taking away the loneliness, the despair...and in their place—*possibility, hope.*

And the man makes a choice. I am going to live! I will beat this illness! I will get well. I will go on.

And he does.

A *transcendent experience,* brought about by the ethereal Beauty of nature, giving birth to *a will to live,* followed by total healing.

The neighbor next door, watching the same sunrise at the same time, notices the beauty of the sky, pauses by the window for a moment and smiles, then looks at his watch and hurries to the kitchen to begin his day.

It doesn't mean this neighbor is an insensitive person. It doesn't mean he missed a grand opportunity to change his life for the better. In fact, it doesn't mean anything at all. For him, it was simply a usual morning with an unusually beautiful sunrise. That's all. Meanwhile, the sick man had what Abraham Maslow called "a peak experience," a transcendent moment that changed him at the very core, giving him the will to triumph over his cancer.

This isn't something that can be planned. It doesn't happen often or to everyone in similar circumstances. But it does happen. To experience transcendence is to be blessed.

*   *   *

TRANSCENDENT EXPERIENCES ARE experiences of surrender. They can come through beauty, and also through pain.

Surrender can be ecstatic, brought about by a sudden burst of joy, or one can literally fall into it from total and utter helplessness. Either way, something in us lets go at that moment, and we are lifted "out of ourselves" and into the bigger, truer part of who we are.

For Eckhart Tolle, the author of *The Power of Now*, awakening happened following an experience of absolute, intense dread. This is what he writes about it:

> *I was gripped by an intense fear, and my body started to shake. I heard the words, 'Resist nothing,' as if spoken inside my chest. I could feel myself being sucked into a void. It felt as if the void was inside myself, rather than outside. Suddenly there was no more fear, and I let myself fall into this void. I have no recollection of what happened after that.*

He woke up in the morning to this experience:

> *...I recognized the room, and yet I knew that I had never truly seen it before... That day I walked around the city in utter amazement at the miracle of life on earth, as if I had just been born into this world.... But even the most beautiful experiences come and go. More fundamental, perhaps, than any experience is the undercurrent of peace that has never left me since then.*

Byron Katie, the author of *Loving What Is*, had once been institutionalized for her fits of rage. And then came one morning when she just woke up laughing. She has been a spiritual teacher ever since.

Here is an example from my own life.

All of my life, above anything else, I wanted to make love work. And yet I was failing at it. My first marriage had ended in divorce. I was in love again, but the relationship had reached an impasse. I couldn't change my boyfriend of three years, no matter how hard I tried. The thought of leaving him was un-bearable. I was gasping for air before I could finish the thought. I was lost. I doubted everything: myself, him, our future together. One night, unable to sleep, I found myself on the living room floor. It must have been close to three o'clock in the morning. Out-side, it was pitch black. No moon, starless sky, no light coming into my window—a quiet time so still I could hear my nails scratching the surface of the floor rug. Curled in a fetal position, I lay without movement. I could not cry. I was beyond tears. It was despair so dark and bottomless, all I could do was lie in this deep black void without hope or thought. Sometimes my fists would clench and unclench. I could feel the dull ache in the pit of my stomach throbbing, contracting—the only physical sensation. I could not pray.

"I know you exist," I whispered to God, to the Goddess . . . "but right now I can't feel it."

"I can't fight any more," I said out loud.

I had not turned on the light and the living room was almost black. My eyes were used to the dark by then, and I could see the outlines of furniture in the room. How long did I stay on that floor, lost to everything but my despair? At some point I drifted to sleep, then opened my eyes again. Empty, spent, I lay there a while longer, then got up and went to bed. My boyfriend, Mykaell, the "source of my pain," turned in his sleep and snuggled up to me. He did not wake up.

I closed my eyes and fell into a deep sleep.

When I woke in the morning, the familiar sense of frustration and pain was gone. I was surrounded in a cocoon of gentleness. I don't think I had ever felt this way before. I felt tenderness toward everything and nothing in particular—mostly toward myself. It was as if all the fight had been taken out of me, scooped out while I was sleeping, and the emptiness that replaced it had not yet been filled. I was floating, I knew not where. I had no expectation and no pain. It was a vulnerable, peaceful space. I thought about

Mykaell. *It somehow did not matter at all whether or not he changed.* He was beautiful just the way he was.

It was a day of soft edges and kindness. I felt wordless gratitude, then sorrow, then quick spasms of joy. At times, I cried and was not sure what I was crying about. When Mykaell came home from work, and we sat down to dinner, it was as if we'd entered a different world, one that hitherto did not exist.

Everything between us felt new, tentative, and real. I knew I was different, *but so was he.* How much had I fought him in the past, trying to get him to *change* and be the way *I* wanted him to be. It had only led to more and bitter fighting. Yet suddenly, without my saying a word, he had discarded the old way of being like an old worn-out coat, never to be picked up again.

*   *   *

Nothing changes, until you do.
—Lazaris

I remember the first time I heard this. How simple it had seemed at the time. How sure I was that I got it, that there was no need to give it any more thought. It was so clear and so obvious that I forgot about it right away. And yet, I would return to it again many times. Because if I wanted my life and my relationship to work, it was imperative that I get it for real.

"Nothing changes until you do." Simple on the surface, this truth — miles deep and anything but simple — is one more thing that has led me to the writing of this book.

So many people — frustrated, disappointed, angry — are stubbornly looking for reasons *outside themselves* to why life continues to remain fraught with problems and relationships remain difficult and often unattainable.

Yet, NOTHING changes, until WE CHANGE.

If these words were understood and followed, we would be living in a different world, leading much happier lives.

I invite you to look to the truth above, perhaps write it down for yourself and return to it over and over again while reading the stories ahead. You will see how powerful and how on target it really is.

*   *   *

The Power of the Possible is not a relationship book per se, though many of the stories and the concepts discussed have to do with relationships. Rather, the issues I talk about are universal, the ones that all of us face in the living of our lives.

The book in your hands is *a book of hope.* My wish for you is that as you read it, your hearts fill with Hope—for yourself, for the ones you love, and for the world we all live in.

It could have, also, easily been called *a book of love.* Everything in our lives begins and ends with love. Love is the subject of every song, every poem and every book that has ever been written. Love's presence or its lack, our hunger and eternal longing for it. This book is no exception.

But above all—this book is *a book of possibility.*

Not the "believe you can do it, and then you can" kind of possibility, which, while true, has become a cliché, but deeper and more, this book is about *the Possibility that lies on the other side of humility*—a possibility of a different future that comes with any true surrender, be it out of joy or pain. In this vulnerable space, with your defenses lifted you can finally be reached. It doesn't mean that you can now get your way. Sometimes the greatest miracle is in *not getting what you've been fighting to get* for so long.

"*More tears are shed over the answered prayers than over unanswered ones,*" wrote Truman Capote.

Once you've let go, the *Power of the Possible* floods your consciousness, and everything changes. New here-to-fore unimaginable scenarios are suddenly *possible,* available—offering new, unexpected outcomes. You will see many examples of this as you read the book.

And one more thing.

My hope is that you will be left with more questions than answers as you enter and exit the world of each chapter. And that those questions will be ones you didn't have before.

This is a good thing. The questions are much more important. The answers will come in time, bringing with them more questions. Because as I said earlier, this road goes on forever. But what a ride!

What Can I Do to Get Him to Change?

To be truly seen is to be truly healed.
> — Marianne Williamson

"*What can I do to get him to change?*" my friend asked me.

We were sitting in an outdoor café on a quiet Sunday afternoon, drinking our lattes and talking.

"*How can I make him understand?!*" She frowned, throwing her hands in the air, spilling some of her coffee onto the tablecloth. She moved the saucer to cover the stain and searched my face. "*There must be a way to get through to him!*"

I knew what would follow next. A heart-felt and angry explanation of why the change is necessary, and how she has tried everything—to no avail. We had talked about it before, many times, but my answers were never what she wanted to hear.

"How can I *get him to see that I am right!? What can I do?*" she insisted. She was at her wits' end. I reached for my coffee.

"How is your father doing?" I asked, changing the subject. "Is he still on the golf course a lot?"

It is a fascinating phenomenon, this conviction that *you know what's best* for another person and that you can actually *do* something to change that person. Who among us hasn't at one time or another felt certain that we have the right to *interfere* with the life of another and *correct* it *for the better?*

Husbands and wives, lovers and friends, partners in businesses and in life, siblings, governments, neighbors...at home and at work...relentlessly, people fight to get others to see their point and change accordingly.

Yet no one does.

Again and again I hear the same old song.

"How can I get Jake to stop drinking? I have tried everything! But he just won't listen!"

"What can I do to get Sara to see that she needs to leave her abusive husband while she is still alive?!"

"How can I get my mother to stop smoking? It is killing her and still she won't stop! Am I supposed to just sit and wait for her to get lung cancer??!!"

A tired, frustrated chorus, determined to get its way, yet never getting it.

"*What can I do to make them change?*" they begin.

"Nothing." I usually say. "*Absolutely nothing.*"

*   *   *

WE'VE ALL BEEN there. We've tried everything — exhausting every means of expression, scratching our foreheads until they bled — but it never made any difference. We kept hitting a wall of resistance. At times, it was mind blowing how impenetrable, how unmovable our loved ones were. Against all logic, contrary to common sense, stubbornly and oh, so stupidly (we were sure) they fought us back every inch of the way. They resisted our pleas and threats. They ignored our cold withdrawals. They were unmoved by our tears and unaffected by our promises to leave. At times it looked as if they were ready to lose everything that mattered to them just so they could continue to act the way they wanted to act.

Have you ever wondered why no matter how convincing you

were, it never worked? Have you ever been dumbfounded by their unbreakable stubbornness? Have you ever questioned their sanity? Or your own? Ever doubted yourself? Cursed the time you met them? Swore to never again fall for someone like that, yet found yourself in the same situation once again — trying to get him or her to change but failing miserably?

No matter how hard we try, no matter how *right* we believe we are, no matter how much we are doing it "for their own good" nor how pure our intention, they never seem to hear us, do they?

Remarkably, however, if we leave our loved ones alone "to their own devises," they often change, mysteriously and inexplicably, when we least expect them to. All these years we've tried to get them to *see*, fought to get them to understand … and now, when we finally drop it, stop badgering them, accept the situation and either leave them or let go of trying to change them … suddenly, after all that time … .who would have thought? … they go and *change on their own!* They do exactly what we've been asking them to do for so long. And why do they do this? Not because of us. But because *they* suddenly *want to* do it.

How do we explain these strange dynamics?
Let me tell you a story.

*   *   *

IT HAPPENED FOUR years ago, in March of 2003, on an especially beautiful spring day. It was the kind of day that fills me with gratitude for being alive: everything seemed right with the world, and I couldn't help but wonder why I ever had any worries when life was so amazing, so rich and abundant, so full of promise.

I was about to go into my home office when the telephone rang.

My friend Jane's voice was hollow, devoid of all expression. She sounded as if all life had drained out of her and it was difficult to speak at all. Still she was making the effort.

"I need to talk to you," she said.

I knew what she wanted to talk about. Jane had been in a destructive, abusive relationship for two years with her boyfriend Clark, who, I was convinced, was a con man, exploiting Jane for all she had. By the time Jane made this call, she had almost completely dropped out of sight, barely returning calls, estranging herself from all her friends. I had suspected she was in trouble and was certain that drugs were involved. I knew that she was supporting Clark, who was not working. I also knew she was hopelessly in love with him, giving him money for alcohol and drugs, paying for his keep in every way. They lived in Jane's studio apartment, which Jane, a woman of exquisite taste, had always maintained beautifully. I couldn't begin to imagine how disturbed she must have been by Clark's constant messiness, even though housekeeping must have been the least of her concerns.

At the time of Jane's call, some of her friends were considering staging an intervention. But I knew from experience that interventions can only be effective if the targeted person is ready to change.

It was a tough call. By then I had had several conversations with Jane, sometimes initiated by her, sometimes by me, but her situation remained the same. I knew that for Jane to change externally there needed to be an *internal* change. There had to be a change in her consciousness, an awakening, a shift in her psyche, and until this happened there was nothing anyone could do.

And so — I didn't try to rescue Jane. I knew what happened in these cases. How many times in the past had I rushed to save a friend? How many times in the past had I felt an urgent, pressing need to get involved, to interfere, to rescue someone whom I believed to be in trouble, to save them from themselves "for their own good"?

But the truth is *"rescuers get slaughtered." Always.* The first time I heard my friend Lazaris say this, I had to pause. It was incredible and yet so simple I could have easily missed it. But the more I thought about it, the more profound these three words became.

Remember the time you attempted to save your friend from

her cheating husband? Did she leave him as you had insisted? Or did she in the end turn against you? Or what about that drinking, alcoholic buddy of yours? Once you explained to him in no uncertain terms where he was headed, did he stop drinking or did he choose instead to end his relationship with you? Remember all the times you've tried so hard to help and instead, the beneficiaries of your care got angry, furious, ungrateful?

And yet you were so sure of what was right for them. It was so obvious to you! If they would only listen to you and change what they were doing... they would be saved from whatever was wrong in their lives. You could see it so clearly! How come it wasn't clear to them? Were they blind? Stubborn? Or just stupid?

Yet in the end, were you able to help? Or did you, perhaps, end up "misunderstood" and "unappreciated" in spite of all your good intentions? I have yet to come across anyone who did not have *good* intentions. Isn't that what the road to hell is paved with? Has anybody *ever* had *bad* intentions?

*   *   *

I HAD NOT tried to rescue Jane because I knew I could not. Instead, I held the hope that the time would come when she would make a different choice, and when it came, I would be there for her.

Perhaps, I thought, listening to her breathing on the other end of the phone, this was the time.

Still I had become weary with her situation.

"I need to talk to you," Jane said. "I know what I have to do."

"If you know what to do, then we really don't even need to talk," I said. By then I thought I had already told her all I could.

"Oh yes, we do," she said with sudden resolve, and I remembered how powerful she could be once she had set her mind to do something. "When can we meet?" she asked.

"Anytime," I said. Such was the nature of our friendship. It was always "anytime," when one of us needed the other.

"How about today?" she said. "One o'clock."

When I picked Jane up near her house two hours later, I was not prepared for what I saw. She seemed to have grown shorter, with a stoop in her posture that I hadn't noticed before. She had gained at least ten pounds and was wearing a loose flannel shirt, shapeless and old, over a long gypsy skirt instead of the tight fitting jeans she loved to wear and always looked so great in in the past. A big straw hat and sun glasses covered her face almost beyond recognition. As she approached my car, she quickly extinguished her cigarette and climbed into the seat next to me. She did not take off her dark glasses. With trembling hands she fingered the edge of her scarf, a scarf she did not need on this warm, sunny day, then wrapped it twice around her neck and reached for another cigarette forgetting to ask me if it was okay to smoke.

"Just keep the cigarette outside," I said softly, as we began to drive down the street.

We were going to have lunch in a downtown restaurant, but in the last minute Jane had called me to change the plans. She was unable to bring herself to go downtown; she couldn't be anywhere among too many people.

"We have all the time in the world," I said. I had cancelled all my plans for that day. "Let's just drive for a while."

I noticed how calm I was. I had no agenda to save Jane and held no illusion that I could do so. But I was there for her all the way. I would go as far as she was ready to go, and no further.

We ended up in a quiet, beautiful restaurant at the Wharf. It was past lunch hour, and the place was half empty. San Francisco Bay stretched outside our window. Azure blue, motionless water, endless blue sky, a lighter shade than the bay, but just as rich and sensuous. There were no clouds. *No matter what happens, no matter what turmoil, what upheaval befalls us, this will always be here, this water, this sky, this peace,* I suddenly thought. *There will always be this respite, this place to fall together.*

Seagulls perched on the backs of empty benches. It was only March, not yet the tourist season in San Francisco. The Wharf was mostly deserted, but for a few passers-by hurrying along the street. Jane leaned back, reached for a glass of water and began to talk.

It was a sad story. Most of it I knew or suspected, though the details turned out to be worse than I had imagined.

I learned that Jane's health was very poor — kidney stones, problems with her lungs, fatigue, lack of sleep, stomach trouble. Several times a week she would find herself on the floor, doubled up with stomach cramps and nausea that lasted for hours, leaving her exhausted and dizzy, unable to function for the rest of the day. Yet she had not seen a doctor and did not know what was causing the attacks. By then she had already lost her health insurance, had absolutely no money, owed everybody, and her fear of Clark was overwhelming. She knew she was being used shamelessly by Clark, and yet she was addicted to him. At times she dreamed of ending the relationship, but was too weak to do anything about it. In fact, Jane lived in perpetual fear of Clark, terrorized by his frequent, out of the blue fits of rage.

As I was listening to Jane, I remembered that Timothy Black, Jane's friend from high school, had called me a few months ago suggesting that all of Jane's good friends get together and demand that Clark leave. I was suddenly seized by a desire for revenge. It was so tempting, so seductive to just go and interfere, right the wrong, punish the abuser, make him pay. We will all stand up for Jane! If we come and throw Clark out, that will show him!

I had to shrug off the thought. It was a familiar temptation. The one that had never worked. Even if we were able to scare Clark into leaving, he would be back the next day. And Jane would let him in.

No. It had to be up to Jane. She was the only one who could change her own life.

We talked for four hours.

Jane felt no need to cover anything up, to make it pretty. She was in love, and it was messy and raw and all wrong. But it was what it was, and it was real. There were times when she was with

Clark and felt more alive and happy than she ever had in her entire life. And it was hard to give it up. A smile, a touch, a moment of tenderness, and then "Can you give me some money? I need a drink." And Clark would go out, cash in hand, not to be seen until the early hours. *Who did he go to?* Jane wondered. *Who would he make love to prior to coming back and falling asleep in a drunken stupor as Jane lay awake all night clenching her fists, hating herself, hating her life, sick with resentment and rage?*

This was the situation she was in, and though I had known some of it from our previous conversations and had suspected the rest of it, I never knew the full extent of her nightmare. Perhaps she needed to hear it herself.

I listened.

"*At least you are not telling me I have to leave him,*" Jane suddenly said. "That's why I stopped talking to everyone else. God! If I hear it again, I'll just scream! Everyone keeps telling me what I already know! I don't need to hear it! And they all hate Clark! I just can't talk to them any more. Even to my sister. I stopped picking up the phone."

Jane reached for her water and emptied the glass in one gulp. I put my hand over her palm. I suddenly saw it as clear as daylight. Two choices lay in front of Jane that afternoon, two roads to travel. But she could only travel one of them. And she was the only one who could make this choice.

"You can do what you want," I said. "No one can tell us what we should do, ever. But if you stay with Clark you are going to die."

I was strangely detached. As if watching both of us from somewhere else while being fully involved in the conversation at the same time. I knew that we were at a pivotal point.

Jane watched me silently. She was letting it sink in.

"That bad, huh?" she said.

"Not bad. Not wrong. Just a choice," I said. But she needed more. "It is okay to die," I said. "It is not bad or wrong. It is simply a choice, and it's up to you. I will miss you, of course, but it is your right, you know that."

Jane closed her eyes for a second.

"Is that what you believe?" she asked.

"Yes. Except it won't be quick and easy. You won't go in your sleep. It will be long and drawn out, with illnesses, pain, poverty."

Was I trying to scare Jane? Was I trying to manipulate her, using fear to get her to see her reality more clearly? Do you think, dear reader, that if I did, it would have worked? Haven't you tried that many times in the past in similar situations? Telling an alcoholic friend that he was drinking himself to death. Telling a smoker that he would die of lung cancer. Telling an abused wife that she should leave while she is still alive. Have they ever done what you suggested? No. They have not.

I was not trying to scare Jane into action. I was simply telling her the truth. I was telling her what I saw. What I knew in my gut, knew intuitively. I also knew it logically. I had no agenda. As I said, I was completely detached. It was a moment of grace. And of total clarity. A moment outside time and space. Nothing else existed between us — only the truth. And that's why Jane heard me.

"That bad," she repeated again.

"Yes. That bad," I said.

There was a pause. A long pause. There seemed to be nothing left to say. Suddenly Jane spoke. She seemed calmer, almost as detached as I was. As if she was simply contemplating ordinary choices.

"You know how I always wanted to move to San Rafael. It is so much warmer there than in San Francisco. And if I moved, Clark could not follow me. He has no car and no money."

"Yes, that would be great," I said.

"But I have no money," she shrugged. "I am in debt to everyone. There's no way I can move. I would need first and last month's rent. A security deposit..."

"I'll give you the money," I said.

I said it so calmly and with such ease, it was as if I had planned it in advance. Though quite the opposite was true, of course. Until I heard myself say it, the thought had never entered my mind. Jane was a notorious borrower and paid back slowly and never on time. I suspected for quite a while that she was doing drugs with Clark and decided not to lend her money again, even if she asked.

But I was not offering a loan.

"It won't be a loan," I said. "It will be my gift. It will give me pleasure. I would love to do it."

It was the right thing to do. And it was not a big deal. I was hoping she'd say yes, yet it was simply an offer. I was not invested in her taking it, though I would be very happy if she did. It was up to Jane, of course. Her desire to move had inspired my offer to help. I wasn't rescuing her, but simply supporting her own choice.

Jane leaned back and stared at me, as if not sure she heard correctly.

I smiled.

"It is not even that much money, Jane."

"You can't do that. No. I can't let you do that. Are you serious?"

"Why not?" I said. "Wouldn't you do the same for me?" It was suddenly very easy. Very clear. I was relaxed.

Jane reached for her coffee, but put it down without drinking. She pulled off her hat, pulled the rubber band off her pony tail, then looked at me again, her eyes wide.

"You would do that?"

And suddenly, my old friend, the excitable, intense, hyper and funny Jane was back there with me, incredulous, stunned, yet unable to contain her excitement as this amazing new possibility was being dropped into her lap as if by magic.

I was excited myself. In fact, I was so excited I had to make an effort not to overwhelm Jane with my own emotions. A miracle was unfolding in front of my eyes. A future that a moment ago had not even been a distant possibility was now rushing in, aligning probabilities, creating circumstances, clearing everything out of its way, so as to fully come into the present and manifest in all its power.

"Perhaps I could have a dog then," Jane said.

"Of course you could," I said. "You could make sure to rent a place that allows dogs."

"And a little yard, so I could work outside in the sun on the computer."

"Certainly. We can look this weekend. That would be a lot of fun."

Looking back later, I wondered what it had been that I'd said to Jane that had made such a difference. What had it been that empowered her to find her voice, to find the strength and the resolve that she needed to change her situation?

Perhaps, I thought, it was not so much what I said, but how I said it. Perhaps, it was the fact that she found herself not being judged, but accepted instead. Maybe something happened between the words, in the silences that were just as important as the words. Perhaps, she could trust the love and honesty she found herself surrounded with and that was what allowed the transformation. Or maybe she simply needed the space to be heard and seen just the way she was — vulnerable, lost, her wounds open, her pain exposed.

But there it was. In front of my eyes, a new exciting future, born out of the shift of energy, was arriving with full force.

Hold on to Your Dreams

All our lives we have been led to believe the lie that our present reality is the result of what happened to us in the past, and that we are stuck in it. The past, they told us, is what creates the present. Cause leads to effect. The past leads to the present, leading to the future. As you shall sow, so shall you reap. You've made your bed, now you will lie in it.

And we bought it hook line and sinker.

However, quite the opposite is true.

Think about it. The dream you had as a child. Not the one

you've let go of because someone you loved told you repeatedly that you could never have it, but the one you held on to.

Perhaps it was a dream of becoming a doctor. A surgeon saving people's lives. You played it all in your mind, all the wonderful details of it. But when you tried telling your parents about it, they only laughed. "Who are you kidding?" they said. "You know we can never afford it. Who do you think you are? No one in our family ever went to college. You think you are better than us, don't you? Stop dreaming. It will never happen, you will only get hurt." After a while you stopped talking about it because they would always get frustrated with you. Yet you held on to your dream. You refused to accept their logic.

You had no idea how you would do it. And yet, looking back now, you can see it so clearly — nothing could have stood in your way. There was no money for that education. The circumstances were all wrong. Your mother needed you at home, your kid sister was in trouble, your Dad just left the family. Who were you to even dream that you could one day...? And yet, stubbornly, against all odds you dreamt. You hoped. You imagined. You couldn't sleep at night. All you could think about was how in the future, you would be a doctor...how your life would look, how great it would feel to do your hospital rounds in the morning. Oh, you could almost taste it. You could smell the hospital rooms. You could see that old man, a recovering patient whose heart you had operated on just a week ago. How happy he was to see you walk in and sit on his bed. "I am feeling much better, doctor," he was saying. *Doctor.* They were calling you doctor. And it felt good. It felt right. It felt like that's where you belonged.

And where are you now? You are a doctor, a doctor taking a break between patients. How did it all happen to you? How did you, the dreaming child with an overactive imagination, with the odds stacked against you get *from there to here?* What was it that pulled you up and out, first into college, then into Medical school, then into residency to become a doctor?

Oh sure, you can find some very logical explanation about how you worked hard, how you earned all your successes, and most certainly you did. *But what actually happened?* How did the circumstances begin to line up to allow the dream to come into being? *There was nothing in your past to suggest this future. There was, however, the future about which you dreamt.* And it was strong. And it was powerful. And it was gathering momentum. *That's* what pulled you. That's what created all the rest of it . . . *Suddenly things shifted, a possibility* appeared for a scholarship or for a job that could make it all work out, or a magical benefactor showed up, or something else happened to pave the way.

The future, born out of the dreams of a child who refused to give up, the future, created in the early hours of the morning, when you lay awake imagining yourself in the operating room, scalpel in hand, just like you saw in the movies. That future was so powerful, its energy so strong . . . it threw you a grappling hook. You caught it and it pulled you towards it.

All the events that happened between then and now were the result of that energy.

My friend Jane had a dream as well. She didn't like the cool weather of San Francisco and dreamt about leaving the city some day and moving to the sunny climate of San Rafael. She also dreamt of having a dog, something she was not allowed in her San Francisco apartment. She and I talked about it many times, imagining her sitting in her sunny garden with her dog by her side, working on her computer.

The dog, the house in the sun, the garden . . . it was all a dream, an improbable dream, many would say, given her circumstances. She had no realistic way of getting there. She had difficulty paying rent on her studio apartment even before her troubles with Clark began. But the dream lived on, fantasy or not. And in the realm of The Possible, *the future was born.* The future that could one day become a *probability,* leading to *possibility* and finally — to *actuality.*

Just think about it. Just allow yourself to play with the idea for a moment. Doesn't it make much more sense than everything else we are used to believing? And how exciting, how liberating it is to know that *our past does not have to define our future. It merely influences it, and only to the degree that we let it. It is actually possible to leave the past behind completely, to transcend it, as if it never was.* Few have been able to do it, that's true. *But it is possible.*

All kinds of realities can be dreamt into being through continuous, focused imagination. Our imagination carries an immensity of power—the power that can bring you the things you dream about—the wonderful ones and the darkest ones, and everything in between.

But who, you might ask, would dream of creating a dark future? Who would be lying awake at night imagining, feeling, tasting the nightmare?

Who indeed?

How about the nights when you couldn't sleep for fear of losing your job? Or were consumed by your hatred of the boss? Being eaten up alive by jealousy? Terrified of having a terminal illness? How about the endless hours people spend hating, blaming, reliving the pain, re-playing the dark scenarios, filled with fear, imagining the worst, like Jane did for months? What happens to all that energy? To all the negative, dark futures that are born of these feelings, of that imagination?

By hanging out there, in the darkness, we are consciously giving life force to potentially dark and dangerous futures, increasing the chance that they will manifest in our lives.

So which one will it be? The dream or the nightmare? *The choice is yours. You are the author of your life,* but *you need to have enough of yourself present* in order to make the right choice. And if you give too much of your energy to self pity, resentments and fear, you may not have what it takes to reach for and grab hold of the future of your dream.

That's why it is so vitally important to *develop the spiritual disci-*

pline of *being conscious* of where you put your *attention,* your focus, your thoughts and feelings. Of being conscious of what you are *imagining.*

"But what if I feel I have a real reason to be afraid? To fear all these possibilities?" you ask.

That is when more than ever, you need to have the discipline to refocus your attention to the positive outcome.

Trust the Power of the Possible

Imagine healing. Imagine change. Believe that even though you can't possibly see a solution, there is one. In fact, there are many and you don't even need to know what they are. You just need *to trust that change is possible,* that it can happen. Fight your cynicism. *Refuse to be hopeless.* Start dreaming against all odds. *Dream of unexpected, magical solutions.* If you can't imagine them, *hope for miracles, expect things to work out* no matter what. Allow hope to take you over. *Allow hope to reign.*

There is tremendous power in hope. Hope is never the last resort. Hope is an immensely powerful tool of manifestation. Learn to hope. And then hope some more. Make it a part of your life. *Feeling hopeful.* Even in the darkest moments. That's powerful. See things shifting, changing for the better. Trust that there can be a positive outcome. When things are dark, when there seems to be no way out, that's when, more than ever, you "can't afford the luxury of a negative thought."

Don't be a realist. Our world needs dreamers. Be an incurable optimist! *And see your reality change.* See it change beyond what *you* can imagine. *Allow the Universe to take care of the details.*

*   *   *

FOR AWHILE, JANE and I just sat in the restaurant silently looking at the view.

"Is it all right with you if we go now?" Jane asked. "I feel over-whelmed. I think I need to be alone."

"Certainly," I said and looked at my watch. "My God! We've been here for four hours!"

"Have we really?" Jane laughed. "Though you know, it feels like we could have been here for a year. I feel like...I actually don't know how I feel. I think I'd rather just walk home if it's okay with you. I need to clear my head."

"I think it's a great idea," I said. I could see she was exhausted. "Go. I'll take care of the check and go home. I am tired myself."

We smiled, hugged, and she was gone.

It was up to Jane now. I was not sure what she was going to do. I trusted that the change that happened at the table was real, and that I would know soon enough.

I hadn't been home for more than two hours when the phone rang.

"You want to know what happened?" Jane asked.

She had left the restaurant dazed. Too much had happened during the hours we had talked. No one had tried to change her. No one had told her what she should do. She had felt loved and known. She had felt seen and accepted just as she was.

"To be truly seen is to be truly healed," I once read in Marianne Williamson's book *Enchanted Love*. Jane had spent an afternoon with me, her friend, who had not judged her, but had not lied to her either. What she had heard was painful, hard to bear—but it was real.

It was her wake up call. The one she was able to hear because there was nothing for her to resist. I did not make her wrong. I did not pressure her to change her life.

She had needed time to assimilate. To just be with what she was beginning to see clearly. For the first time in the two years she had been with Clark, Jane let herself feel the immensity of her rage.

Rage is an emotion different from anger. In times of physical or emotional abuse, when we feel devalued and powerless, when some-one attacks us, frightens us, insults our dignity, shatters our confidence, demeans our character—we feel rage. Condensed, bottled up, determined and deadly. When we swallow the abuse unable to deal with it in the moment it happens, we also swallow the rage—the poisonous, often silent rage—that, from that moment on, eats away at our organs, affecting everything we do, weakening us in every way. It is the cause of so many illnesses. It's what's behind our exhaustion and our chronic fatigue. It brings with it lack of sleep and lack of motivation. Rage is a destructive force that never sleeps and never lets go. It's a force we can tap into at a moment's notice.

Today, sitting alone by the water, Jane saw how disempowered she had become in the relationship, how little she had been valued by both Clark and herself. It was a hard and painful realization. It was also sobering.

All the time she had spent feeling sorry for herself, feeling victimized by Clark, resenting the mess she was in, resenting Clark and everything he came to represent, yet never allowing herself to really feel the actual horror of it. She had chosen the numbing balm of self pity and martyrdom to anaesthetize herself against any true feelings—against the only thing that could set her free.

She saw it all clearly that afternoon, and she cried for her pain and found a level of compassion she had never felt before. Compassion for Jane and for the humanity of it all. She felt her pain fully and completely, not afraid to go where it took her, and she came out cleansed, released. And in that place where rage and resentment had lived side by side for such along time, a new resolve was born.

A resolve that washed away the fear of losing Clark and being alone again. A resolve that left no room for fear of Clark's outbursts, which suddenly seemed petty, ridiculous, weak—no more frightening than a temper tantrum of a spoiled, out of control child. The fear was gone and in its place came courage born of self respect.

As she was walking home that early evening, not knowing what time it was, not knowing how long she had spent alone by the water, the sky growing darker, dusk setting in, she did not think about what she was going to say to Clark once she saw him. She was not indignant any more nor consumed by rage. Instead, she felt the cold fury of resolve that had lifted her off the bench and onto her feet and was now propelling her forward, making her move faster, carrying her home on a resolute wave of clarity.

She did not rehearse her speech. When she walked into the apartment, she calmly switched off the TV and turned to face Clark. The words she spoke came from a woman Clark had not known before.

She didn't blame, insult or accuse. She didn't raise her voice nor lose her temper. When she laid out the facts of their situation, she was honest and clear and direct.

Looking Clark straight in the eye, Jane spoke it all—the good the bad and the ugly. Clark's breaking of her trust, his stealing, his lying and his manipulation.

She spoke about her own weakness, how lonely she had been before meeting Clark, how much she grew to enjoy his company and their rare moments of tenderness, and how dependent she had become on them. She had been hopelessly in love with Clark, and she had refused to see what was going on. She had supported Clark financially and pretended to believe he was incapable of making an income. But this led to her current financial nightmare.

There were no victims in their relationship, only perpetrators. Different roles had been played. And if Jane looked a victim, in truth—she was not. She had volunteered for her role.

"I am just as responsible for what happened between us as you are," she said. "I allowed it, encouraged it, and went along with it. And—it's over."

Shaken and stunned, Clark looked at his feet. He was suddenly small, pathetic. Jane almost felt sorry for him, but she knew better.

"I will move out tomorrow," Clark whispered.

Jane looked at him and saw a shell. An empty shell of a man

lost to himself, beaten by his own addictions. Was there a flicker of remorse in those pale blue eyes, the eyes that had once made her sick with love, ready to give up everything? Or was it simply defeat and shame and the desire to flee? To get away from the raw pain she was exposing, holding in front of him like a mirror?

"He just left," Jane said to me on the phone, "And you know, I feel nothing, but relief. I know there will be more pain to go through later, but I am so clear, so relieved. And it is over. I don't even know what I feel for him right now. But even if he were to change overnight, I don't want him. Whatever I had for him is dead. Funny, this morning I couldn't see my way out. I was so stuck, I hated him and couldn't live without him. And now it was so easy. So clear and so easy. And I know he *will* move out tomorrow. He won't dare. You know, it's like I am a different person."

"*Nothing changes till we do*," I said, "Remember?"

"My favorite quote," she said. "Why do I always forget it?"

"So shall we go looking at places to rent this weekend?" I asked.

"But how can I? I am broke."

"I said I'd give you the money, remember?" I said.

"Boy, miracles just don't stop coming, do they?" Jane laughed. "I had forgotten your offer completely. I was so focused on Clark. You know how long I have been dreaming about moving out of the city?!

"Of course I do."

"I don't know whether to laugh or cry. Too much for one day, don't you think? Okay. I'll check the ads. Let's go looking on Sunday!"

That very Sunday we found her a place. It was the first place we saw. Within two months, Jane had moved, and now a year and a half later, she lives in a bigger house with a beautiful yard and a dog she adores. In addition, her income has almost doubled, she has given up drugs and is planning to give up smoking entirely, though to be honest, she is rather slow about that one. But come on, it doesn't have to be perfect, does it? She is free and fully involved in her life, hoping to one day be able to buy her own house. Her health is better, though still not great, and she has not once heard from Clark. In fact, it is as if Clark has completely disappeared from her radar.

The Law of Resonance

The change in Jane at the restaurant and on her walk home was so profound that she and Clark simply did not match any more. This was *the law of resonance — in action.*

The law of resonance is a phenomenon of physics. It says quite plainly that if two sources of energy are vibrating at different frequencies, in time they will vibrate at the same frequency. Either the higher frequency will lower or the lower frequency will raise, or they will both change meeting somewhere in between. This law applies to everything in our lives, be it people or inanimate objects. All of us are sources of energy, and our resonance is the result of all the different energies we carry at any particular moment. From the lowest, imprisoning vibration of, say, loneliness, despair, or hopelessness to the highest energies of love or hope. Whatever it is that each of us is comprised of, all of it must find a way to coexist, creating a unique resonance for each individual. These energies come together within us — canceling, amplifying, diminishing and augmenting each other. When, in the end, they coalesce, a standing wave of energy — a resonance — is formed.

It is important to understand that *our resonance is not static.* It shifts and changes with our moods, with our thoughts and feelings, for they too are energies, or vibrational frequencies. But *the main tone of it, its predominant note, remains.*

*   *   *

THE SHIFT IN Jane's resonance, and the transformation that happened to her as a result of it, was so powerful that all of a sudden Clark's resonance was repelling to her. In one sweep, Jane's transformation had wiped out the possibility of the two of them staying together. Ending the relationship became an organic, natural thing — it was the only thing that could happen. Clark knew it instantly as well. He had nothing in common with this new Jane. He left the next day.

That's how the law of resonance works. It not only affects every area of our lives, it affects us all the time.

Positive, optimistic people, the ones who expect things to work out no matter what, the ones everyone likes to be around because they somehow begin to feel better just being in their presence, are the ones whose resonance is very high and who won't lower it regardless of what happens to them at different times. Sure they sometimes feel upset or angry or frustrated or afraid just like anyone else, but the predominant optimistic attitude they carry does not waver. They remain who they are regardless of the circumstances.

We all know people like that. We marvel at their strength of character, at their perseverance, at their positive attitude. How can they always be so optimistic? They can. It is who they are. *It is as natural to them as flight to an eagle.* It is their grace. They don't know how to be any other way. Somewhere deep inside they carry a level of trust that to most other people is unfathomable. They *know* the universe is a benevolent place, and that they will be all right no matter what.

You want people like that around you. You want to be in their orbit, just because when you are around them, some of it may rub off on you. And it usually does. It is inevitable. You spend some time with them, hear them talk, and suddenly you find yourself feeling better. *Your resonance rises, being pulled upwards by theirs.* "My dreams *can* come true as well," you suddenly think. "Maybe I can do it. That thing I always wanted to do. Maybe I can have it. Maybe there is a way." Sometimes just being with a person with such high resonance is enough to change your life.

I have always had a positive attitude towards life, and I am very grateful for that. For as long as I can remember, I have been called "an optimist." Sometimes it was said with approval or admiration or even with a touch of envy, and sometimes with dismissal and contempt. Sometimes it sounded like an accusation. If I refused to accept that a situation was hopeless, some received this with irritation or anger. Somehow it meant I could not be taken seriously because I would not "see the reality," the gravity of events.

Although my natural state has always been to expect the good, I have experienced times when it has been hard to do so — when I couldn't see my way clearly and was plunged into the depth of despair and pain. At times like that, if I had had a friend who was able to believe for me in what I was unable to believe myself, a friend who would absolutely know that what was happening in my life was only temporary and trusted that I would come out of it with more healing and wisdom and clarity than before, if I was lucky, so very lucky to have a friend like that — and sometimes I was — it was much easier for me to deal with the despair and pain, so much easier to find the way to heal. *Because my friend would hold her resonance strong. She would refuse to lower it no matter where I was with mine. And it would pull me toward it.* Hope would return, bringing answers, solutions, new possibilities. My natural resonance would be restored, creating the space for healing and with it — for change.

This is what I was able to give to Jane.

People travel to far lands, to India for example, to just sit with a guru. And if the guru is a real one, they change. Sometimes, when they are on their own again, their resonance drops. They are unable to hold it without the presence of the Master. People like listening to motivational speakers for the same reason. Listening to them lifts their resonance, makes them feel better, more hopeful, more alive. But how long after the speech is over will they be able to hold their raised resonance? It differs with each of us. Some may have been permanently changed, some changed slightly because once we are on our own, it is up to us to keep our resonance high — to refuse to return to the old way of being. *That's why it is so important to be as conscious as possible* of your own resonance.

*   *   *

BE AWARE OF your thoughts, of *where you focus your attention*. Decide to guard your resonance, to protect it from negative influences. Choose to surround yourself with people who have positive, optimistic attitudes about life. Stay away from those with the victim mentality. Stay away from people who love to blame everyone and everything. Protect your resonance from them, for they will bring it down, just as Clark brought Jane down with him for two years with his addiction to drugs, his cynicism and absolute refusal to take responsibility for his own life. The longer she stayed with him, the harder it was to disengage, as she was sinking deeper and deeper into the fog of Clark's low resonance.

Become conscious of who you allow to be in your environment. This decision will have a profound effect on your life. If you don't want to be affected by the negative energy of a particular person, you must leave their vicinity. Otherwise — you *will* be affected. Even ten minutes in the company of a mean-spirited, pessimistic person will affect how you feel. Seek to be around the people who make you feel better instead of worse. Wouldn't it be more fun?

Spend time with someone who simply emanates success out of every pore of their being, and you are going to want to be more successful. You will start seeing the possibilities. Have you noticed that somehow successful, trustworthy, positive people always attract loyal, trustworthy, positive and reliable friends and employees? Because it just works this way. If, per chance, someone with a different vibrational frequency manages to get into their circle, they either change or won't stay around long. There is no other option. *The law of resonance is simply that — a law. It works regardless of whether we believe in it or not.* If it is something you never thought about before, start paying attention to it, and you will see how the shifts and changes in your daily resonance influence your reality all the time.

For example, you may be in the midst of a conversation with a friend, and everything is going great. You are having a wonderful time with each other . . . and then one of you says something that causes the other to become upset, or angry, or to withdraw from you and become silent, and suddenly — what happened to the good time you were just having? Whatever it was that caused the upset, that person's resonance has dropped, changed, and everything at the table you are sitting at is now different. Sometimes it is hard to bring the good energy back. Sometimes it is easy. The point is we know immediately when the resonance changes. We know when it drops, and we know when it rises.

If you want to raise the resonance that has just dropped, refocus your attention on something positive right away. Remember the good things in your life, think of the ones you love, and let the memory fill you. Continue to focus your attention this way until you feel an internal shift and see your friend's resonance begin to lift to match yours.

There are people whom we call "positive" and those we call "negative." There is also everyone in between. *What matters is how strong their resonance is,* wherever it falls on the continuum.

The stronger it is, the more power it has to impact us. Some people stand out for all of us to see. They are the heroes, the saints, or the villains of their times.

On the one end of the spectrum — the Dalai Lama, Dr. Martin Luther King, Mahatma Gandhi, Buddha, Jesus Christ. On the other end — Hitler, Stalin, Saddam Hussein, Osama Bin Laden.

There is a Russian saying "Tell me who your friends are, and I will tell you who you are." There is wisdom in this proverb. *Be aware of who you spend your time with. Always — be careful of the company you keep.*

The Resonance of Hope

During World War II, England was in grave danger. London was being bombed. People were dying. Food was rationed. The German U boats were surrounding Britain. Most families had someone fighting in the war.

Every morning people turned on the radio to listen to Prime Minister Winston Churchill. Keep in mind that Churchill was a notorious drunk. There probably wasn't a time when he was not drunk, be it morning, noon or night. He slurred his words. Often you could not make out what he was saying. Yet every morning the nation turned on the radio to listen to his booming voice announcing that *he would never surrender.* And as they listened, something happened to them. *Something good.* After the speech was over, they invariably felt better. They knew they would go on. They would persevere. And they would win!

So high was Churchill's resonance, so strong his conviction, his belief and his determination, so powerful was his will and his vision — it was enough to lift the nation, to give them hope, to lead them to victory. *Hope entered the rooms of England on Churchill's booming voice.* Hope filled the hearts of people and gave them strength to go on. It didn't matter that they couldn't make out the words of his speeches. *It was not in the words.* His power, his resolve, his unbending will was in the energy that drifted thru the radio waves and penetrated everyone listening. *He would not lower his resonance.* He refused to do it. Or perhaps, he simply could not.

Some of the best leaders in history were like that. Some were loud and overbearingly powerful, like Churchill; some were quiet, with a will of steel like Gandhi; or strength of vision, like Dr.

Martin Luther King. What is common to all of them is their amazingly high resonance.

We want to emulate these people. We wonder how they got there, what we can do to be like them.

Becoming conscious of the phenomenon of resonance is the first step.

The Resonance of America

Have you ever wondered why American films almost always have happy endings? Because Americans don't like the unhappy ones! They have been raised on films in which everything works out in the end. It doesn't matter how impossible this may seem in the beginning or the middle of the movie. *In the end—it is going to be all right.* The good guys always win. And thus the belief is bred into our children early on: *the good guy will win.*

This is the kind of movie my husband and I love to see. We look for films daring enough to show that no matter how difficult events and situations are, we are left with hope. We see triumph of character, the possibility of change, and the victory of the human spirit in the face of tragedy. No matter how much I may cry during this type of movie, I leave feeling cleansed, uplifted, renewed.

The same with good comedies. We love them because we can always use wonderful laughter. It is one of the best, most powerful resonance lifters.

Over twenty-five years ago, when Dr. Norman Cousins, a prominent journalist and peace advocate, was diagnosed with a life threatening tissue disease, he made it a point to watch Marx Brothers movies every day for hours. He noticed at the time that even a few minutes of hearty laughter gave him at least an hour or more of pain free sleep. Refusing to accept the fatal outcome, he laughed and hoped and laughed and hoped against all odds. *"Hope, purpose and determination are not merely mental states,"* he wrote later. *"They have electrochemical connections that affect the immune system."* Cousins laughed his way to complete healing. So strong was the resonance of a good belly laugh, that the disease, brought about by an emotional pain, had no choice but to dissolve, as he was lifted into a higher vibration — that of 'non disease' and of restored health.

No matter how scary things get in an American movie, no matter how terrified we may feel for the heroes, we know it will all work out. Such is the overall resonance of the American people, that no matter what, they just can't bring themselves to have a movie end badly. It is not shallow, nor is it superficial. It is our saving grace. As an immigrant from the former Soviet Union, it has taken me many years to understand this.

When I first came to America and was exposed to American films, I was very surprised to discover that the movies would invariably have some version of a happy ending. I thought it was artificial, unrealistic and untrue. I was irritated and annoyed by it. I thought I was not being taken seriously as a viewer. Did the makers of the movie think I was so naïve? Didn't I know that in life things go wrong and often don't work out? Why was I always being shown this Pollyanna, sweetened version of life? I was indignant. I was contemptuous. American people are naïve, I concluded. They are just like children. They want to live in a fairy tale land instead of the real world.

I learned that many people new to the United States have had similar reactions, trying to find an explanation for the predominant optimism of the American people, their vibrant spirit and an absolute expectation that the right thing will be done.

American troops stationed in Europe after the end of World War II changed the face of Europe for good with their high resonance of optimism, freedom and hope. There was something so different about the way they viewed the world, something so powerful in their attitude. Most people in Europe had no experience with this type of resonance. Impoverished, ravaged by the horrors of war, they were lifted by the American spirit, by the light of freedom American soldiers carried in the very core of their beings. Children of the Land of the Free and the Home of the Brave. These concepts, sacred, instilled in them since birth had an amazing impact. The kids, raised on movies with happy endings, children who have been told again and again that "you could be whatever you wanted to be, that it is all up to you, what you make out of your life"—the spirit of those soldiers entered the hearts and minds of the people they liberated and changed them forever.

This phenomenon is uniquely American. Those born and raised here do not recognize it as special. To them it is normal. As normal as water is normal to fish. I came here with no money, no connections and no knowledge of this way of life. But I experienced it myself in the most powerful and astonishing way: Americans will cheer you on. They will support your success, proclaim it, talk about it and write about it, and—they will love it! Receiving this attitude, this reaction from total strangers, is worth every obstacle you encounter along the way. It has made all the difference for me.

In this country, regardless of the circumstances under which they grow up, children are told again and again that they can become whatever they want to become. They hear it everywhere. *If not at home, then at school, if not at school, then through the media.* It is in the air. It is what our air is made of. It is a powerful, positive force that distinguishes us from any other country in the world. Hope and a predominant belief in goodness permeate everything: magazines, ads, commercials, the lyrics of songs. There is a message: *the future is your hands.* And you have to actually fight this message, if you want to escape it.

It makes some people angry. People who love to blame rather than take responsibility. The very concept of choice is infuriating to them. But—*it is always our choice,* and there are plenty of role models who have risen to the top against all odds, just on the power of their will to do so.

After World War II, Europeans recognized the different spirit of the American soldiers temporarily in their land, and were changed by it. Similarly those who've moved here, almost always change. They become more optimistic, more hopeful. The great majority of them would never go back to their own countries, except to visit. When they do, they discover that they don't fit in anymore. Their resonance has changed. They have become different people.

I smile when I remember how I used to think. What seemed to me "naïve and childlike" about America isn't that at all. It is a resonance of a very high octave, something I wasn't exposed to before. It is the "American spirit." It takes my breath away.

Hitting Bottom

I said to my soul, be still and wait without hope,
For hope would be hope for the wrong thing,
Wait without love, for love would be love of the wrong thing,
There is yet faith, but the faith and the love and the hope
are all in the waiting,
Wait without thought, for you are not ready for thought:
So the darkness shall be light and the stillness the dancing.
　　　　　　　　　　　　　　　　　—T. S. ELLIOT

IT IS NOT TRUE THAT PEOPLE DON'T CHANGE.

They do. But never when we ask them or tell them to.

People change when they *want to change,* and *only* when they want to change. The more we insist, the more they will resist us every way they can. There is a saying: "What you resist — persists." I changed it to: "*What we insist on — resists us.*"

As long as we insist on changing someone — we keep them from changing of their own free will.

Let go of your demands and it is up to them. Now — they *will* or *will not* change on their own. *By not insisting — we have set them free.*

No one has ever changed for somebody else. On the other hand — one person can be someone's *reason* to change. There is a profound and fundamental difference.

Let me explain.

Remember Jack Nicholson's character Mr. Udall in the movie *As Good As It Gets?* When we first meet Mr.Udall, he is an obnoxious, rude and unbelievably self-centered eccentric, diagnosed with obsessive-compulsive disorder. He derives perverse pleasure from insulting and shocking people, and he is incredibly good at it. Udall manages to insult and alienate everyone he comes into contact with. He is also very intelligent, remarkably, completely aware of his behavior. But he doesn't give a damn. The only person important to Mr. Udall is Mr. Udall.

As the movie unfolds, however, we discover, that there is someone else that matters to Mr. Udall. It is the waitress Carol (played by Helen Hunt) who has been serving him breakfast in the restaurant every morning for a very long time. In fact, it is beginning to look more and more like he is falling in love with her. In an unusual twist of events, Udall and Carol find themselves on a dinner date. True to form, though probably unintentionally and due to his nervousness, Udall insults Carol. Instead of an apology, Carol demands a compliment. And is has to be a real one.

The situation is critical and Udall knows it. He is an inch away from having Carol walk out of the restaurant. He concentrates, thinking hard. He knows this is his only chance…and then he tells her something unexpected. His doctor has prescribed him a certain medication that he must take every day to help him with his condition.

"I *hate* pills," he tells Carol. "Very dangerous thing — pills. *Hate*. I am using the word *hate* here. About pills." He then reminds Carol of a recent encounter they'd had and what she had said to him when she arrived at his door in the middle of the night, soaked with rain, but determined to deliver her message: I will *never* sleep with you! (making him realize how repulsed she had always been by his obnoxious behavior). He looks straight at her. "My compliment is," he says, *"The next day* I started taking the pills."

But Carol doesn't understand. What does this have to do with her compliment? Udall pauses…and then explains.

"You make me want to be a better man," he says.

And she melts. "That may be the best compliment of my life," she says and smiles.

Anyone who remembers the movie and remembers Jack Nicholson's character knows what an immense effort it was for Udall to begin taking his medication. And, of course, had Carol asked him to do so in order for him to behave in a more acceptable way, he would have absolutely refused.

He did it on his own. He did it *because* of her. She was *his reason* to become "a better man," but it was *his* choice.

The Wife of an Alcoholic

I want to tell you a story of a woman whose husband was an alcoholic. For years she had been fighting with her husband to get him to stop drinking. She had tried everything — from pleading to reasoning to threatening to begging. She cried, she yelled at him, she left him, she came back.

She knew she couldn't go on like that. And yet she could not leave him either.

Her husband was stubborn, she always thought, *but so was she.* She was determined to triumph over his drinking, find a way to change him, so that he would wake up one day, hear her, and become the guy she once knew, the one she fell in love with so many years ago. It was unimaginable to her that there was nothing she could do to bring her guy back, nothing she could do to have their old life return. She never stopped loving him. She probably loved him more now than she did when she had married him twenty-five years ago, when they were barely out of college.

He had always had to have his liquor. But it didn't seem to matter in the past. Over the years, however, what used to make him funny, what seemed cute and adorable had turned into something else, something ugly. It wasn't funny any more.

Oh, how she fought the very notion. How much she refused to

believe he was an alcoholic. How much she tried to reason with him, talk to him. She accepted the truth eventually, unable to find another explanation for his drinking, and it made her fight harder to save him.

And just as hard he fought her back.

As their children were growing up, as they were getting older—he was drinking, and drinking, and drinking more. It was hard to remember him sober—hard to remember when last they had a good time together.

Now they were on their own again, the children gone. A friend suggested a therapist, Brian, who she said could be very helpful. The woman made an appointment hoping for a solution, hoping to learn how to influence her husband, to discover the way to be, so that he would finally understand and take her pain into consideration. Perhaps Brian would teach her how to convince her husband to go to AA?

But instead, the therapist told her to *disengage.* He had been telling her that at every session. Once he had even refused to see her again. He had nothing else to tell her, he claimed...She fought him. That bottomless anger she had been living with all those years, she unleashed onto her shrink instead of to where it belonged.

She apologized later and asked to come back.

He let her come for another session.

"I hide the keys to the car when he drinks," she said.

"Don't," said Brian.

"But he is not just a danger to himself. He can kill somebody else as well."

"There is nothing you can do to stop him," Brian said again. "His life is his. You have to decide what you can live with and what you can't. And you *must* disengage."

It was the last session they would have, only she didn't know this at the time. When she spoke to Brian later, he told her he wasn't sure whether or not he had been able to reach her. He noticed that she had been quiet, more subdued than usual. She listened, but didn't say much at all. He said he felt there was something different about this particular session. When she said good bye, she made no other appointment.

*   *   *

She had no words to explain what exactly had happened to her at the last session. Except that for the first time since she had begun working with the therapist, she had let herself *hear* what he was saying, *rather than resist it or fight against it.*

"There is *nothing* you can do," Brian's words reached her and stuck. "Nothing *anyone* can do but him."

"And he doesn't want to do anything . . ." she finished to herself silently.

It startled her, and she let it in deeper. Admitting to herself finally what she had known all along but had been refusing to accept.

How clear it suddenly was. How absolutely and shockingly obvious. Brian kept talking quietly, but she had stopped listening. All she could do was just sit there in stunned silence, her body lifeless and still, her hands wasted on her lap.

She was powerless to save her husband from drinking.

She swallowed, fighting the urge to throw up, looked at Brian, then looked away. Suddenly dizzy, she leaned forward, her hand to her throat, steadying her breath, willing the nausea to leave.

"Are you all right? Would you like a glass of water?" Brian asked. She swallowed the water without tasting it, squeezed the arm of the sofa and sat up.

"I don't know," she said, not looking at him. "I don't know."

*   *   *

"There is nothing I can do," she thought, walking back to her car.

It was freeing to say this even in her own mind. She let it sink in. Strangely, inexplicably, there was a sense of lightness to the throbbing pain in her heart.

"Nothing," she repeated out loud this time, as if testing her voice, checking to see if her own mouth was able to speak the word. She put her hand to her throat.

"Can this be true?" she spoke again, a statement more than a question, addressed to no one in particular, but needing an answer nonetheless.

"Yes," she nodded and kept on walking. It was astonishing, and yet beyond question.

She was *powerless* to save her husband.

The truth staring her squarely in the face had to be spoken out loud, so that she herself would hear it and let it stay. The words caught in her throat making it hard to breathe. She crossed the road to where she had parked her car — ages ago it seemed — but didn't stop there and picked up her pace. At the corner, she turned and stumbled, losing her balance. Someone's hand, strong and steady caught her by the elbow just in time.

"Lady, are you okay?"

"I am okay, thank you," she whispered and looked away.

The kindness of strangers, she thought, wrapping her coat around herself and blinking the tears away. Then, she turned and hurried back to her car.

The lights came on, washing the street in the glow of a winter evening. Clutching the key in her hand, she let herself into the car and locked the door.

She leaned back on her seat and closed her eyes. "So this is it," she whispered and touched her stomach, then let her hand drop on her lap. She reached to roll down the window, but stopped. It felt safer to just stay like that, hidden away in the dark car with the windows closed.

Memories came, pulling her back in time into the years long gone.

Her son's terrified face, smeared with snot and tears, floated up from the past, stabbing at her heart once again. No more than six years old, clutching at the handrail, refusing to go to bed. "Is Daddy okay, Mommy? Is he okay? Why did he fall down? Is he okay?" Grabbing the child in her arms, carrying him to bed and staying in his bedroom that night with the door locked, on the hard fold out sofa and just a thin throw to cover herself with... How many nights had she slept there? After that first one? She started keeping an extra blanket in her son's closet just in case. That's how she came upon a bottle of vodka in the back of the top shelf one night. Hidden away where her son couldn't reach it.

How many more bottles, all hidden in strange places, did she stumble upon over the years? Endless bottles of vodka. Each one poured out into the kitchen sink with delicious vengeance... but to what end?

She found two bottles stashed in the far corner of the down-stairs storage, and it led to an ugly scene. Didn't he have anything sacred? Hiding his booze behind her old wedding dress?! Next day he brought her a bunch of red carnations, something he gave her every Christmas. "Christmas came early this year," he said and kissed her on the lips. She touched the flowers to her chest. She always forgave him so easily. She was in the kitchen at that time, baking chicken, chopping onions and carrots. Was it the onions or the carnations in which she buried her face that had made her cry?

She turned away quickly, reaching for the kitchen towel. Her parents were in town and were coming over that night. She had been cooking all evening. Cooking and praying silently for the dinner to go well and for her husband to not get drunk. But he did. And they fought after everyone left, alone at the kitchen sink amid his drunken slur and her tears.

The memories kept shifting, some lingering, others leaving fast. It seemed that her thinking had stopped at some point, and she was floating somewhere in the nothingness, in the nowhere of space, unaware of where she was. Time stopped as well. As for her senses, they were a whirlwind of moving pictures with wave upon wave of feelings so powerful and shattering she was lost to everything else. Then—with a startling shudder—she was back. Nowhere and then now here. Returning from the weightlessness and back into her body, like waking up from a deep sleep.

She rubbed her eyes and sat up. Then she rolled down the car window. The evening air was soft and pleasant to her face. It relaxed her, and she leaned back closing her eyes again.

She remembered the therapy session she had had that day. It seemed as if it had been ages ago.

She looked at her watch. In an hour, her husband would be home and expecting dinner. She adjusted her seat and started the car.

"I will tell him tonight," she thought. "Tonight at dinner."

She noticed how calm she was, how collected.

"I am detached," she thought and smiled. "Just like Brian has been telling me for months."

She put her hand to her cheek, touching her skin lightly.

"How will I be on my own?" the thought came. "I will have to learn," she said out loud and began to drive home. She pulled into her garage ten minutes later.

When was it she had made her decision? When did it become crystal clear to her that she was leaving her husband? Looking back later she would never be able to pin point it exactly. Was it the moment she left her therapy session? The moment the stranger asked if she needed help? Saying the words out loud? Sitting alone in her car?

She remembered having been almost unconscious, and yet she wasn't at the same time... and then *she just knew.* She wasn't fighting any more. She wasn't frightened either. She was simply leaving.

*   *   *

AT HOME, SHE watched him pour down his vodka, put on his glasses, and reach for the evening paper. Just like she'd seen him do thousands of times, on thousands of other evenings. She got up to make a fresh pot of coffee, and put the dirty plates in the sink.

"Smells good," her husband muttered turning the page.

She poured the coffee into two mugs, placed one in front of him and watched him sip the hot liquid in big thirsty gulps. Absorbed in his paper, he loosened his tie and unbuttoned the top of his shirt. She picked up her coffee and sat down at the table again.

How aged he looked. Dark yellow circles under his eyes surrounded in heavy bags of soft flesh. His hair — almost all grey, thinning at the temples, exposing the pink shiny skin.

She hadn't noticed any of this before. To her he had always been the most handsome man ever.

The love of her life.

She swallowed the coffee, burning her tongue, and put the cup down quickly. Then she moved it away and leaning on her elbows looked at her husband again.

"I love you," she said. He looked up. It was her voice. Something different in the way she said "I love you." Without the usual "but..." or "if only..." that had always seemed to be there in the past.

He cleared his throat, tried to say something, but couldn't. He put down his paper, and it slid onto the floor with a rustle. He let it stay.

Slumping in his chair, he was suddenly tired. Too tired, perhaps.

He looked at his wife again and read what was coming before she could say another word.

"I will be leaving you," she said quietly. "I just can't be around your drinking, that's all. I won't leave tomorrow. I have nowhere to go. But I will take care of things, and as soon as I am ready, I will be gone."

He must have forgotten how to speak. His lips moved, yet no sound came out. He folded his napkin, got up, then sat down again and buried his head in his arms. He sobbed silently, hoarsely, his big body shaking uncontrollably, as she stroked his hair and held him, tears running down her cheeks, tears she brushed away as she held him tighter.

They didn't speak again that night. There was nothing left to say. But the following evening he came home later than usual.

"I went to AA," he told her and looked at his feet. "I think I will have to go every night."

This happened many years ago, and it still is one of my favorite stories. It has a happy ending.

You guessed it. She did not leave after all. She didn't have to, because her husband never had another drink.

* * *

HOW DID IT happen? Why then? What made that evening, that dinner conversation so different from all the other ones?

It is obvious, isn't it? As you are reading this, imagining them together, hearing her speak. It's obvious that the conversation they had at dinner was so profoundly different from all the hundreds of other ones they had had over the years. All on the same subject, all leading nowhere.

It was different this time because *she* was different.

All those many years, her entire energy, the entire focus of her attention had been directed towards trying to change her husband. All the years spent arguing, blaming, fighting. Her mind running in circles, trying to find a way out, looking for what she could do to make him stop drinking.

Oh, how she hated it. How much she hated what their life had become. It was because he was weak! So selfish! So self absorbed! No one mattered to him. Just his booze! She wanted to smash all those bottles he kept bringing in and hiding from her. All that vodka, stashed everywhere. Who did he think she was?! A fool?! Of course she was! More than a fool, a spineless doormat for staying with him all these years! It was all those guys he so loved to hang out with at the bar next door. It was their fault as well. Perhaps, if they moved to a different city? She felt some relief when she could blame others. It gave her a kind of strength, a hit of power. Took her away from that dull ache in her chest she got so used to living with over the years. And so she blamed him more, and she kept on fighting... anything, just so she could go on another day. Just so she wouldn't feel the depth of her despair, the harrowing emptiness of her loneliness... never really letting herself *feel her pain*, the real horror of what was happening, the pain of seeing where he was headed, the pain that became so much a part of her she couldn't remember when last she didn't have that tightness in her chest that was making her inhale deeply from time to time just to make sure she still could.

She had learned to ignore it. It was her natural state by then. The anger at seeing his drunken stupor, the rage that squeezed her lungs every time she tried to speak to him... and then the sadness, so deep she thought she was drowning, gasping for air just to stay alive. It was scary to let yourself drop down into this bottomless, swirling pool of pain. And so she would stop. Not allow it. She had to be strong. She could not afford to fall apart like that. What would happen if she is was no longer the rock of Gibraltar, the pillar of strength that held her family together? What would happen then?

Her loneliness was overwhelming. But she could persevere, she told herself. She could hold it together. Hold it in tightly. She was in control. Not the one to give up. She would continue to "work on him" until he gets it. Until their life returned. She had a mission. She was saving his life. She didn't have time for herself. How could she just take time to be alone and simply let herself feel her despair like her shrink was suggesting? She wasn't frivolous. She wasn't weak. She had a real cause, and that cause defined her very existence. *If I let myself feel all that's inside me, I'll lose it*, she thought. *I need to be strong. I can't fall apart.*

All the while falling apart more and more.

And then one day with Brian, it was as if the blinders she had placed over her eyes years ago and had fought tooth and nail to keep in place had been suddenly — inexplicably and forcefully — pulled off. There was nothing obscuring her sight, nothing to hold back the truth. In a flash she saw it all. How pointless it was. Like hitting her head on a brick wall. It stopped her breath for a second. She felt as if she was falling down into the abyss with no safety mat to catch her as she hit the bottom. Her body went into a spasm and she had to clutch at her stomach. She didn't think she could get up, walk to the door, say good bye, make it home.

A powerful shift in the entire perception of her life was shattering everything she had believed to be true, breaking the last of her resistance, leaving her *powerless*, naked, exposed. This shift left her no room for maneuvering, were she to try once again to bring the illusion back. It left no wiggle room for explanations, excuses and delays. What she saw, she saw in bright Technicolor. Vivid and clear as day.

Her husband was an alcoholic who wanted to keep on drinking, and there was nothing, absolutely nothing she could do to change this fact.

Everything in her life looked different suddenly. The way she saw herself, the way she saw her husband and their continuous, never ending battle of wills, the way she had been experiencing their relationship and her role in it. She couldn't save him from his addiction. She couldn't enter his world and pull him out by the strength of her love. She had a will of steel...and yet it meant nothing, as far as his drinking was concerned. All the years of fighting, trying so hard to make him stop...how useless it all seemed now. How futile. Doomed from the start.

Something was happening to her. Something she had no control over any more.

It came upon her like a flood, like a tidal wave so huge it was useless to try to fight it. She lost her balance falling head first into the swirling darkness, losing the last of her control, letting go finally, perhaps for the first time in her life.

She was not prepared for this, and so had no way of handling it. It was bubbling up to the surface from such depths, she was lost to everything else. The things she did that she could never undo... the loneliness so abysmal she felt like dying. And then the hurt, alternating with anger rising from deep inside her belly, from her heart so filled with sorrow, so filled with loss. In her throat, where for such a long time she had had a constriction that would make her voice hoarse...she felt it releasing, opening up.

She didn't care about anything any more. What did it matter? She was losing it all. Just like she had lost her husband to drink. If this was what it felt like to die, it was okay.

When it was over and she opened her eyes, she realized she had no knowledge of how she got to her car from the therapist's office, nor how long she had spent sitting there with the door locked. She noticed the softness in her body, the way her hands were resting lightly on either side of the wheel. She wasn't gripping it tightly, like she used to in the past.

A knowing of what she was going to do filled her, making her straighten her back, adjust the seat of her car. She leaned forward slightly as if trying to see her new future, then took a deep breath and started the engine.

Her husband's face floated before her eyes.

"I love you," she said out loud and kept on driving. She was at peace with her decision. *She was setting both of them free.*

Transcendence

"Illumination," said Martin Buber, "*cannot be achieved in any other place than in the abyss of 'I with me.' This in its realest sense is not even a monologue, much less a real conversation. All speech is exhausted here. All that is left is a muted shudder of self being.*"

You lie awake staring into nothing as the realization of your defeat slowly sinks in.

You have failed to change the one you love. Lost the battle the two of you have been locked in for so long. You *accept* it now. This is the end of the road. You can go no further. There is nothing else, it seems, to hold on to, to grab, to pull yourself up. Your thinking stops. And with it — time. There is just you and the night, and the pain in your gut. Raw and alive, like you've never felt it before.

And then — there is nothing.

You must have fallen asleep. For it is morning now, there is light outside the window. You open you eyes, you blink, you remember.

"He can have it his way," you hear yourself thinking. But there is no usual tension in your chest as this comes to you. Instead it feels like you are *setting him free*. Letting him just be for the first time ever. "He can have it his way," you think again. Or maybe not think it — just know it. You are empty now. Empty in a way you've never been before. Empty, but free as well. The weight that was inside you all this time, his weight that you were going to triumph over — it's gone now. With nothing to replace it. Except maybe — this *peace*.

"Why was I holding on to this fight for so long?" you wonder in a detached sort of way. It was wrong. It feels now like *a violation*. The thought comes and goes. A thought that belongs in a different time. In a different life. You get up. You take a few steps. Your new life has begun.

The moment of surrender is a transcendent state.

It is a state in which you die to your old way of being, so that a new you can be born.

Many have tried to describe it, always finding themselves at a loss for words. There are no words for it. Our language is not equipped to define the unfathomable.

People talk about becoming unconscious, or falling somewhere they knew not where, or seeing the bright white light filling their space, or losing all sense of time... but these words always fail to describe the actual experience. What remains is the knowing: they have been changed.

Irreversibly, irrevocably changed. Transformed forever.

You cannot get there by *trying* to let go.

"Then what can I *do?*" people ask.

Nothing.

This *is not* something that can be *done.*

Transcendence happens with true surrender, not an attempt at it. The only way to get there is *to fully accept your pain.*

Accept your circumstances and just let them be what they are.

For most — this is the most difficult and the most frightening thing of all.

With this acceptance, comes both the pain and — eventually — the *freedom* from this *pain.* When we accept, it is often the first time we actually *feel* the depth of our despair.

At this level of pain there is no more blame, no more denial, no more fighting. Your sorrow engulfs you as you drop deep down, and then deeper still.

When *we accept our pain* fully, accept it without fighting it, without explaining it, without apologizing for it or trying to make it better... when we simply *face the truth* no matter how unbearable, how ugly, how humiliating... and *feel* the despair, the hopelessness, the sorrow... the fact that we truly *are powerless* to change the situation... when the frantic, desperate thinking stops running in circles trying to find a way out... because it can't, and we have finally accepted it ...

The powerlessness we are left with is perhaps the most powerful state of all.

In this state of total surrender, *not submission, not giving in,* but really just *letting go* — something happens to us. It is as if a hand reaches down wiping the sweat off our brow, drying our tears, surrounding us with peace.

Split open, all defenses gone, we can finally be reached and can be lifted into The Possible. We've "let go and let God."

How long does this state of surrender last? No one can tell. It could seem to last forever.

Then suddenly, out of nowhere — this lightness, this neutral place. And then — *clarity.*

When did you make your choice, you might wonder? Yet it feels as if it has been there all along. It just bubbled up to the surface from somewhere inside of you. And it is the *only* choice. There can be no other.

A choice that prior to that instant was impossible. No matter how appealing, no matter how logical, no matter how obvious to other people. To you — an impossible choice to make. That's how it had been for so long. That's how it had been for eternity, for all the time you struggled and fought hard against it. Now suddenly — *the only thing possible.* Clear as day. All obstacles removed. Perhaps the most difficult thing in your life. Yet made easier by the knowing — this is what you will do. You are not sure how, but you know one thing: you *will* find the strength. You will find the way. You don't know how you know it. You just do.

This is when an alcoholic knows he will never have another drink. This is when the wife of an abusive husband knows she is going to leave. This is when a mother calmly asks an adult child to get his own place, and he does. Without argument.

Suddenly, you are doing something that until that moment you could never muster the strength to do. Leave that dead end relationship, quit the job you have hated for so long and step into the unknown of your dream. Whatever it is you could not do before. You are doing it. And you are doing it now.

Letting Go of Control

It seems so simple, so obvious, doesn't it? Why is it then so hard for most of us to understand and to follow?

So afraid are we to feel our pain, so afraid of how much it will hurt to actually experience it, that we go to any extent possible just so we can avoid it.

And then there are the hidden agendas, the undercurrents that drive us. We don't just want to change that particular person. We want to get vindication as well. We are not ready to just let them off the hook so easily. Sometimes it is the vindication for all the time we've suffered at their hand. Sometimes we just want recognition. See, I told you, didn't I? We want them to see how wrong they were, while we were the ones who knew it all along.

Behind most of these personal agendas is one thing and one thing only—*control*. We want control.

She wants him to change! He will be damned if he does!

Insidious and impenetrable, control keeps both people locked in the prison of their own creation, made even more seductive by their need *to be right*.

If we are right, we are in control. In fact we thrive on knowing what's best for other people. We think we know it better than they do, know it better than anyone else. We know it better than their Souls and even better than God.

But do we?

Because as long as we are in control, insisting that *we know what's best*, we *block off* all other *possible* outcomes. The *endless possibilities* that lie beyond our control, beyond what *we* can imagine. The outcomes that exist in the realm of The Possible, where miracles are waiting to happen to us if we would just get out of the way.

Oh, the many voices in our heads telling us how someone else should be. I know these voices well. Mine used to be very loud, and I listened to them for years and then wondered how come happiness continued to be elusive. How come relationships remained difficult.

There were many wake up calls that I had. Some of them loud, and a few that I eventually heard.

When I look at photographs from those earlier years, the photos in which I'd always believed I looked so good, I am shocked by the hardness in my face, by the stubborn angle of my chin with its tightly clenched, controlled jaw.

My face in those photographs is that of a woman trying so hard to hold it together. To make it look like she was okay. But she does not fool me anymore. I can see her pain in the way her hands are folded across her chest. In the way she smiles with her lips closed, in her eyes that don't brighten even when she tries to smile.

This is my past. It is someone I no longer am. I love her and I thank her for her perseverance. She was there for me until I found my way. I bless her and I let her go.

As I began to heal, I was told a number of times how different I was beginning to look. "What happened to you?" I was asked many times. "I took the weight off," I would answer.

And though people would immediately look at my body, to check for weight loss, this was not the weight I was referring to. The weight I was gradually taking off was the weight of the pain I had been carrying and the weight of my control.

A Mother's Story

To break the circle, you can interrupt it at any point.
— LAZARIS

The Shock

The telephone rang at four in the afternoon, just as Maya was getting done with her work.

She picked up the phone expecting it to be her boyfriend Daniel.

"Mom?" Her son's voice, low and hoarse, reached her and she sat down, pressing the phone into her ear.

"What's wrong?" She knew instantly. Heard it before he could finish his sentence.

But he didn't continue. He seemed to be waiting.

She leaned forward, elbows on the desk, gripping the phone tightly. Was there a way for her not to hear it? It was in his voice. She touched her stomach.

"What is it? Tell me."

"Mom..."Alan spoke again. "Please...don't be mad." He was crying now. Twenty years old and crying on the phone.

"What happened?! You are scaring me to death."

"I am in a Nevada jail, Mom. You need to bail me out, please. It is five thousand dollars."

She answered, measuring her words, biting on her lower lip, "Why are you in jail, Alan? What did you do?"

"Nothing, Mom. I didn't do anything. We were celebrating Dustin's twenty-first birthday. We were in Lake Tahoe staying at the casino at the hotel. We had marijuana with us. And when we checked out we forgot about it and left it in the room. Well, I went back to pick it up later, but the police were already there and I got arrested. The hotel overlaps the borders of California and Nevada. Our room was on the Nevada side. They took me to jail in Nevada, and the bail is five thousand dollars." He stopped, waiting for Maya to say something.

"Mom? Can you hear me, Mom?"

"I can hear you," she said. She leaned back crossing her legs.

"Why are you not saying anything?"

"Perhaps, you should stay in jail this time."

"Mom, please don't . . . please." He was sobbing now. "You have no idea what it is like here. This is Nevada. It is a felony here. Please, we'll talk about it when I am out. I promise you I will change."

"How will you get home?"

"Dustin is here. He would have posted the bail for me, but he only has forty-six hundred on his account. It's not enough . . . and I'd rather he didn't have to do it. . . . He is waiting for me. As soon as you send the money by Western Union he will drive me home."

At least he had a good friend. Dustin. Maya hadn't met him but had heard the name many times.

She was touched.

"Give me his cell phone number and put an officer on the phone," she said.

"You will do it then? Thank you, thank you, Mom, I promise."

"Okay," she said. "We'll talk when you are back."

How many more times??!!

She was in her car on the way to the post office to wire the money. How many more times until something really serious...?

How much longer will I be rescuing him? Saving him from the crazy things he gets himself into? Crazy!? They are not just crazy! Dangerous! Did he say felony? He did say felony. I must call his lawyer.

Yes, Alan was twenty years old and he already had a lawyer. In fact, he had had his own lawyer since he was fifteen years old.

He was not a "delinquent" child. Somehow, Alan's teachers at school had liked to make that distinction, though Maya had never been sure what exactly that word meant. He was a difficult child, a problem child, always walking close to the edge, always testing the boundaries, always checking how far he could go in breaking rules, how much he could get away with.

And he didn't get away with much. He seemed to have a gift for getting caught. Other kids would do the same things and nothing would happen. No one would ever know. But not in Alan's case. Besides, he was always the first to admit what he had done. And he would never, ever point to anyone else who was involved in the same prank.

At the interview with the Head of Admissions of an elite private high school, he had mentioned as he was about to leave the office, "By the way, I am a discipline problem." When he told Maya about it, she was sure he would never get into the school. But the man was touched by Alan's honesty, so he was accepted.

There was an innocence about her son. A lack of cunning, and it never changed. It was a part of him not everyone knew. But Maya did. At times she wished he would not be this vulnerable with others, that he would learn to protect himself better. But deep inside her heart — she knew this was who her son really was. Good, loving, caring and sensitive. Not the "I can do whatever I want" persona he chose to show to the rest of the world.

It was hard to concentrate while filling out the paperwork for the Western Union. She finally managed to complete the forms. She sent the five thousand, grateful that she had the funds and that she could do it so easily, and went back to her car.

She started to drive, but had to pull over by the curb side. Her heart was beating too fast, and she put her hand to it and kept it there, covering her chest as if trying to calm it down. She made herself pause and just stay in the car for a few minutes. It was all too fast, the events of this evening, with her only son locked up somewhere in Nevada like a criminal. *What am I going to do?* she thought. *What am I going to do about him?!*

And when is it going to stop?!! She unbuttoned her coat, pulling it off her shoulders completely.

She was hot. Too hot even in her thin sleeveless tee shirt. And too restless. She started the car again, now anxious to be back home. How long had she been angry? For how many years? There must have been a time in the past when she could think about Alan and not get upset within minutes. She wanted to remember it now, to help her calm down, but instead scene after scene of endless memories of times when she had had to pull him out of trouble were playing in her mind's eye, culminating in tonight's call from a Nevada jail.

She got used to constant calls from his elementary and middle school, but it started for real in his freshman year of high school. He had been on probation several times, and before the school year was over, Alan was placed into a special program away from school and allowed to return in September. He had to finish the freshman academic courses in a summer school.

But before the sophomore year ended, he was expelled. They didn't want him at that private school any more. "Disruptive behavior. We can't have him in class," they said. Alan had a reputation by then. "A class clown, a prankster, a trouble maker." Maya used to dread the calls from school. They were inevitably about something that Alan did. One more thing to tell his parents about.

It often seemed to Maya that ever since her son had been born, he was mysteriously governed by one particular agenda. This agenda was to always resist every possible rule and every possible authority. He had been this way since he was a tiny infant, and they got used to that. He was the only child. They didn't know anything else.

Friends began early on to ask Maya and Rick to leave their child with the baby sitter when coming to their parties even if it was on a Sunday afternoon and other children were present. Alan was always a disruption, always demanding extra attention, always up to one mischief or another. Climbing onto roofs, hanging off a tree, and then jumping down and scaring everyone. Climbing up the library ladder to pull up books from top shelves, getting too close to the burning stove. Maya would be exhausted just watching her son, making sure he didn't hurt himself or break anything at their friends' houses.

He was a kid who thought it was funny to spray water onto the newly painted ceiling at the dentist's office while waiting in the dental chair. He ruined the fresh paint job, and his parents had to pay for the repair.

He must have been no older than thirteen or fourteen when the police arrested him on Halloween together with his friends for spray painting the garage door of a girl from school.

He was fifteen when he was arrested at Disneyland for trying to get in without a ticket. He had a ticket in his pocket, but it was more fun to try to sneak in without it. His parents found out when notified of the trial in Southern California.

Over time, what had begun as innocent pranks turned into something else, something threatening and dangerous. It was as if Alan was on a course from which he could not escape.

Now it ran his life. "I am the one who gets in trouble" had become his identity, functioning seemingly on its own.

At sixteen he was arrested again one sunny Sunday afternoon

while sitting on the grass waiting for a bus and examining a toy BB gun he had just bought at the flea market. Drivers of the passing cars saw a teenager with a rifle in his hands and called the police. He was handcuffed and brought into the station. They kept him handcuffed until his parents picked him up.

He was arrested once more while driving with his friends at night in a tough city neighborhood. It was past curfew, and the police spotted teenagers in the car and stopped them. His parents were convinced he was asleep in his bed, but he had climbed out the window and gone off to join his friends.

In his freshman year of college, he was arrested and taken to jail when he and his friend, having parked their car in the teacher's spot at the college parking lot, were smoking marijuana in broad day light. Maya bailed him out that time with a thousand dollars. She and her husband paid for the lawyer.

Parked in the teacher's spot in broad daylight? He must have been screaming to be stopped. Except no one knew how to do it.

At seventeen, he crashed his car but was miraculously unharmed. They learned about it when the phone call woke them up at six in the morning. Their son was okay but he was at the hospital. He had fallen asleep at the wheel. The car was totaled. He was supposed to be staying over at his friend's but he had decided to drive home and sleep in his own bed instead.

Pale and shaken, they brought him home as they let it sink in. They could have lost him. He could have been dead.

This was the picture. And it was a grim one.

Are you thinking perhaps, that Alan grew up in a horrible family, had a nightmarish childhood, and thus was angry, rebellious, fighting everyone and everything like so many teenagers do, their hormones raging, making everything worse?

The answer is — no. But no with an explanation.

His was a "normal" family. If a thing like that even exists. While his parents had their own difficulties and dysfunction and were by no means perfect parents, they were good people, and they loved their son. Perhaps they loved him too much.

If anything, they had failed to provide Alan strong and healthy boundaries, something he must have needed. His parents were not good at tough love. They had made their son the most important person — more important than they were to each other, more important than each of them was to him or herself, more important than their marriage.

It is not easy for any child to be growing up in our modern world. And certainly the family dynamics had its negative influence on Alan, but his choices were his own. He never doubted his parents love for him. He always knew how much he mattered. And while he loved them both intensely and hated causing them pain, he was in his own trajectory, driven by forces they could not understand.

*   *   *

THEY STARTED LOOKING for help early on. When he was nine years old, there had been a succession of therapists, all giving up in frustration. There were behavioral pediatricians, private schools with stronger supervision, endless talks between parents and son, alternating punishment, and more talks. *But they were failing at changing his behavior.* Alan continued to resist everything, setting himself up for more and more trouble.

When was he going to stop? Where was it all going? These were the questions without answers.

The parents fought over how best to raise their son. They blamed each other. They blamed themselves adding even more stress to their marriage which was already falling apart.

"If things don't change between us, I will leave in two years," Maya had said to her husband when Alan was sixteen. They got worse, and she moved out when he was eighteen.

She tried so hard to understand her son.

"Why?" she would ask Alan when he was a little boy. "Why?" she would ask him when he was older, a teenager, a young adult. "Why are you doing all this? Tell me why."

But he couldn't tell. "I don't know," was all he would say. He looked as confused as she was. They would hug, they would cry, she would ask, he would promise — nothing would change.

What have I done so wrong? What are we both doing wrong? She used to cry by herself, her mind racing, trying to find the answer. What's making him do it? How can I help my son?

It was her mantra for many years: *How can I help my son?*

She would talk to him again, asking the same questions, explaining, pleading, threatening. She would get furious, lose her temper, scare him with the intensity of her anger. She would punish him, ground him for days, then get upset with herself for being so harsh. She'd let it all go, one more time, and forgive him. They would hug, relieved it was over, have a great time with each other . . . and soon be back at it again.

He would be sent home for two days of probation for yet another prank. *Why should I punish him more?* she'd think. *The school has already punished him enough.*

Then Rick, his father, would come home from work and ground his son anyway, and Maya would fight with him behind the closed doors of their bedroom or agree with him depending on the occasion.

It was a never-ending roller coaster of crying and laughing, of punishing and forgiving, of being at once too close and too distant, loving and sweet, then frustrated and angry again.

His grades, previously quite high, began to be a problem in his sophomore year when he was fifteen years old. He didn't seem to care any more. Alan's therapist at the time suggested testing him for drugs, but he tested negative. He tested negative every six months, every time he was tested. Why then this sudden lack of motivation? It was something no one could answer. They hired a private tutor, and he would come to the house every week night just to make sure Alan did his homework. But Alan would lean back in his chair, put his feet on the desk and pretend to be falling asleep. The tutor resigned, and they hired a new one. They changed the therapist, hired a different one again.

Now Alan was twenty years old and Maya had just bailed him out of a Nevada jail.

She had called his lawyer before leaving for the post office. Overwhelmingly angry at her son, she had considered letting him stay in jail overnight, but the lawyer had been adamant. "You don't want your son in jail in Nevada on charges of felony, Maya, believe me."

The next day Alan and his parents learned that the minimum sentence for possession of marijuana in Nevada was six months. Alan stood to be sentenced to spend six months to three years in prison with six months being the best case scenario. There was going to be a trial, and the length of the sentence would be up to the judge. Nevada code of law had no other options for this type of crime and no loop holes either. No hope for community service to replace prison time. It would have been a different case, had this happened in California where they lived. In California it would have been a misdemeanor. But in Nevada it was felony.

Alan had finally done it. He would be very lucky if he were to get six months only in Nevada prison. "Good thing his previous record of misdemeanors was expunged when he turned eighteen," his lawyer said. "Had this not been the case, we would be looking at a different sentence this time."

Prison, not jail.

She couldn't think straight. "What do you mean 'prison'?" The lawyer explained the difference. He spoke for a while longer, but she could not follow, could no longer understand what he was saying. Everything was blurred now. The changes were happening too fast. The demand on her for action, for some kind of decision, was too urgent, too strong, too much. All of it—it was all too much. And she was paralyzed. She simply could not move.

The entire day prior to Alan's call receded into a distant, far away past. It seemed ages ago when she was happy, when her life was working, when everything was okay. To think that she could have been upset about the small things that used to upset her!

How different everything was now. Now her son was going to prison. This much looked like a certainty. Her gentle, handsome boy was going to be locked up with the criminals, and the only question seemed to be for how long?

She hung up the phone.

It could not be. It just could not.

She grabbed a coat from the coat closet, threw it on and walked out of the house. She lived at the end of the street on a steep hill, where the view of the city below was the most astounding. Tall buildings outlined against the sky, surrounded by the deep blue of the San Francisco Bay. She liked to just pause there, take in the beauty, the magnificence of it all. It filled her with gratitude, made her smile, brought her a sense of peace. No one owns this view, she would think. It belongs to no one and everyone. And so it is always mine as well.

Not tonight. Wrapping her coat around her body, she lowered her head against the wind walking past her favorite place without pausing. *Become invisible,* she told herself, hoping not to run into anyone she knew. She began to walk fast, crossing the street to the park around the corner. To be alone, to gather her thoughts together and think. That's what was most important right now. Slow everything down. Clear her head.

There must be a way out of this. There always is. What does the lawyer know?! She and Rick can hire a new one. Alan—a criminal!

They are making him a criminal! That's not even ridiculous! That's crazy. Yes. Crazy. And stupid! Stupid, stupid, stupid! How stupid can he be?!!! Returning to the room to claim his stupid drugs!

She would have laughed, had it not been the reality. Had it not had to do with her son.

The lawyer's words from the morning conversation were like a nightmare she could not shake off. "Look, Maya. They have the evidence in their hands. They have a brown paper bag full of grass. They can test it and see what it is, and we know what it is already, don't we? They also have Alan returning to the room after checking out of the hotel to claim his paper bag with what he called his 'medicine.' He admitted in front of the housekeeping and police that the paper bag and its contents were his. Your son never denies anything. You should know this by now. He is always the first to turn himself in. He believes if he tells the truth, they will treat him better, be more lenient. Not this time. There is no way around this one, Maya. I am sorry. I wish there was. I already spoke to the judge, and this is going to trial. It doesn't look good at all. They are really getting down on this kind of thing in Nevada."

It was like a bad dream that kept getting worse by the second.

She wasn't the kind to just accept things without fighting though it looked like there wasn't anything her fighting would achieve this time.

And who would she fight? The Nevada code of law? Some unknown judge? Could she stage a break in and destroy the evidence they have against her son? Bribe the witnesses? Fight for her son Alan one more time? She clenched her fists just thinking about it. Replace Jack Walsh, the lawyer? But he was the very best.

It started to rain and she turned to walk back home. In her kitchen, she boiled water and made herself a strong cup of tea. But she was restless. *I can't sit at home, I can't think straight and I can't do anything to change things*, she thought. *And I can't accept this.*

I must do something. She leaned back on the sofa and closed her eyes. She wanted to cry, but couldn't. She put the tea down unable to drink.

The telephone rang and she answered. She couldn't afford not to. It was Rick, her ex husband and Alan's father. But they couldn't help each other. It was too much this time, and they were both lost.

Rick's voice was low. She could barely make out the words. She knew that voice well. It was telling her what she already knew. They had a real problem. Different from what they were used to in the past.

This one was beyond anything they could control.

This one was incomprehensible.

"I feel like such a failure," Rick said.

"I do, too," said Maya. "I just want to shake him. Squeeze him and just shake him up! So stupid! So idiotic!"

"It's too late for that. We've done all the shaking we could."

Rick stopped and she thought he was crying. "Sad, isn't it?"

"Yes," she whispered. "Yes."

"I don't know what to do," she said.

"There isn't much we can do. Jack is working on it. Pulling all the strings he can. He knows the people in Nevada. He spoke to the judge already. If we are lucky, Alan will get the minimum. Then it will be six months."

It wasn't like Rick to give up either. They were so used to pulling their son by the ears out of all his messes.

She couldn't listen any more. She wished he hadn't called her. "We'll talk later," she said and hung up.

She cried then. First silently, then out loud. Wordless despair, caught in her throat, trying to escape. Her voice, shrill and raspy, cutting through the empty living room, breaking the silence of the house. Hitting the floor with her fists. No!!! No! No! Like an animal wounded. In agony. Caught in a trap.

She didn't want to talk to her son. Couldn't look at his lost face. And what would he say to her? One more time—I don't know why I do it? One more time—I am sorry? "My heart is breaking," she whispered. She knew what heartache felt like. It was physical, the pain, the heavy throbbing inside the chest. It started earlier in the day and was getting unbearable. She touched her hand to her heart.

He is so good looking, she thought, Alan's face in front of her eyes. So young and so innocent in many ways. In spite of all the constant troubles. Always admitting to what he did, expecting to be treated fairly. Not a cunning bone in his body. What would happen to him in prison?

But it was getting worse.

Alan's attorney, Jack Walsh, flew to Nevada the following day and called with more bad news. There were Ecstasy pills in the brown paper bag as well as marijuana, Alan had told him. The contents of the bag were being checked at the lab and soon the prosecution would have the results. With this new evidence, there was little hope for just a six months sentence.

Maya called her therapist. "Would you see Alan and me together?" she asked. "He needs help as much as I do right now."

"I don't want to see Alan," the therapist said. "But I do want to talk to you. You alone. I can see you this afternoon."

Hoping against hope, she arrived at the therapist's office. Perhaps she was missing something. She might yet be able to help Alan were she to have more clarity.

"How many times have you rescued your son?" the therapist asked when she sat down. But he already knew the answer. "What I am going to tell you, Maya, may sound harsh," he began, "but please listen. Here you are, making yourself crazy, trying to save Alan one more time. And this time it is serious. This time he may be going to prison. Say, you succeed. Pull him out again. Find a magic trick and do it. What then? We are talking six months to three years now. What makes you think he would not do something worse again? What is it going to be next time? Haven't you noticed he's raising the ante? It is not school pranks any more.

And you can't stop him. No one can. And yet he knows — no matter what he does, his mother will come and get him out of it. It is a dance you two have. An unhealthy dance. And now — a dangerous dance. As long as you are there, he doesn't need to grow up. He doesn't have to become responsible for his life. And why should he? His mother will always take care of things, won't she? He is how old now? Twenty? Not even eighteen anymore. You've done the mothering, Maya. However good or bad — it's done. And you've done a pretty good job overall, damn it! And now — it's up to him. It is his only chance.

"Step off the dance floor, and let him be. You can't change his behavior. You can't change him. And he — he never felt he needed to. Maybe this is what he needs right now. To actually go to prison. So he can wake up. Become an adult. God knows, nothing else has worked so far. It is his life and his lessons."

The therapist paused, but Maya was silent.

"Does he have any money to pay for the attorney?" he asked.

"He has some. He has been saving all the money he got from everyone in our big family for each birthday. They have all given him money instead of gifts for years. I don't remember who started the tradition. His Grandmother, I think."

"Well, entertain the idea of not even paying for his attorney. Let him use his own money. I am not telling you not to do it, but just think about it. Don't start punishing him suddenly, but consider separating from the process all together. I am positive that *unless you let go, if you were to save him one more time, there will be something worse in the future.* Better now. There are consequences to actions, and he hasn't learned that yet."

It was the longest drive in Maya's life. Fifteen minutes by car from the therapist's office to her front door. Fifteen minutes that lasted a life time.

The freeway traffic outside her windows was moving in slow motion. Cars and trucks gliding by, a surrealist movie on each side of the glass. And in the center of it all—Maya. At the wheel, but absent, aware of traffic and yet far away.

Coming to grips with it. Her son, Alan, was going to prison. It was a fact.

The beautiful golden boy she gave birth to twenty years ago in another life, in another place. Her boy, who grew up to become a teenager and then a young man. A willful child, both loving and difficult, the child she could never quite handle, but who could always pull on her heart with one single look.

She loved him more than she knew how to describe. But for so long now her love for her son had been laced with pain. Anger at the ridiculous things he did, so stupid and dangerous, anger at his incomprehensible stubbornness, and now—drugs??!! How long has he been doing drugs? Was it serious? Or was it just "recreational"?

She had never taken any drugs in her entire life and so had no experience and no understanding. What did this new information mean on top of the fact that he was going to prison?

She was so close to her son, it hurt. But for a number of years now, ever since adolescence, he had been putting up walls between them. He became secretive, stopped letting her in. There were too many things about him she could never understand. Maybe she never would.

If she didn't stop saving him, he would continue to self-destruct.

She heard the words of her therapist. It was nothing new. He had told her she had to let go many times in the past. But she had never allowed herself to actually *hear* it. It never held any meaning. Just words, easily said by someone who had no children of his own. "Stop enabling him," he used to say. *More psycho babble,* she thought. "I am not," she'd answer.

"You are playing with fire, Maya," he said this time. "It has gone too far."

It was chilling to realize what the words meant. She knew *she had come to the end of this road*. She *had* to stop. For Alan's sake. She had to cut him off. The hardest surgery in the world. Yet it was his only chance. His father had stepped off the game board long ago. And it was never about his father anyway. It was about her. Her dance with her son. Their push/pull, their tug of war. *She had to end it. And do it for real.* She could not indulge herself by rescuing him one more time. The stakes were too high.

It seemed for a moment she couldn't breathe any more. To let him just go to prison? *Yes.* The answer formed in her mind. *Yes.* If that's what has to happen — then so be it.

"You've done the mothering, Maya." The therapist's voice echoed in her head. *Oh, Alan!* She thought again clutching at her throat.

She rolled down the window letting in both the air and the freeway noise. But it was too jarring and she closed it half way again. Her mouth was dry, and she reached for the water bottle on the seat next to her, drank some and then kept on drinking. She finished the bottle and dropped it on the floor.

Once again her son's image came before her. His eyes forlorn, filled with sadness. She swallowed hard, biting on the side of her tongue and shuddered as her mouth filled with pain. The sensation shocked her, and she sat up straight, focusing on the road ahead.

And then she made her decision.

"I am not saving you any more, Alan," she said. Said it in her head, or maybe out loud. Said it and meant it with her entire being, body and soul, mind and heart, her every feeling and every thought. The clarity was astonishing. *She was setting him free.* Free to live. Free to be. To mess up his life or to exalt in it. To soar or to fall and to do everything there was in between. "You have always fought for that, Alan," she said again. "And I have always stepped in, tried to do it for you. It is yours now. Your life. I wish with all my heart that things weren't the way they are for you right now, but you will have to deal with them without me this time. From now on — you are on your own."

It was a place she had not known or been to before. A place both dark and light. A place of clarity born of despair and resolve. There was no room in this place for doubt, confusion or questioning. They too were a luxury, belonging in the far away past. She felt suddenly alive in a way she hadn't felt since Alan's call from Nevada. All of her senses — sharp, at attention. It felt like she could see forever, so good was her eye sight, unobstructed and clear in the light of late afternoon. She straightened in her seat, focusing on the road ahead and took the next exit.

She would have fought for him till her dying days. She would have fought all his wars and all his battles, and then would fight some more.

If it was *her* life that was at stake.

But not when it was his.

In the fading light of the day, she made her decision — made it with the finality and certainty of a death row inmate whose last appeals have been exhausted. Alone in her car, with the sun setting on the distant side of Mount Tam and the freeway roaring outside her half open window, lost to the world, caught up in the wordless, messy entanglement of her feelings and thoughts, she had closed one door and opened another.

Fully aware of what it meant, she accepted the harsh reality of her situation. *There simply was no other way.* Not for her. Not as far as Alan was concerned. She was backed against the wall, forced into her choice by the course of events she could no longer control. A decision long overdue, and yet more timely than ever.

She took a deep breath, squeezed the wheel with both hands — and cut her son loose.

This is what happened next.

The Shift

Maya needed to take a bath. To be submerged, let go of everything, feel the heat of the water on her skin, feel it penetrate deep into her body smoothing out her raw, tangled nerves, rocking her into peace, transporting her to some place far away.

There would be nothing else then, if only for a brief moment. Just the water, scalding hot, high up to the tip of her chin, calming her down, restoring her, bringing her back to herself.

She always did this when she was in pain. Step into a bathtub filled with hot steamy water and just stay there, cocooned in the heat, isolating herself, forcing herself to slow down.

The magnitude of her decision had not yet sunk in, but the decision was made and like a child first learning to walk, she would take her first hesitant steps.

She filled the bathtub, dropped her clothes on the floor and stepped into the water. She was still in the bath when the telephone rang.

"Maya?" she heard Rick's voice.

"Yes, Rick."

"What are you doing right now, Maya?"

She shrugged. "What am I doing? . . . I am taking a bath. Why?"

"You are not going to believe it, Maya."

Something had happened. That much was clear. She sat up, adjusted the phone to her ear. "What happened? Tell me."

"Jack just called. He got a call from Nevada. The judge threw the case out. It is over, Maya. There is no more case against Alan."

"What???!!!"

"That's right. He just threw it out. No explanation. Jack doesn't understand. Never had anything like that happen before. Ever. No one has any idea what went on there. But — it is over. No case. Nothing."

"What about the evidence? The bag?"

"I have no idea. And neither does Jack. All he said was that the case was thrown out. Dismissed. There will be no hearing, no checking of anything, nothing. It is done, finished."

"Oh, my God."

"I don't know what happened there, Maya, but we have been very lucky. Very, very lucky. I am having a hard time believing it, but...I sure am not going to question it, right?"

Rick paused, catching his breath. "What are you thinking?" he asked. "Are you relieved?"

She would have answered but for her lips which seemed to have a mind of their own, twisting and stretching, forming into a broad, enormous, oversized smile — the biggest smile she had ever had, followed by tears of astonished gratitude.

"Relieved???!!!" She blinked the tears away.

"Are you crying, Maya?"

"I am smiling, Rick. I am smiling. Laughing and smiling."

"I don't know what happened," Rick said again, as if talking to himself.

I do, thought Maya, *I do*.

It was too big to comprehend. She wanted to dance, to embrace the whole world, let her gratitude spill into the streets of the city, overflowing it, bathing everyone in its golden glow. She closed her eyes stretching her legs under water, knowing she couldn't move.

She was still in her bath when Alan called.

"Mom?"

"...I know, I already know. Dad called me."

"I can't believe it, Mom. I just can't...I am not going to jail. I am still shaking after Dad's call. Are you crying, Mom?"

"I guess I am, Alan. I am crying and laughing at the same time."

They talked and talked. Like they hadn't talked to each other in years.

"I have been smoking pot since I was fifteen," Alan said. "I was never not stoned, Mom. I slept through most of the classes at school."

So that was the reason for his sudden lack of motivation.

"What about your urine tests?"

"Come on. You have no idea how easy it was for me to cheat on these tests. Every kid at school knew how to do it. I will tell you one day. You are not going to believe it. It was a joke, the tests Dad had me do. But I am stopping it, Mom. I am stopping everything. I won't touch it anymore."

"You won't?"

"That's right. Please, believe me. Why would I be telling you otherwise?"

"Okay," she said. "Okay, honey. That's really great," wiping the tears, hanging up the phone, closing her eyes and slipping deeper into the warmth of the tub to lie there still, slowing down her heart, shutting everything away.

It was a miracle. A miracle of her own design. Better yet — it was a miracle beyond her design and beyond her imagination. No explanation was ever given to make logical sense of the events, but the entire reality of her son's looming trial followed by the inevitable prison time had been obliterated, never to be heard about again. It was as though everything that had taken place — starting with Alan's call from a Nevada jail and ending with Rick's telephone call of good news — had never happened.

It was the very last time Alan had any altercations with the law.

He stepped out of the life of a trouble maker like stepping out of an old worn out suit he had no use for anymore, and at the time of this writing is a successful entrepreneur living a full life in New York City.

Breaking the Psychic Contract

Why then was there this sudden and unexpected reversal? What caused the seemingly inexplicable change?

Have you ever paused to consider how strongly we are connected to the people in our lives? *They are in our energy field all the time, just like we are in theirs.* Whether we love them or hate them, as long as we have intense feelings about them, the connection is always powerfully present. It never sleeps. It never takes a break. When something happens to that person, we are often aware of it instantly. And though it is mostly unconscious, the transmission is received. We know something happened because we feel it. A premonition, often confirmed when the news arrives.

How greatly do we underestimate the power of our communication with each other that has nothing to do with the words we say. Yet it is on this level, that we are heard most clearly and most precisely. The wordless communications, instant and concise, get to the one we are close to faster than the time it takes to formulate the thought in our minds. Whatever it is that we feel at a given moment—if it is felt intensely—reaches the ones we love at that very moment, sending them a message of what's happening with us. Perhaps the best example of this are stories of mothers, miles away from their sons or daughters, knowing instantly that something horrible has just happened to their child.

In the same fashion, when one of us changes in a profound, fundamental way, the other one knows it right away. The energy field in which our relationship exists is suddenly different. The old patterns are dropped, and new ones come into being.

In the story I have just told, the relationship between Maya and Alan included the energies of Maya's frustration, anger and disappointment, which had to be supported by Alan's continuous behavioral problems. When Maya withdrew her need to be her son's constant savior, the existing energy field between them collapsed, reorganizing itself instantly into a different field, the one that did not include those components. They now had a new, very different relationship, and in it the constant problems Alan used to have simply did not exist.

We do not need to hit rock bottom, as Maya did, to finally accept the truth. But most of us do. We fight the facts till the very last minute. Till we reach the limit of our pain and wake up. Till the voice inside our head says *Enough.*

Sometimes all that is needed is being *willing to do what it takes.* If the willingness is real, then the lesson is learned, and you don't need to actually live through the experience.

Why then had she waited that long? Until it was almost too late, and her son was one step away from prison?

We are ready when we are ready and not a moment before.

The process of change and our readiness for it is one of life's great mysteries. The information, the hints, the clues, the whispers and even the shouts are always there for us to hear and see, presented with continuous regularity, and yet...we look the other way...we block our ears and shut our eyes, fight against the obvious, refuse, deny, delay...until it hits us. Until we finally reach the point where we've had enough.

Where exactly is this "point"?

It differs for each of us. It may take days, week or years. For some it may take a lifetime.

On her way home from her therapist's office, caught in the whirlwind of thoughts and feelings and lost to everything else, Maya was able to see her relationship with her son in a way she never had before. She saw the pattern that had begun when Alan was very little, intensifying with time, until their roles were established—Alan's that of a difficult, problem child and Maya's of his stoic, long suffering mother, always there to save him from trouble. It was a *psychic contract* signed by both of them, holding them to the roles they chose. And though it appeared that it had always been Alan's doing, Maya was just as much a part of the game.

It takes two to tango, as we all know. And it took both of them to dance their particular dance. Always playing with fire, always playing on the edge. Coming close to the abyss, looking down and quickly stepping aside in the last moment, never actually falling in. A titillating and dangerous drama that finally went too far.

It was an old dance, and it wasn't fun anymore.

It functioned automatically following a program written too long ago. The contract held them to their roles as the years went on. What seemed to be relatively harmless — a mother with a tendency for drama who also needed the validation of being a good parent, and a child learning about rules and boundaries — turned into something serious that was threatening disaster. It was a contract that outlived its usefulness long ago, and it had to be broken.

When Maya made her decision privately in her car, the message was sent and received. "You are on your own," was the message, spelled clearly and with no fine print. The truth sank in. "I am on my own. And I am facing a prison sentence. Wow."

The shock of the impending catastrophe was electric. It brought Alan back, out of the stupor he had been in for several days and into the bleak reality of tomorrow.

Going to prison??!! Like hell I will!!! If Mother is off the dance floor — then I am, too.

And he made his own choice.

Both mother and son — changing with the choices they made, discarding their old agendas, canceling the old contract, erasing it completely from the blackboard of their lives.

And reality turned on a dime.

In one reality, the bag with the drugs was in the lab for inspection and Alan was going to prison, and in another reality, there was no bag with drugs, no lab and no prison.

Prior to the moment she had made her choice, Maya was a mother with a problem son. And after the choice was made, she had a son who never had a problem to begin with.

It doesn't have to take hours or weeks or months to make a powerful choice that will turn everything in your life a hundred eighty degrees. It can take but a second.

What makes a difference is the *intensity* with which the choice is made.

Intensity is a word that is often misunderstood. Intensity is not loud or frantic or in your face. On the contrary, the energy of intensity is often very quiet. It is condensed, focused and directed.

Nothing exists, but that moment. You are alert, with all your senses sharp, activated and alive.

It is a state of consciousness where there is no room for anything else, *but the present.* The clarity you've been seeking is suddenly yours, and you know what you need to do.

The choice becomes obvious, and you make it there and then, and with such power of will and spirit, you literally become a different person.

It is hard to fit this phenomenon into a linear explanation of things.

It is not "A" leading to "B" leading to "C"...and so forth. Instead — it is more like in one moment you are an "A" — and in the next moment — you are a letter from a different alphabet, or, if it is the same alphabet, then you are suddenly — a "Q." Skipping all the letters in between. A caterpillar that becomes a butterfly. Not an improved, better version of a caterpillar, but a different species all together.

Our reality is not a result of endless causes leading to consequent endless effects.

Scientists have known now for a hundred years that Newtonian physics is wrong. And it has been fifty years since they have *proven* that it is wrong. That, in fact, Newton's approach — causes creating effects, colliding, creating causes that are creating effects — is *not* how it works. And still it doesn't seem to matter. Because it is easy to imagine a billiard ball hitting a billiard ball, hitting the next billiard ball and so on. That's what we were taught at school, and it has become so deeply engrained that most people never question it.

In truth, however, *our reality is a product of our choices.*

There is no such thing as objective reality. We each have our own unique subjective realities and sometimes they overlap each other. Reality is not solid. It is mutable and pliable, and it changes as we change and to the degree that we change. Sometimes the change is subtle; sometimes it is dramatic. Sometimes the change is *fundamental* and the entire reality "flips" and becomes something else.

It is *choice* that determines what happens and what does not happen in our lives. *Choice is pivotal to the creation of every realty, without exception.*

If your mind is racing for a rational explanation every time you hear about something unexplainable, just let it go for now. Give it a well deserved rest and instead *stay with the impact* of the story. Let it open you to *what's possible. To the Possible that defies linear understanding and brings us unimaginable outcomes and miraculous shifts.*

Let the *Power of the Possible* fill you. Allow your imagination to take you places you have not been to before.

Perhaps it is the artists who understand this best. They have no fear of stepping outside the "norm," into the "dew line" of reality. It is the place where their genius dwells, the place where it is at home. They step outside, they dip, and they return — bringing back the magic. They have no words for it, but they know where they've been. And they express it through their art.

"Everyone tries to understand art," says Picasso. "Why not try to understand the song of a bird?"

Magic means *changing your reality at will*. In *accordance* with your *will* and your *choice*. But *not* at the dictation of your ego. Magic will always be more than what you or I can imagine, if we but just stop trying to control it, stop trying to figure it out and have the *humility* to allow it to come to us. Ours is to do our part. Learn our lessons and then receive the bounty.

Allow *this truth* to change you. Think about it for a moment. How empowering, how liberating to know that it is our *choices* that determine everything in our lives.

Just be with it. Let it wash over you like a gentle rain. A gentle healing rain on a sunny afternoon. See the rainbow in the sky. A full rainbow. See the glow of light behind the mist. It always makes us feel better, seeing a rainbow in the sky. We smile, we are moved in ways we can't explain.

Something we've always known stirs inside us awakening ancient memory. Some things just *are*. They do not need an explanation. There is a knowing we have that transcends our need to have everything fit neatly into a straight line. This knowing is innate, it just drops in.

We hear truth spoken, and we know it without knowing how.

Honor this knowing. Let it be enough. Enough for now. Enough to open the door.

The Son Who Forgave His Father

You may call God love, you may call God goodness, but the name for God is compassion.

— MEISTER ECKHART

FORGIVE ME FOR STARTING THIS CHAPTER with an old joke, but it is simply too appropriate to pass over. "How many psychiatrists does it take to change a light bulb?" "Just one. But the light bulb must *want* to change."

What is it going to take to finally learn the simple and obvious truth that has been staring us in the face all our conscious lives? *Trying to change another person is a hopeless and pointless task. It doesn't work. It can't. And it never will.*

Yet even with the evidence stacked up against us, we don't give up easily. So sure that we know *what's best*, we make our displeasure known one way or another. Sometimes we don't say anything at all. Just wish silently and desperately for the person to change, unaware that an energy field forms between us with each wishful thought and each hopeful feeling. An energy field that lets the other one know we disapprove. An energy field against which he or she will now bounce.

It is an energy field of resistance — to us and to our desire to change them.

Whichever way we go about trying to control their behavior — from verbal confrontations to silent sighs of unhappiness, to quiet expectation, to obvious disapproval, whether we talk about it constantly or never say a word — it really makes no difference.

The field is there. They know it. And they resist.

In fact, the more you push them, the harder they will push back. At some point it won't even be about change any longer. *It will be about fighting you.*

The field of resistance between the two of you will become *the barrier* to the very change you want to happen, keeping you both stuck on either side of it until you won't even see each other any more. The colored prisms of your control will be distorting your view and blocking out everything that is real.

As long as one of you insists, the other one will resist it. Some can go on like this forever. Sometimes — they actually do.

Insisting that someone changes, and resisting making that change, are the opposite sides of the same coin. Is it any surprise that nothing changes at all?

If you remove your need for other people to change, the field of resistance between you collapses. The barrier is replaced by a mirror, leaving them face to face with themselves. With nothing to fight against, they are forced to make a choice.

They can choose to change or *they can choose not to.*

It is their right. Not yours, not mine, not anyone's.

Whether they are your lover or your spouse, your parent or your child, your friend, your colleague or anyone else — this right is not negotiable.

Freedom can mean different things to different people. But among the many things freedom is, and among the many choices it brings us, one choice stands out.

This choice is *our right to choose for ourselves whether to improve or to diminish our lives.*

This choice is our inalienable right as human beings.

It means that at any given time every one of us is free to make a choice that to anyone else may look bad, wrong, ridiculous and crazy. And yet it is still ours to make it. Ours and ours alone.

WHEN WE ACCEPT the fact that a person is the way he or she is, and there is nothing *we* can do to change this, when we stop imposing our choices for them upon them — the energy field of resistance between us disappears.

It does not mean we have to suddenly agree with the way they are.

It simply means *we let go of trying to have them be different.* We stop fighting it, hating it and resisting it, even though we may not know what will happen next.

In this new state of emptiness, with no expectation and without the interference of our control *we have surrendered to the Power of the Possible,* and with it to limitless outcomes and endless options.

We have been blocking this door for so long....Leaning on it with all the weight we could muster, insisting on getting our way, thus holding off all other possibilities.

Now we have swung this door open.

We've made space for magic to enter our reality.

Don't plan for it, don't expect it and don't try to figure out what it might look like. Let go of trying to control anything.

Free all this energy and *turn it towards living your own life.*

By setting free the one you have been trying to change, you successfully free yourself.

*   *   *

Robert's Story

A young man I once knew talked to me about the hatred he felt for his father. He likened it to a rubber band that held the two of them together. No matter how far he moved to get away from his father, the rubber band of his hate would always pull him back. It was a magnet. An energy field he could never escape. He would leave home, move to a different town, but he would always come back, return to the "battle field," drawn to his father by the hate he felt, a force from which he could not break free.

It was palpable, alive — as alive as he was, maybe more. And it consumed him. It fueled his every action, fed his every thought. He lived it with each breath he took. "It was visceral," he told me. "I could feel it on my skin."

He had reasons — real reasons — for hating his father. His father had beaten him severely all through his childhood getting more and more inventive with his punishments. But the emotional abuse had been even worse. His father had a genius for it, and he had used it expertly, aiming to take away the last shreds of his son's dignity.

Had he done it consciously? Probably not. He had been too drunk for that. In fact, he was always drunk, often too drunk to stand on his own two feet. Robert's mother drank as well, and so did his older sister.

If you can't beat them — join them. Robert became an alcoholic by the time he was twelve. Many people expected him to kill his father one day. No one would be surprised if he did. But he knew he never would. Just as he knew his hatred was killing *him*, turning him into someone dangerous and destructive, someone people stayed away from, sensing the secrets in the darkness, not wishing to know.

He did not expect to live long. Could not remember a day he wasn't drunk. And since everyone in the family was an alcoholic, it was okay. No one cared, no one paid much attention. He would throw away the articles a friend would bring him from time to time. Articles about sons who killed their fathers. If he were to kill anybody, it would be himself. He tried that when he was little, but like his father told him, he "couldn't even do that right."

There were car crashes, many of them, but he always came out unscathed as if protected by an invisible hand that would pull him out of danger each time.

He had very few friends. He was a loner, living behind the glass wall of pain, looking at the world with the eyes of an outsider.

"I would have died young, had I not stopped drinking," he told me. "I was absolutely sure of that." But he stopped. At twenty-six, he woke up one day and just knew he would never drink again.

It was the turning point in his life. He dragged himself to AA and began the slow process of recovery. He never touched another drink.

*   *   *

OUR LIVES ARE rich with examples of triumph of the human spirit. Alcoholics and drug addicts finding the strength to end their addiction, often dedicating their lives to service, inspiring others with their own example. And while all this is actually true of Robert's life as well, there is much more to his story.

One morning when he was twenty-eight years old, he woke up with a distinct feeling that he needed to forgive his father. The urgency he felt grew and intensified as he was trying to go about his day, a persistent pull dominating everything else. *Go home, forgive him. Forgive him today.*

It was an instant, out of the blue obsession. It was all he could think about.

There was no time to lose. He was sure of it without knowing how he knew this to be true. Over time, he had learned to trust his feelings and his intuitive sense. He never questioned this.

His father was fifty-one at the time, though, looking at him, he might as well have been eighty. Haggard, unkempt, grey stubble covering his unshaved face, his eyes pale and lifeless. His stoop had gotten worse over the years. He had difficulty walking and had to hold onto the walls to keep himself from falling. His liver was as good as gone. He did not have long to live. No one ever dared mention his drinking in his presence. He ridiculed his son for being sober. "So you think you are too 'clean' now for this family, don't you?" he used to say.

"I must forgive him," his son thought that morning.

It was an especially cold winter in Minnesota. The roads were icy and dangerous, and it was snowing hard. The son lived three hours away from his father, but nothing was a problem that day. He got into his car and started driving.

What happened to the hate he had been living with for so long?

It seemed to have been suspended, lifted into some place he could not access. That morning—it didn't matter. It was a moment of grace, the only thing he could feel as he was driving home breaking every speed limit was his intense need to forgive and, with it, a wave of absolute compassion for his father.

"I would have never survived the childhood *he* had," he told me. "Mine was nothing compared to his."

*   *   *

HE ARRIVED AT his family home in the early afternoon.

"What are you doing here, Mr. Saintly?" was his father's greeting. But it was like water off a duck's back. The more his father tried to taunt him, the less it mattered. He was immune to his insults. There was no hook inside him to which his father's darkness could attach itself. And so it slid off him without having any impact.

Imagine a situation where someone suddenly accuses you of something that is so out of the realm of the possible things you could ever do, that even getting angry at the accusation would be ridiculous. Wouldn't your first reaction to that accusation be to laugh at it? Would you even bother to argue? Would you bother to defend yourself? Wouldn't you just shrug it off? Walk away? Dismiss it because whoever was saying it must be crazy?

Now imagine someone accuses you of doing something that is, in fact, quite possible for you to have done, but you didn't do it. Now — you will fight. You will argue. You will try to prove your innocence. You will get very angry. You will get indignant. "How dare you?! How dare you accuse me of this?! I would never! I would hate to think!!!"

Why such different reactions? It is quite simple actually. In the first call — you do not feel vulnerable to the accusation, and so it doesn't stick. There is no hook for it inside you.

It is a very different story in the second case. You have been accused of something you could have easily done, but didn't this time. Now, the vulnerability, the weakness is there, and it trips you up. You can't stay calm, can't just laugh off the accusation. You lose your temper, you start acting as if indeed you are guilty. Crazy, but true, the more you defend yourself, the less believable you sound.

Similarly, as long as Robert was consumed by his hatred of his father, any ridicule or insult from him would bring out a violent, angry response. But on the afternoon of that day and for the first time in his conscious life, he was able to see his father through the eyes of compassion only. He saw a frail, very sick man desperately trying to hold on to his last bits of dignity. He saw a man who was scared and lost, too weak to walk on his own, doling out insults more out of habit and fear of dying than out of any real malice. He could not get angry with this man, no matter what he was saying. In fact, he barely heard him. He was detached in the truest sense of the word. He also knew he could be seeing his father for the last time.

The old man grumbled on for a while and then stopped and looked at his son.

"I must stop drinking," he said suddenly, then quickly looked away.

If lightning were to strike in the middle of a bright sunny day, it would have been less unexpected and less unimaginable. Yet there it was, a taboo subject, never to be mentioned for fear of death itself, and he was bringing it up himself.

"Sounds good," his son said calmly. He had spent years in AA and knew better than to try to force anything. Any overt interest on his part would guarantee an opposite reaction from his father.

He got up to make himself a cup of coffee, reached for the coffee maker, poured the water into the pot. The old man shifted in his chair, coughed loudly and spat the phlegm into the ashtray by his side. He lit a cigarette, inhaled and then put it down. Something was making him uncomfortable, and he couldn't put his finger on it. He got up, walked to the window, and leaned against the windowsill.

"You making coffee?" he asked his son without turning his head. "I'll have a cup."

It was snowing hard all day, and Robert was glad to be inside, in the old kitchen once again. He poured the coffee into the cups placing one in front of his father.

"I'll start the fire," he said and leaned by the fireplace to arrange the logs.

If one didn't know better, the scene in the kitchen was a picture of quiet domesticity. The crackling of fire in the fireplace on a cold winter day, father and son having coffee in the afternoon with the son resting his feet on top of the coffee table looking through the newspaper.

"Still sober?" his father chuckled, knowing the answer in advance. He wanted to add something else, something mean and sarcastic, but found himself at a loss for words. It wasn't entertaining anymore to be his old nasty self, and it bothered him. He finished his coffee in one gulp and pushed the cup away. Something was different about his son, too different, and it was throwing him off guard, making it difficult to relate to him in the old way. He prodded some more, looking for the familiar resistance, but the wall was gone and his barbs just flew through the air and landed on the floor.

"What are you up to these days anyway?" he asked. They talked for a bit about nothing in particular, a simple conversation, something they hadn't done in years. They ate some pie, then Robert fixed the broken drain in the sink.

Several hours had passed since Robert had arrived, and he was deciding whether to spend the night. It was still snowing, the days were short, and it would get dark soon. He had never felt so peaceful in his parents' home. There was hardly a time in the past when he wouldn't be seething at the very thought of his father, anticipating his attacks, ready to fight in an instant. Now it was as if he had simply dreamt his horrible past, as if the man in front of him coughing noisily into his big folded palms was someone else, someone he was just beginning to know.

"It will be dark soon," his father said.

"Yes, it will," said Robert.

"I am sick and tired of this cough."

"I know," said Robert.

He looked at his father. Bending over the sink, the old man was splashing water onto his face. He reached for the kitchen towel, put it to his cheeks.

"Perhaps I should go and check myself into a rehab center," he suddenly said.

"It would be good," responded his son.

There was a pause. A long pause. No one spoke again for a while. Robert got up and added some logs to the dying fire. It was soon ablaze again.

"I can't do it today," the father spoke again. "I promised Mother to take the books back to the library. They are past due."

"I'll take them for you, if you want," his son said, not turning his head. The sound of a siren broke the afternoon's quiet as a fire engine sped by the window and disappeared.

"Linda!" the father yelled. "Linda, come here this minute."

"What is it?" Robert's mother entered the room. "Why are you yelling? I am watching a show. Where do you think you are going in this weather?"

Reaching for his hat and gloves, her husband turned and looked at her without blinking.

"I am checking into a rehab right now, Linda. Put your coat on. You will drive."

And that was it. That was how it happened.

* * *

STAYING IN THE rehabilitation clinic had begun the process, which led to AA and to many months of painful but steady recovery. As it turned out, the haggard, beaten down man still had some fire, and his will was stronger than his addiction. Once he had made his choice, he stuck with it. He stopped drinking on the day his son came home to forgive him, and he did not drink again.

I met Robert at a friends' Christmas party in New York. By then he was thirty-eight years old, married and had twin sons. While in New York on business, he had been buying Christmas gifts for his family. He showed me a wonderful thick woolen sweater he had just bought.

"Who is it for?" I asked. "Is it for you?"

"It's for my Dad," he said smiling. "He rides his bike in pretty much any weather. I thought he could use something like this."

I sensed the warmth in his voice when he spoke about his father, and it touched me. "You must be very close," I said.

"Yes, we are," was all he answered.

Robert told me his story years after we met and gave me permission to share it. It is a magical story — a story of kindness and love — a story of the incredible force of forgiveness and of one's courage in the face of pain.

Not once in the many years after he had stopped drinking did the father acknowledge how abusive he had been to his family. It was something he couldn't do. But he lived his love for them with every breath he took. His dedication was total. And so was his loyalty. Without the alcohol in his blood, he was a new man.

"I never had a better friend in my life," Robert told me. "He is my best friend, and I trust him with everything."

The Gift of Forgiveness

To forgive is to set the prisoner free. And then to
discover that the prisoner — was you.

At the depth of forgiveness lies the magic of healing. Its workings are not ours to understand. The miracle of forgiveness heals our very Souls, steeped as it is in the purest, cleanest waters of love.

When you have an impulse to simply forgive someone, do not ignore it. Do not dismiss it, and do not postpone it.

A friend once quoted me something I found to be very powerful.

"If you suddenly learned that you have one hour left to live, who would you call? What would you say? *And why are you waiting?*"

Most people would call the ones they love, and the only regret they have is that they haven't told them more often that they love them. Some recognize they have to make amends. There are still things left in their past for which they need to seek forgiveness. Yet others realize it is time *to forgive,* to let go of the past and *to set themselves free.* They have been carrying the sword for too long, and it has become too heavy.

It's time to set it down and to let their wounds be healed.

The impulse to forgive comes from a sacred place. It is presented to us at exactly the right time, placed in front of us by our Souls and, if followed, has the power to change not just our lives, but also the lives of others.

Trust that call. Trust the knowing you have. Call it intuition. Call it instinct. Call it a hunch. The label is not important. What is important is *the more we trust it, the stronger it gets.* The stronger it gets, the safer we feel relying upon this knowing, so it can finally lead us to where we need to go.

I once asked a friend of mine, an enormously successful New York lawyer, how he chose the cases he represented. What was the final criterion in his decision? He answered quickly and without a hesitation: "Intuition."

Trusting his intuition, Robert got into the car and drove for hours in the snow to forgive his father. He did not postpone it till the weekend. He did not tell himself he was busy and had to go to work and that the weather was unsafe and that he should wait until the storm passed. He got into the car and started driving. And when three hours later he had arrived to find his father drunk and mean and barely walking — the way he had been for so long — he had already forgiven him. Forgiven him without any conscious knowing that he had done it.

There is a mystical quality to choice. *When it is made unequivocally and with absolute clarity of will, it will override all our conditioning, all our previous choices and all the beliefs we hold.* At that level the choice we make can transform and change anything.

Propelled by his strong need to forgive his father, the son made a powerful choice. "I will forgive him" was his choice, followed by "I will forgive him now."

The intensity of his choice had urgency and momentum. It seemed his entire being was being rearranged in that instant, as if a tightly held lock had just been unhinged, letting in the light for the first time ever. He felt a movement inside his chest, but did not pause to analyze what it was. He simply knew he had to go, knew that it was important, and he followed what he knew.

The process of change had begun and nothing could stand in its way.

When I imagine that day, I see the events lining up in a beautiful curve, or better yet — I see them moving in a wavelike motion — an undulating wave of change comprised of several smaller waves, all—parts of the whole, all flowing powerfully and decisively towards the shore of healing.

The Mystery of Change

With the choice to forgive came forgiveness itself. And with forgiveness came change. And nothing in the life of that family was ever the same.

Did it happen in the early hours of the morning, when the thought of forgiving his father first came to Robert and he did not dismiss it? Did it happen as he was getting ready to leave, hastily throwing a change of clothes into his backpack? Or during the hours he was driving, trying hard to stay on the road, fighting the blinding wind-driven snow? Somehow, somewhere in-between the thoughts and feelings he had about his father, his hatred lifted, suspended just long enough for forgiveness to slip in.

We can never pinpoint the exact moment when we have changed. We just know we have, because we feel it. We act differently, we feel different feelings, we think different thoughts. "You are different, people tell us. You have changed." And we know they are right. It is true. We are no longer who we used to be.

Change is a mystery, and so is forgiveness. And mysteries they will always remain—not to be solved and thus stripped of their magic, but received, like treasured and precious gifts, healing us in an instant.

By the time Robert arrived at his parents' door, he had already forgiven his father. *The moment it happened—his father knew.* It wasn't conscious knowing—and yet he knew. And when his son opened the front door and entered the house, this knowing was confirmed. It wasn't something the father could articulate or explain, but it was unmistakable, and it threw him off guard.

He looked for the hatred he had always felt from his son, but found kindness instead. There was something peaceful about the way Robert was which made him feel uneasy. He tried to resist it, looking for the familiar tension between the two of them but could not find it. And he had no idea how to be without it. He tried to pick a fight, used a few of the old tricks that had never failed to make his son angry in the past, but got no reaction. He tried again, half-heartedly this time, but had to give up. He was lost. Irritated, annoyed, thrown off balance, he felt like a grumpy old fool. There was simply no way to have a fight with Robert, try as he might. His son had not come home for that. He had simply come to pay a visit.

He looked at Robert again, stealthily. Saw how handsome he was. His eyes clear, his face bright and clean shaven, the very skin radiating good health. No longer the pale shadow of a youngster who wouldn't look him in the eye. He could tell Robert hadn't been drinking in a long, long time.

He actually felt a twinge of pride for his son, something he could not remember having felt before. "Good for him," he thought. "He beat it, didn't he? But it's too late for me." He looked at his son again. A quick glance. Turning away at once. *Maybe it isn't,* the thought came. *Maybe I still could.*

When he was in the car three hours later, his wife at the wheel, taking him to the hospital for detoxification, he had no idea how it had happened to him. But he was going, and that was all there was to it. He had given up. He was not fighting any more. He felt his son's forgiveness — offered freely and without condition — and it had brought down the elaborate bastion of the old man's resistance. That fortress had taken decades to erect and fortify, and yet it crumbled with the slightest touch. With no one to resist him, the fighting became meaningless. The walls came down, and with them the roof, the ceiling and the locks on the doors. And into the place where darkness, self loathing and hate had lived side by side for so long, light could penetrate again. And with it — a flicker of hope, a touch of love. A new possibility.

Until that moment—beyond the imagination. Now suddenly—a reality. Approaching faster and faster as he was being taken away, down the freeway to the rehabilitation center.

*   *   *

AT THE ROOT *of all destructive behavior lies pain and our inability to deal with it.*

Whether someone is hurting us, or themselves, it is important to understand that *pain* is the *primary reason* behind their actions. It doesn't make their behavior okay. We don't have to stick around and continue to suffer the consequences of their pain. Understanding why they act the way they do *does not excuse* it, but it makes accepting the facts and forgiving them more attainable.

If you are sincere in your desire to help the ones you love, stop talking to them about it. Stop saving them. Stop trying to convince them that they really need to change. They already know it. *They cannot hear you.* Not under these conditions. Not as long as you are on the other side.

Try seeing it through their eyes. What are you seeing? It's a life of me against them, isn't it? And the "them" is simply everyone. *Including yourself.* Because "you don't understand." That's why insisting that someone changes does not work. You simply become one more person to rebel against.

Remove your need to have the person be different. Remove your resistance to the way they are. Remove that barrier. Stop trying to have them *get it.* Accept that they are exactly where they need to be, however detrimental it may look on the outside. Have the humility to trust that you don't know or understand everything.

It doesn't mean you have to stay with them. But if you want them to have a flicker of a chance—*accept them.* It doesn't have to be perfect. It doesn't have to be a hundred percent. Do the best you can. Accept them the way they are. Hold the hope, hold the light of your love for them, but *do it from a neutral place.* Honor them in this way. *Respect their freedom of choice.* Allow them to just "be."

* * *

THE PATH OF one's Soul is a mystery. Its plan is often invisible and not for others to comprehend. The Soul will stop at nothing to bring us the healing we need. *The Soul has just one goal* and one goal only. *And it is that we grow.* Grow spiritually. Grow as human beings. And if we don't yet know how to grow through love — then we will grow through pain. But grow we *shall.* That is the ultimate purpose of our being here, whether we know it or not. That is the absolute, highest truth; that is our only reason.

It is not for us to judge the way others choose to grow. Nor for us to decide what one should or should not do. Ours is to be understanding. Ours is to carry compassion in our hearts. Ours is to forgive.

To Stay or to Leave.
Forgiving the Unforgivable

I said to the almond tree, "Friend, speak to me of God,"
And the almond tree blossomed.
— Nikos Kazantzakis

"All happy families resemble one another, but each unhappy family is unhappy in its own way." These words of Leo Tolstoy have stayed with me since I first read them as a teenage girl in Russia. I kept returning to them over the years, marveling at the depth of Tolstoy's observation, as my own "picture perfect" marriage was falling apart, as other marriages of people I knew kept ending in divorce, the ones we were all expecting to go on forever, while yet others, often "the bad ones" — the marriages that everyone thought could never last — kept going strong.

It was humbling to accept that no matter how close we were to the people whose relationships or marriages we were trying to understand, we would never know them in their entirety.

What happens between two people belongs with the two of them. No one looking from the outside can ever assess the immeasurable number of nuances that play in the relationships of others. No one should ever try. Not friends, not strangers, often — not even therapists.

Most of the time, we see things *through the prism of our own perceptions,* which has little or nothing to do with what's real. Often the two people themselves are so caught up in layers and layers of feelings that they have been pushing away and refusing to deal with for so many years that even they are blinded to the truth of their situation.

Lost, angry, frustrated, and confused, they try to decide whether *to stay or to leave* their relationship, unable to find the answer, never quite knowing what they really want. Haunted by this uncertainty, they go back and forth, weighing the pros and cons of staying versus leaving, never reaching the peace that comes with making a decision—*the decision that is right for them,* regardless of how it may look to other people.

Sometimes it is right to stay, and sometimes it is right to leave. And there is no one who can tell us which one it is. This decision is up to us alone.

*   *   *

I want to tell you a story. It is a story about a woman and her marriage. I heard it on one of Caroline Myss's tapes many years ago and was profoundly moved by it.

The story takes place at a workshop given by a medical intuitive on the subject of *depression and forgiveness.* Among the participants of the workshop was a woman in the last stages of cancer. She was very sick and obviously in a lot of pain. She had difficulty sitting and needed pillows to lean on, so she could make it through the workshop. The cancer had metastasized and was now everywhere in her body. She had but a very short time left to live.

The workshop lasted a week and concerned itself with *the role forgiveness has in the process of physical and emotional healing.*

Before long, the workshop participants got involved with the material being discussed, forgetting about the sick woman. Propped up by her pillows, she appeared to be barely conscious, sitting very quietly with her eyes closed.

In the middle of the week, the workshop leader took everyone on a guided visualization. When it was over and it was time for a break, someone noticed that the sick woman in the back of the room was not moving. Had she died? She appeared not to be breathing. The teacher rushed to her side, took her pulse. She was alive, but had entered a state of deep trance. He decided not to disturb her and just wait for her to come back on her own. He stayed with her, as did everyone else in the room, and after a while the woman opened her eyes, looked around and sat up.

She had to take time to adjust. The light was too bright, too many eyes were upon her, searching her face, wondering. What was she doing in this strange room, surrounded by all these people? Slowly her memory returned. She straightened in her chair, and feeling uncomfortably warm opened the top buttons of her blouse. Then she turned to the workshop leader. "Thank you," she said touching his arm lightly. "Thank you."

"Are you all right?" he asked.

"I am." She nodded smiling, reaching for her purse. "Yes, I believe, I am fine."

What happened next left everyone speechless.

The woman stood up, hand-pressed her skirt, and refusing help from anyone, grabbed her coat and walked out of the room.

Outside, she hailed a taxi and went straight to the airport. She flew home that very day.

As Caroline Myss would learn later, it was a total, spontaneous healing. The woman's cancer was gone. Everyone in that room had witnessed a miracle.

A miracle that happened at the workshop on forgiveness.

Captivated, I had listened to Caroline Myss tell the woman's story. I let my imagination fill in the missing details, watching the woman's life unfold in front of me like a movie.

Closing my eyes, I could see her clearly. A young bride on the day of her wedding. So alive, so radiant, her eyes glowing, her face flushed. She is wearing her mother's wedding dress, saved for her with tender care so she could wear it this one special day.

It fits her perfectly, its soft creamy lace brushing the floor just barely, as she glides down the isle on her father's arm. It is four o'clock, and the late afternoon sun is streaming through the mosaic of the church windows, leaving patterns of colored light on the floor, making people shade their eyes as they smile and watch her reach the altar where the groom is waiting.

Standing in front of the altar now, pressing the bouquet of tiny white roses to her chest, a string of pearls around her neck reaching to her collar bone...she swallows, tightens her grip on the bouquet, blinks, then looks up.

She can barely contain herself. How can I be so lucky? *I should just pinch myself,* she thinks.

She closes her eyes for a second, a soft smile on her lips. Why me? All this happiness, all for me alone...what have I done to deserve this?

Fighting tears, she repeats her vows. "I do," she says, trembling. He puts the ring on her finger. She closes her palm. A wife. His wife. Thank you, God.

"You may kiss the bride," says the minister.

He takes her in his arms, draws her close. All that for me...

Down the aisle they walk hand in hand. She seems to be floating, walking on air. The music, the laughter, her mother's face.

And then the reception at her parent's house. So beautiful, awash in more white roses.

She must have had too much to drink. She barely had any food that day, and so she got tipsy, giddy with the excitement of the evening, laughing, hugging everyone. She was dancing so much, she lost track of her husband. Wasn't he just here, dancing next to her with her aunt? Where is he anyway? She looks around the room. Where can he be? She searches the dance floor with her eyes. Not there. Not at the table either. He must be outside, having a cigarette, she decides. She really shouldn't have had so much wine. *I'll run upstairs, check my face and then go out and get him,* she thinks. Panting, she runs up the steps to her old bedroom, passing the door to the guest bedroom. She hears sounds behind the door and comes to a sudden halt. She swings the door open. She freezes. Then turns and runs away.

How quickly she lost it all. Her laughter, her innocence, her dream...Her future. It hadn't even begun, and already it was over.

This was the beginning of the marriage that was to survive for the next twenty five years. Like a nightmare she could never shake off, the memory of what she had seen that day would haunt her, spreading inside her like cancer. There was hardly a day when she didn't relive the scene in that bedroom. Her husband's flushed, fear-stricken face. His tussled hair, unbuttoned shirt. Her girlfriend's skirt pulled up, exposing her long tanned legs.

She never saw her again. As for her husband...she wanted to leave him, but...couldn't.

"I was drunk," he said, crying, begging her. "Please, just give me a chance...please."

And so she stayed, hating herself for staying, unable to forgive his betrayal or forget the image of that bedroom, the scene playing and replaying in front of her eyes like a tableau. Within days, she discovered she was pregnant. *She now had a reason to stay.*

*   *   *

HER TRUST HAD been destroyed but the love lived on — the love she would grow to hate for not being able to expunge it.

Something had broken inside her, something she didn't know how to mend. A different woman emerged out of the wreckage, bitter and silent. Gone was the innocence. Gone was the effervescent joy that used to spill out of her for no reason at all. It all died in that moment when, paralyzed, she had watched her husband hastily zip up his pants and push her girlfriend away.

Her life became a constant, vigilant watch for signs of his infidelities. A silent agony of hate, despair, self ridicule and blame. She searched his pockets and drawers, shuffled through the papers on his desk, stiffened when he lowered his voice answering the phone in the other room.

She had plenty of proof. No need to look for more. What was wrong with him? All these women. Why did he need them? Why wasn't she enough? What was so wrong with her that he would keep cheating on her, and that she would still stay with him year after year?

"I need to stay until my son grows up," she told herself. "A boy needs a father."

Then she was pregnant again and had another boy. Two sons. "How can I leave my husband now?" she would ask herself. I will wait a little longer, until my children go to college. Then I will leave him for good. It's just a few more years, she would promise herself, as her boys were growing up. Just a little bit longer.

Relentlessly, her husband continued to carry on. So many women. Some she knew about, others she suspected. There was hardly a time in all the years of her marriage that she would let herself forget the terrible compromise she had made.

How much longer can I go on like this? she would ask herself.

The sleepless nights with clenched fists. Tears of rage on her pillow. Eyes swollen in the morning after a night of crying. He, gone on a business trip, and she knowing who went with him. His new flame. Whatever her name was. She pitied them. Fools, all of them. Hoping for something they will never get. But who was she to judge them? She who had stayed with him in spite of it all.

How can I be so spineless? she would ask herself. Putting up with this? Crying over that bastard! Get up, pull yourself together, get a good lawyer. Leave! But how can I? she would answer. I promised myself to stay. For the boys. Not for me. For them. I must be strong.

But oh, how she hated herself for staying. For not having the guts . . . for being so weak. Her self loathing had a life of its own, it seemed, with its own voice taunting her, calling her names. She never touched alcohol, not since her wedding. To soothe herself, she ate instead. A roller coaster of raiding the fridge in the middle of the night, then dieting on no food at all.

Gaining weight, losing weight, overeating then starving herself. He didn't seem to mind. "I like you whatever your weight is," he'd say. She shrugged it off. He didn't mind because he didn't care, she was sure. She would turn away, walk out of the room.

It was always the same. He would return from a business trip, swing open the front door, filling the house with his roaring laughter, raising the temperature in the room from mild to hot in an instant. A burst of sparkling energy, like a fire she wanted to warm her hands by and never leave.

He would open his arms, grab his youngest and throw him up in the air, catching him just in time. With a twinkle in his eye, he'd toss a wrapped package to the older boy. "Dad! You didn't!"

"Well, open it up and let's see!"

He'd gather his wife into his arms, and for a moment she'd let herself believe it could be all right. That he still loved her. Why would he be with her otherwise? Then, instantly, she would remember his most recent transgression, hear the old voice in her head, "Pathetic coward...don't you know where he has been? And with whom?"

She'd stiffen in his arms. He'd let go. They would turn away from each other. The moment would be gone. He'd busy himself with the children.

"Are you staying for dinner?" she'd ask.

"I have a meeting at five o'clock," he would answer quickly. "I may or may not be done on time. Don't wait. I will call you."

"Don't bother," she would reply, walking away, picking up the torn wrapping paper from the floor.

In the silence that would fill the room, the boys would gather their gifts and climb upstairs to their bedroom. She'd walk into the kitchen and put on a pot of water for tea. Breathing sharp, shallow breaths in an effort to calm down, she'd repeat to herself the promise that fueled her life: "I'll wait till the children go to college, and then I'll leave."

She had made this promise for the last six years. And would continue doing so for the next nineteen.

*   *   *

Was there ever a time he did not cheat on her during all the years they had been married? She was not sure. It seemed there was always somebody in the background. She'd find lipstick traces on his collar from time to time, answer telephone calls with silences on the other end. Somebody hung up every time she picked up the phone.

But she would wait until her sons grew up. At least until both of them graduate from high school. They would be stronger by then, better able to deal with the pain of their parents' divorce.

Then it was time for college. One after the other, they were both accepted to schools on the East Coast. How could she leave her husband during that sensitive time? When the boys had to have stability back home, a family that was proud of them, hoping they would do well, study hard, not party and drink and smoke instead? She knew what college time could be like. She still remembered her own.

Just wait a few more years, she told herself. What's that in comparison to how long she had waited already? She would count the days, she told herself.

But she didn't count on Vietnam.

The draft came just as her oldest had graduated. Within weeks he was gone, fighting the war she hated, risking his life every day. For what?!

And then her other boy. They had to have him as well.

With both her sons gone, her life was all about waiting. Waiting for the letters. Waiting for good news. Praying for them. Hoping they were unharmed. She needed to have a secure home for them to come back to. Not a broken one. No. She wouldn't want to put that kind of strain on her boys. Her sons who looked death in the eye every day. Their home must remain their safe harbor. Nothing, she decided, would change in their home until their return.

Mercifully, miraculously, both her sons were spared and came home at war's end. She cried, filled with gratitude and relief. They were men now, not boys any more. One, silent and pensive, with eyes of steel blue just like his father's. The other one, more like her in frame. Slender and tall, easy going and fun to be with. Always the heart of the party. They both moved out soon, setting up homes of their own.

I can leave now, she said to herself. There is nothing to keep me here anymore.

Then suddenly, out of the blue — this strange ache in her back. A sharp pain that made her grab onto the table. "Go to the doctor," her husband said. "Have it checked." She went. And then — the news. The worst news of all. Cancer everywhere in her body. In most of her organs, her blood, her brain. "Too late to operate," they told her. And what would they operate on first?

They gave her two months to live. Maybe six weeks.

That's all?

The news left her numb. She couldn't feel a thing when she left the doctor's office. It wasn't happening to her. It couldn't be.

Removed from the events, as if watching a movie about someone else, she stayed calm as she began taking care of business. She didn't know how to fall apart. An internal mechanism installed ages ago and functioning still kept it together as she organized things for her family. Photographs, letters, documents.

Then came the day when she couldn't get out of bed.

"I am dying," she said out loud. It was ridiculous. Crazy... "I am dying," she said again, testing her voice. Something moved inside her chest. A sound came out, hoarse and agonizing, the call of an animal trapped, filled with terror. She couldn't fight it if she tried. She had been fighting it forever. It shocked her, breaking apart the control that had made her "keep it together" for twenty-five years—not letting her extend herself any compassion, any kindness. Everything was fast now, a movie of her life on fast forward. A kaleidoscope of shifting pictures. Images moving in front of her as if on their own.

I am dying and I haven't even lived, she thought. *I spent my life hating my life. And now it is too late.*

Her sorrow was overwhelming. It hit her hard. Hit her like a freight train. And she unraveled, falling into the abyss, black as the night, darker than black itself. Inside this darkness, she shed the last of her control like a snake dropping off its old skin. She had no use for it now.

Her husband wanted to take her away. Spend time together, go where it's warm, anywhere, just to be away. He didn't have much time left with her, he told her, but as much as there was, he wanted it all. She was confused. He seemed devastated by the prospect of losing her.

But she was too weak to sit through hours of flight and too weak to analyze his behavior. She was bedridden most of the time and took morphine to help with the pain.

One day, an old friend stopped by to visit and mentioned a workshop on forgiveness that she was attending the following week.

"Could I come with you?" the cancer patient asked.

*   *   *

PROPPED UP BY her pillows at the back of the room, she listened to the man talk about forgiveness. He was about to take them on a guided visualization. She closed her eyes, followed the man's instructions and entered a deep meditative trance.

She was reliving her life again, all of it, starting with the day of her wedding. This was the turning point—the time when everything stopped and her pain was born, the pain that was killing her now.

Was it all his fault?

She married the man who could not, would not be faithful. She knew this so early on. And yet she chose to stay, finding reasons for why she couldn't leave. Making excuses for herself, so she could live with her decision. But what kind of life was it? What price had she paid for her sacrifice? *Were her sons better off in the end, having grown up in a household of hostile silences and polite conversations? Having grown up with a long suffering, stoic mother and an absent father?*

He had lied to her once. After that he didn't need to because she knew. She had been lying to herself all her life. All at once, the astonishing truth was staring her straight in the eye making it impossible to turn away.

She didn't stay because of her children. She stayed with her husband because she simply wanted to stay. She did not want to leave him. She never did. Not because of her sons. Not because of anything. He was the man she loved, and she wanted to be with him even if it meant him sleeping with other women. There was something between them that had connected them viscerally, on the soul level. A tie, stronger than she could ever put into words. A *knowing of each other* that transcended all else.

This intimacy, in spite of all that was wrong... how could she ever explain it to anybody? But did she need to? Her life was her business. Hers alone.

In the background, the man was talking about forgiveness. The miracle of it. Its power to transform, to lift, to heal lives.

Her husband's face floated before her. His eyes, so concerned about her lately, looked at her without blinking. An instant, wordless communication. More real than if he were right there by her side.

Her love for him shot through her body. The love she had fought against ever since the fateful day of her wedding. It made her hot, as if the thermostat in the room was suddenly turned up to a hundred degrees. Deep in her trance, she wanted to move, do something, step outside into the rain, lean against a tree, feel the raindrops wash over her hot face.

Something was letting go inside her body. It was a physical sensation, as if a tight grip was being released, a knot untangled and let loose somewhere between her stomach and her heart.

The relief of finally letting it be okay to just love him. To remain his wife regardless of how he was with other women.

She did not need anyone's permission. Good or bad, right or wrong — the very concepts seemed to belong to a reality she wasn't part of anymore.

She wanted to hug herself. To hold her body tight in her arms until it stopped its uncontrollable shaking. "There, there," she was whispering softly, imagining she stood behind the woman in the chair, her arms crossing over the woman's chest and stroking the elbows, then down to the trembling hands.

What have I ever done that I would treat myself so badly?

Through her tears, she could feel her face softening, her body relaxing. She touched her cheek gently and felt a tear roll onto her finger. She took it to her lips, its salty taste — like the salty almonds she used to sprinkle on her sons' cereal — filling her with tenderness. What have I done to myself? What have I done?

It was as if there were suddenly two of them in the back of that room, the one on the chair and the one asking the questions. But this new other one was soft and kind, *accepting her with all her mistakes.* She wasn't judging her harshly, mercilessly, the way she had always judged herself. Instead — she was filled with a beautiful sadness, a caring born of deep and profound sorrow.

She was free to love him now, to love him without fighting herself. She was finally done fighting.

How overwhelming to know that you can love that intensely, to be free to love without being a hostage to it, to feel your love without the pain that had attached itself to it so long ago. How much of herself had she given to hating this love of hers so that her hatred itself had become an entity, poisonous, resilient, and willful?

What did it take to deny a love that would not die no matter how much she had tried to kill it? What steely determination, what condensed focus, what immensity of will? All that energy directed towards self-recrimination and blame. And it was killing her now.

If you can hate with great intensity, then you can love just as strongly.

Hate is so close to love it could be its dark twin sister. Not the opposite like most would have us believe. *The opposite of love is indifference,* and she had never been indifferent to him. Not for a moment in their entire life together.

She loved him with everything she had. Loved him totally and completely. Only him, all of her life.

Did he love her back? He did. Not the way she loved him. But in his own way, different from hers, he loved her, too.

She could see it clearly now. He loved her the way he could. It was a different kind of love, not the one she wanted, but the one he was capable of. Perhaps, it was all he had to give. Less than what she had dreamed of, but all of what he had. If his heart could ever belong to one woman, then she was that woman. As for his body, it would always belong to many. It didn't mean anything, he had always said.

Submerged in the deep trance of her meditation, she saw her husband with the objectivity afforded to the dying. *There is nothing wrong with me,* she realized, startled. Nothing at all. He would have been unfaithful to anyone. If he hadn't met me, if he had married somebody else — anyone, any woman at all — he would not have stayed true. He would not have been faithful to one woman. That's the man he was. That was the way he chose to live. It had nothing, nothing whatsoever to do with me.

Suddenly — it didn't matter. Suddenly none of it mattered. She opened her eyes. The room was quiet. Everyone's eyes were upon her, expectant, searching her face. It took a moment to concentrate and bring herself back to this reality.

She touched her forehead lightly. The skin felt cool to her fingers, a soft, pleasant touch. She stretched her feet and stood up holding onto the back of the chair, smoothed her skirt across her knees, removed the bobby pins from her head. Her hair fell down onto her shoulders framing her face in soft curls. She had refused the chemotherapy treatments her husband had been insisting on, and so her hair was intact, as full as ever. Moving a loose strand away from her eyes, she reached for her purse.

I'll fly home as soon as I get to the airport, she thought. She couldn't wait to be in her own kitchen. She was going to make herself a cup of good strong tea as soon as she got there.

"Are you all right?" the workshop leader was asking.

"I am." She nodded. "Thank you. Thank you," she said again and smiled. Then, scanning the room one more time, she walked out.

The Process of Healing Has Four Phases: Realization, Feeling, Forgiveness, and Change

To heal ourselves, we must first *realize* the role we played in our pain. Then we will be able to *feel* the pain and the sorrow of this realization, deeply and completely. Only then can we *forgive* and accept *ourselves*, allowing us to authentically forgive *others*. Out of this healing process, comes the clarity that gives us the answers we need to make the right decision and to fundamentally *change*.

Let's take a look at what happened in the story I just told you.

Realization

The sick woman had asked to be brought to the workshop hoping to find a way to forgive her husband before she died. And then something else happened. Something she did not expect. She discovered that *there was more to forgive than just her husband*. There were *two* players in that drama called her life. Two principle actors. And she was one of the two. More than forgiving her husband, she needed to forgive herself.

With astounding clarity, she saw their silent pact for the life to-gether — the choices they each had made and had lived by. Her husband's — to keep sleeping with other women, and hers — to stay with him anyway.

He hadn't forced her to accept his choice. He hadn't forced her to live with him all these years.

The choice to stay had always been her own.

She had chosen to stay, and also to hate herself for staying.

All her life, all her misery — was her own doing.

It was as if a lightbulb had just gone on, altering everything she had believed to be true. Taking apart in an instant the elaborate, meticulously constructed story she had been telling herself all those years to protect herself from feeling the pain. Now, the dam was broken and nothing could stop the flood of feelings that rushed through her like a wild river.

There was too much to feel and too little time to feel it. Twenty-five years of hiding. Taking all that anger, all that desperate rage and stuffing it into her body, tucking it deep into her organs, away from her sight. They would lie there awaiting their time, petrify-ing into resentments, turning into cancerous cells, feeding on her relentless hate — of herself, of her husband, of their life together. She had judged herself with more harshness and more determina-tion than anyone else ever could. Did she have to be dying to let it be okay to love her husband? To finally take herself off the hook?

She could never bring back all those years or undo what she had done. Sorrow — dark, wordless — *the pain of the unforgivable* — was lifting at the back of her throat threatening to choke her with its im-mensity of feeling . . . overwhelming, but *real*, for the first time.

Feeling the Sorrow, Feeling the Pain

Sorrow is an emotion so profound it reaches the very depth of one's Soul. It is the pain of the unforgivable in us, and it changes us forever. These are the skeletons in the burial places of our past.

The skeletons that won't be buried, *the things we did that we would do everything in our power to take back, and can't.*

The woman's sorrow: decades of self-recrimination and hate. Punishing herself, feeling worthless, lying to herself, denying herself the right to love the man she loved, regardless of the circumstances...a quarter century of self abuse. And then — cancer.

The skeletons of the unforgivable. They roam the grounds in the night, keeping us awake, reminding us of what we did, holding us prisoners. They need to be put to rest. They have rumbled too long. They, too, are tired and ready to be laid in the ground.

"But how?" we ask. Again and again we try to lay them down, failing every time.

After all, we have deemed them "the unforgivable," and it seems beyond our power to simply let them be gone.

How harshly we judge ourselves. How much easier it is at times to forgive another than oneself. How inventive we have become at the self punishment we inflict. Keeping the pain alive, stirring the memories like embers of the fire that is never allowed to die out. And yet — it is this pain that has opened our hearts to see others with the eyes of compassion and to be more understanding.

Compassion is a caring born out of our sorrows, out of the tears we cry for things we cannot undo.

Our sorrow is not determined by the severity of our crimes, but by the *level of pain it has caused us* and by *how heavily we have judged ourselves* for what we have done.

It could have been something minor, something someone else would have dismissed and forgotten long ago. To us, however, it is a source of continuous pain, a reminder of everything we hate about ourselves.

I remember a fight I had with my son once. He must have been thirteen or fourteen years old. He was acting out, wanting something I wasn't letting him have. The details are gone. I can't remember a thing about that fight. But what I remember vividly, and what has turned into one of my most painful memories, is how I slammed the door of my car and drove off to work, knowing I wouldn't see him until the evening, wanting nothing else but to punish him in this way.

His face filled with fear and pain and he was instantly sorry for what he had done. He saw I was ready to leave and had wanted to rush to me and make up. We were very close and I knew he wanted to apologize and not let me go like this... but his friend was there watching the scene, and so he held himself back — acted like it didn't matter. I saw all this in an instant, but would not relent... and so I slammed that car door and drove off.

My day was ruined, of course, and when I came home from work in the evening, we made up, and everything went on as usual.

What was the big deal? I am sure my son would not even remember that fight. He probably forgot about it the next day. It was one of so many we had at the time. As for me, it is difficult to write about it even now. I have tried to forgive myself for it endless times. Sometimes, I remember that morning, without the usual tension in my stomach that accompanies it. But I did feel it now, while writing about it. That memory is one of my sorrows. Something I did that I can never take back. Made stronger by *the significance I gave it*. For me — it meant I was not a good enough mother. For me — nothing was worse than that.

We are our own severest judges. Giving ourselves life sentences for things for which we would easily forgive others.

Yes, I know sorrow well. It's been my dark companion for a great number of years.

But not everything we regret doing will become our sorrow. There are things I did in my past that were certainly far more serious than that fight with my son. Many of them became my life lessons, but not my sorrows. I have felt remorse. I regret the circumstances, but I am not really sorry.

It is a paradox, and it is the truth. A part of me knows innately that these incidents had to play out that way. I am sorry for the pain I caused others, but not sorry I did what I did. Out of the rubble of those experiences, a me emerged that eventually became what I am today. Would it have been better to learn the same lessons differently? Perhaps. But I didn't. And I forgave myself for them. That past has no hold on me, and I am richer for having lived it.

There are other things in my life that have turned into my sorrows. Most I've been able to put to rest. Some are still not quite gone, though their voices grow fainter and fainter as my heart heals and I forgive myself at deeper levels. I know the day will come, and it will be soon, that these memories will lose their hold on me. One day they will fade away forever. I will be free.

Not everybody carries sorrow in their hearts. To some, forgiveness of self comes easily. It is part of their grace. They have an ability *to feel remorse and then to simply let go.* Some have a gift, a natural ease with self forgiveness. Some don't.

And then, there comes the forgiveness of others.

Forgiving the Unforgivable

Forgiveness. We give so much lip service to this word, using it casually and often without real understanding, thus making it less attainable, stripping it of the immensity of its power.

Forgive, we say, often without thinking. *I can never forgive,* we say just as often. Not realizing that by saying this, *we are giving a silent consent for pain to lodge itself deeper and deeper into our psyche.*

As long as there are people in our past we have not forgiven, we are not free of them. They are with us at all times, forever close, breathing down our necks, whispering into our ears, mocking us, threatening our peace of mind, a constant conscious or unconscious reminder of our pain.

If you were to stop and think about it for a moment, aren't there people from your recent past or from times long gone with whom you are having silent dialogues? Arguing, proving your point, fighting back, never succeeding in being heard, always ending the conversation angrier and more frustrated than when you started? Thus keeping the conflict that might have happened twenty or thirty years ago as fresh and alive as if what had caused it happened yesterday?

The father you have not forgiven for what he did to you when you were a junior in high school—he is right here, looking over your shoulder, telling you you'll never amount to anything. Just like he did when you were seventeen.

But I haven't seen him or spoken to him in twenty years! Doesn't matter. He is still here. You have not let him go. And everyone in authority over you, real or perceived, becomes "the father," the one who would *never approve,* the one who would always bring you down, the one you need *to rebel against,* or *seek acceptance* from or both. And what's most frightening—you don't even know it. And now you are thirty seven, a father yourself, still having problems with authority figures, fathers, all of them. You are not free to respond to them as an adult. Instead, you are at the mercy of unconscious reflexes, an adolescent in a body of a grown up man.

Yes, we carry the ones we won't forgive on our backs, whether we know it or not. And only forgiveness will bring an end to it.

"But if I were to forgive," some say, "then I will forget what they did to me. And I never want to forget that. There are things that were done to me that I can never forgive. Never ever. I won't forgive them. I can't."

I understand. Murder, rape, incest, physical and emotional abuse, cruelty to children...the list is long. The list is endless. That's true.

And here lies the paradox of forgiveness.

There truly are things that appear to be unforgivable, and yet we must forgive to be free of them.

Advocates of the death penalty, and those friends and relatives of the victims who are sure that witnessing the death of the murderer will bring them a measure of release from the pain of their loss, have discovered that this is not so. The completion they had hoped to find did not come with the death of the one who took the life of their loved ones.

In many cases, it was simply the end of the first phase of their grief.

The only way they could cope with the tragedy was to focus all their energy on justice. Finding the murderer, wishing for the death sentence, watching the unfolding of court proceedings — anything, anything at all that could take them away from fully feeling the unimaginable horror of their loss. To feel that would be to die themselves. Often they wished for that, often their pain was more than they could bear.

That initial phase of grief, lasting at times for very many years, would keep the survivors of the tragedy locked in their bottomless anger, wishing for revenge, fighting for it, hoping, believing that only revenge, once it happens, would bring relief to the unutterable pain they were living with every day.

And then the execution takes place, the murderer's life is taken, but the hoped for completion does not come. Instead, there is an emptiness that does not alleviate the pain, but brings it more to the surface. An emptiness the survivors did not expect. Nothing has changed. The pain is as strong as ever — maybe stronger — because there is nothing there anymore *to distract* them from feeling it.

In some cases, this becomes a doorway to finally *being able to feel* the immensity of their loss, followed by a degree of healing, perhaps even forgiveness and change.

There are also those who remain locked in their pain, *nursing the hate* for the ones who caused it and thus *staying connected to them* (dead or alive) for the rest of their lives.

"But I have every right to hate them! Don't tell me not to hate!

Don't talk to me about forgiveness! I am right! And I know it. I will hate them as long as I live!" Yes. You have every right to hate them. And if you do, they have not just taken from you the life of the one you loved, they have also effectively taken yours.

The healing of your pain *cannot happen* with the fulfillment of your dream for revenge. But it *will* happen with *forgiveness.* Once you consciously take your energy away from hate, you may at first experience disorientation. This is what happens as one is about to come out of their grief. In essence, it is a kind of *letting go,* like opening a tightly held fist and releasing the pain — not to forget it, but *to be free from it.*

You may not even be aware of having forgiven the one who took what was everything in your life away from you. But there is no familiar gripping in the pit of your stomach when you think about that person. Now even his image is fading and drifting away. You think about the one you lost, and you know nothing will ever take this love away.

You will never forget what happened to you. How can you? Your loss has become part of you and it has changed you forever. It has changed the direction of your life, but it doesn't have to de-fine you. You have been stopped. The future you believed you had — it is gone. But there is a different future that can be yours. A depth of Soul, a level of compassion, and with it — a new light. Your loss is woven into the fabric of your being, and yet — you are free from its hold on you.

We don't have to forgive *what* was done to us, if we can't. We may never forgive that. But we must forgive the *why* of what they did.

The famous words of Jesus Christ: "Forgive them, Father, for they know not what they do" is a phenomenal example of a great Soul forgiving the unforgivable.

What does it mean to forgive the *why* of what was done to us, even if at times we can't forgive the *what?*

Most will agree people are not born monsters. Yet, sometimes, they turn into one. Things happen to them in the course of their lives. Bad things. Terrible things. Pain gets inflicted, causing rage, humiliation, hurt, shame. Often it is *not* so much *what happened to them*, but *how they dealt with it*. Some are better equipped to deal with pain than others. The same event in the same family may turn one brother into a criminal, while the other will go on to become a great humanitarian teacher.

It is not for us to judge the effect of the experience on another human being. We are all different, and so are our abilities to cope and the choices we make.

The fact that people have suffered crippling emotional or physical pain, causing damage they have not found a way to heal, does not then give them a license to continue to perpetrate the same or worse crimes upon others. But understanding these causes helps us forgive the "whys" of their behavior.

Jesus calls on the Father to forgive his torturers while in the grips of unimaginable pain.

Why?

Because he has a profound understanding that those who did it to him, *did it out of their own pain, ignorance and fear.* Their *own* Souls had been damaged by what had been done *to them*. That's what made them capable of such cruelty.

Only forgiveness has the power to break this chain of pain.

To refuse to forgive is to always live a slave to our impulses. The dark impulses born out of our rage and shame, out of our hate and self-hatred.

Jesus became a teacher of a different way of being: turn the other cheek, forgive, walk away. And humanity has been struggling with the concept ever since.

I came from an atheist country and an atheist family. My father's relationship with God was that of denial. My mother prayed secretly and as a last resort. My spirituality bears no connection to any religion. But I am greatly moved by the story of Jesus Christ. It matters not whether you believe these were actual events or simply mythology. There isn't a more powerful example of a call for forgiveness and of the explanation for the reason to do it.

Forgiveness Is a State of Grace

Certain *misconceptions* about forgiveness make it harder to understand it. Some view forgiveness as weakness. Others are unwilling to forgive out of fear that they would have to resume a relationship with the people they have forgiven, something they have no intention or interest in doing.

Neither of these assumptions is true. *The only reason to forgive is to set yourself free* of your past, so you can step into the myriad of available futures that you can't see through the eyes of pain. Forgiveness swings open the door to the Power of the Possible and delivers you to the other side.

There, on the other side of Forgiveness, the most unimaginable scenarios lie waiting for you to show up and claim. You've stepped through the looking glass and *anything is possible*. On the other side of Forgiveness, your sight is clearer, your perceptions uncluttered. The people you used to hate may surprise you with kindnesses, or leave your life so utterly, you'll wonder if you didn't just dream your past. You may also discover there is *more* to forgive than just them. You may discover, just like the woman in the story I told earlier, that *the person you need to forgive most is yourself.*

Forgiveness is a state of grace.
I said it earlier, but it bears repeating: Forgiveness cannot be *done,* but only *received.*

It is, in a sense, our rain dance for freedom. When it doesn't rain in the desert, the natives dance. They dance "a rain dance" so that it will rain. And then, at some point — it does. Does it rain because they danced? Would it have rained even if they hadn't? "Of course," we say. The weather does not depend on a dance. Maybe so. But does it matter? They dance anyway. They dance so that it will rain. And then it does.

We take the steps to forgive, we dance the dance of forgiveness, and then at some point what we used to feel about that particular person — we don't feel anymore. It is simply gone.

How did it happen? I have tried to forgive many times, but every time I did I would just clench my teeth and my stomach would get tense and I would need a glass of water and then the telephone would ring and then I would have to deal with things... and I just couldn't... It was the same every time. But I kept trying. Just like I was supposed to... And then one day, or one night, as I cried myself to sleep one more time... I just don't know what happened... I woke up different. I looked for my anger and it was gone. The hate? I hadn't had a minute without it as long as I could remember. Where was it? Gone. You look for it in all the familiar places, you bring back the familiar images, images that used to make you cringe, but they don't make you feel the way they did in the past. Now it is like watching a cartoon. They have lost their power, and you simply turn them off.

What happened? When? When was it taken? *Does it matter?* Maybe your *intention* was all that was needed. Forgiveness comes from the realm of the miraculous. It's a magic that cannot be put into the words of our language. It defies our logic; it is beyond our intellectual understanding. Whatever we believe we understand about its mechanism doesn't begin to touch it. *Forgiveness is a gift.*

Once we experience it, *once we are touched by it, its grace changes us forever.*

A cancer, spread through the body of a dying woman — gone in an instant. A miracle? Absolutely.

But a true story never-the-less. It is one of many. Not as many as we would like, but it did happen. And *if one crow is white then not all crows are black.*

She went on to live a life she had never let herself live before.

She saw the truth of her situation, she felt her pain — and *she forgave herself.* Forgave herself for all the years of self-loathing and self-deprecating hatred. And then — *she gave herself permission to live the live she chose.*

For the first time ever, she didn't need permission from anyone else. And *she forgave her husband.* She saw him in all his complexity and she just let him be. And it was okay to love him and to stay with him even if he would never be faithful. Her choice to live, propelled by the power of her *acceptance of herself,* was all it took.

Accepting Yourself

There is tremendous power in accepting yourself. And yet, the very concept remains foreign to most people. It is not something we are taught as children growing up. Not at school, not at home, not anywhere. Maybe because those who are supposed to teach us not to demand perfection of ourselves, to be forgiving and kind to ourselves, to have the patience and the understanding that making mistakes is part of what makes us human — don't know it themselves. So many cultures are based on the demand for perfection. A demand that can never be attained, but is never-the-less ingrained into the very fabric of our being, having been spoon-fed to us since we were born. By the time we can walk and say our first words, it is already done. We know it is not okay to make mistakes. And when we do — we will be severely punished for them. No wonder we grow up to become our own worst judges, refusing ourselves the compassion we may willingly extend to strangers.

There are *four main principles of self-acceptance.* These principles, once mastered, can make the difference between a life of continuous self judgment, self punishment and blame, and a life of reflection and understanding, deeply rooted in compassion and healing of the heart. Print them out, put them on your bathroom mirror or any place you can see them every day. Read them again and again. Make them an integral part of your being.

Four Principles of Self-Acceptance

1. Realize that you are a human being and as such *you can and will make mistakes.* (It is not a crime to make mistakes, it is simply a fact of life.)

2. For these mistakes—*you can be forgiven.* And you can forgive.

3. *Sometimes you are prepared for life and sometimes you are not.* And that's how it will always be. (This means that there are and will be situations in your life where things will happen, for which you will not be prepared. And so you might act in ways that, had you been better prepared, you would not have acted. It doesn't mean that you are a bad person. Again, it is just—a fact of life. You can be forgiven for these actions, and you can forgive yourself.)

4. *Your needs and wants are important,* though they may not be the first priority. That they are not the first priority does not mean they are not important. They matter. You matter. You are important.

Stop here for a second. Let these words sink in: *you matter. You are important. You have a right to have your own needs and wants. And they are important.*

When I heard this the first time many years ago, it turned my world upside down. Such a simple statement. Such an obvious thing. Why then was I sobbing? I didn't even know that I thought I didn't matter before. I simply never thought about it. So many things mattered to me. My son, my husband, my family, my business...But myself? Wasn't it selfish? To think about yourself? To make myself important?

I am aware that some may read this and shrug. If you were raised to love yourself—great. You have been lucky. But in our world today, sadly you are a minority.

I learned the principles of self-acceptance years ago, and understanding them was one of the turning points of my life.

To me—they were a revelation. I could be forgiven? It was actually okay to make mistakes? And not just that. It was a given that I would make them again? I never thought about it in the past. I simply knew I had to be punished. And if not by others, then by myself. The harsher—the better. A mechanism that started soon after birth and had become an innate part of me. It took me years to undo it. It is something I still remind myself of at times. I hope the day will come when self- acceptance will become for me as automatic as punishing myself had been for so long. There are times when it already is.

The dying woman in the story had an epiphany. In deep meditative state, she saw herself in a way she had never allowed herself before. And *she accepted herself* with all her vulnerabilities. She let it be okay to stay with her husband even if he was never going to be faithful to her. She let it be okay to love him anyway. *So profound was her acceptance of herself that the self-forgiveness was its natural by-product.* So profound was her awakening to the truth of herself, that the wave of self love that washed through her body dissolved the cancerous cells in that very instant.

Making the Right Decision

The right decision is a decision that is *right for you*. Not for your friends, not for your parents or your children and not for anyone else. What's right for you, really *right*, will also *in the end be right for others*.

But you must know what it is first.

Thinking and *using logic and reason alone* won't get you there. Nor will the usual *substitutes for real feelings: self pity, avoidance, resentments, denial, blame.* And you will be stuck in indecision for years, or make a decision you may later regret, never quite certain it was the right one. Or lie to yourself about what you really want, just like the woman in the story, *refusing to feel* until an inch away from death. She had an awakening in the last minute, and she had a miraculous healing. Not everyone does.

I know it is scary to look inside and discover what you really feel, especially if you have been avoiding it all your life. But there is no way around it. You *must* lift out of *the entanglement* of your feelings, so you can see clearly.

If you don't know how, find the way. Nowadays, help is available in many forms. There is therapy, counseling, support groups, friends. I teach this at the workshops I give and you may find the information about them on my website: *www.powerofthepossible.com.*

One way to go about getting in touch with what you really feel is to write a letter addressed, for example, to your partner. It will be a letter that *you will not mail.* Write it and *make it real* for you. It doesn't have to be fair or right or justified. The only reason to do it, is to get it all out. If that's what's inside, you want to be free from it, so it doesn't continue to poison you. If you want to blame, or curse — go ahead. If you feel too sorry for yourself and just want to stop, write just that, and keep on writing. Don't evaluate what you write, don't analyze it, don't pay attention to grammar or punctuation, just keep going. At a certain point your walls will break down, you will drop the pretense and the real you will come out. Remember: this is a letter no one will see. You will not mail it. But it is your ticket to freedom. So write. And as your hand moves down the paper, everything you hold inside will start flowing out. Don't let your tears stop the writing. You want to feel it all. Only then can you get to a neutral place — the only place from which to make a decision.

Once you are done with the writing and there is nothing more to add — fold the letter and put it away for a day. MAKE SURE that no one finds this letter. You don't want anyone to come across it and read it. *Ever.* Especially someone mentioned in the letter. This could be a very hurtful and punishing thing, and it may be very damaging to your relationship.

Next day — re-read the letter slowly, add to it or make corrections to make it stronger. Then fold it and put it away again.

On the third day, re-read what you have written one more time, slowly, without adding anything. After that, BURN THE LETTER page by page. This is very important. You are giving your subconscious mind a clear message: *I am letting go of this anger. I am done with it.*

Having worked with many people to whom I had given this technique, I have discovered that burning the letter sooner than three days doesn't work. One woman told me that she had experienced great difficulty burning the pages even on the second day.

"Was it because the fire would keep dying, or because it was hard for you to do it emotionally?" I asked.

"It was not the fire," she said. "It was me. I felt tremendous resistance. I just *didn't want* to burn these pages."

Yes, holding on to old angers has many pay offs: blaming, being right, self pity, righteous anger to name a few. And while they may not feel good, many keep taking these pay offs because they are as addictive as any drug — addictive and very dangerous, often leading to a serious or fatal illness, as we have seen with the woman with cancer who had denied her true feelings for twenty-five years.

Trying to answer what may be the most difficult question in your life while avoiding feeling the pain that this is causing you is like trying to see through fogged glass: everything is blurred.

The answers you are seeking lie on the other side of the wall of your feelings. This wall will melt and dissolve once you allow the feelings to flow.

If we were to liken our emotions to a deep pool of water, the answers to our questions wait for us at the bottom of this pool. You *must find the strength* to step into that pool and then to dive in.

Try the following visualization: imagine yourself a scuba diver wearing an oxygen mask and all the necessary equipment, so you can breathe under the water. Begin to slowly float down, towards the bottom of this *pool of emotions.* Now—forget about everything else, and focus on what you are feeling. Imagine the things that are causing you pain and let yourself *feel what comes with all the intensity you can muster.*

At first you will probably feel *anger.* Anger is usually so close to the surface, that it is easy to tap into. Anger may switch to *hurt,* then to more anger, then back to hurt. You may come upon *rage, fear, sadness, shame, sorrow, remorse.* Feel them, and let them go. Right, wrong, justified, unjustified, easy or hard . . . stay with them and keep sinking deeper. Resist the urge to get the hell out of the pool. That's what you've done every time in the past. When it felt like too much. That's why you are so clogged, searching for answers and never finding them. Do it differently this time. Have the guts to stay with your feelings no matter how difficult it is and how scared you are.

The deeper you go—the more you will find.

And not more pain—*more beauty.* The most beautiful emotions have *substance and weight.* They don't float on the surface or in the upper layers of the pool.

Love, hope, happiness, joy, forgiveness, peace . . . they all are waiting for you on the way to the bottom. You can't get to them without first wading thru everything else that's in your way. They also hold your answers.

Too many times, having made it almost to the bottom, a voice whispers in your ear: *that's too much, you can't take it anymore.* This is a voice that has led you down the wrong path every time. A voice of *your negative ego, an enemy inside you.* But instead of dismissing this voice, the voice that has never ever told you the truth, you respond to it and rush all the way up, back to the surface. Not reaching the bottom, not finding the freedom, not finding the release.

There was just one minute left. Maybe even a second, no more...but you didn't trust what you knew. You allowed yourself, once again, to be seduced by your ego. And instead of coming up cleansed, pushed upwards into the clean, fresh air of knowing, you experienced a partial release only and are still left without the answer you sought.

Think about it. Isn't it fascinating? Why is feeling pain so terribly frightening to people that they will go to any length to avoid it?

Let me give you another example of this.

A young man who was sick with cancer was working with a psychotherapist. Sometimes he would come to the therapy sessions with his mother, often too weak after his chemotherapy treatment. Knowing that at the root of every physical illness lies emotional cause, the therapist was trying to help the young man get in touch with his feelings. In the process of their work together, the therapist discovered that the young man's father had died years before and that the son had never grieved his death.

"Next time, when you come, why don't I help you get though your feelings, so you can grieve your Dad's death," the doctor suggested. The young man's body stiffened. He looked at his feet, folded his arms across his chest. He reached for the glass of water. The therapist waited.

"No," the man broke the silence. "No. I'd rather keep doing chemotherapy. *I only vomit for four hours after the chemo. I can deal with that.*"

And yet, frightening or not, feelings are simply that — feelings. They fluctuate and they change — high-tide, low-tide, storms, fires, droughts. Small children before they've learned to adapt and to imitate adults are a good example. Crying one moment, laughing happily the next. Feelings come and go. Teach yourself how not to stuff them. *Feel them, and release them,* so you can be free. Because as long as they are in the way, you will be run by them. And eventually — destroyed by them.

Unexpressed, unattended constricting feelings are the time bombs ready to explode. The clock is set, but the time is unknown.

*   *   *

AT THE ROOT of cancer lies anger. Old, petrified, unexpressed, and now deadly. *It is the anger that we are sure is too late to do anything about.*

There is nothing I can do about it, it happened too long ago, it is too late now is the message we give our subconscious again and again. Sometimes the anger may indeed be so old, we don't even remember it. We have succeeded in tucking it away, hiding it even from ourselves.

But it is there. As alive and potent as when it was first born, and it is doing its deadly job. *The subconscious gets the message: it is too late.* The subconscious does not judge or evaluate. It simply follows the given program. The body follows as well: it is too late. And a person gets a deadly illness. Designed to get him out of here because it is too late *for here.*

It is not too late! And this bomb slowly ticking away inside often can be stopped. So many have done it successfully. None of them without getting to the bottom of their feelings and freeing themselves from their constricting grip. Having a life threatening illness was their motivation. It doesn't have to go that far.

Self pity, being sorry for yourself, *is not a feeling,* but a mood, a condition. It *is an anesthetic* that keeps you stuck, and so does *blaming* — yourself or others. They are the "drugs" to alleviate pain, and just as addictive. The drugs that don't heal you but kill you instead. Killing you slowly, or on the spot, like an overdose.

With a heart attack or a cancer or a severe depression.

What is depression? Imagine gauzelike strips of anger laid upon each other one layer at a time. A slow process, building up with the years, eventually creating a thick, impenetrable brick, hard and dark and solid, that is now pressing onto your chest. Composed of all your angers, big and small, gathered over the years. All of them—unattended, stuffed together, so many it is impossible to pick apart. And you are doing nothing about it. Just letting them build. Until one morning you can't get out of bed, and you can't explain why. Or something very minor happens—a colleague at the next desk at work laughs too loud, again (!!!!) after you've asked her so many times not too ... and you *can't take it anymore.* That was the last straw. You snap. You see no point in living. That's depression. Now you are a prime candidate for real drugs—antidepressants which you hope will make you feel better. But they will do nothing to take away the original cause.

The rate of cancer is increasing. Depression is on the rise. More and more, we hear of people dying of heart attacks in the prime of life. An athlete, a young man who seemed to have nothing wrong with his health at all, suddenly drops dead on a tennis court. A heart attack at the age of forty. But there was nothing wrong with his heart before?! Are you sure? What determines whether or not something was wrong with one's heart? Does heartache qualify? A heartache that is not measurable by means of traditional medicine? But men must be strong, they must "bear it like a man," ignore the pain of the heart and keep "handling it."

Do they?

In many cases, the first symptom of a heart attack is death. Happening to people too young to die. What's going on? A heart too full of pain can bear only so much. And it gives up.

If you are in the medical profession and are reading this, don't dismiss it too readily. Don't dismiss the increasing number of healings that defy medical explanations either.

I have great respect for our Western medicine. My life was saved at least twice when I had internal bleedings that I was not aware of until too much blood had been lost. Why was I bleeding internally? Bleeding high up in my stomach, so close to the heart?

What was it that I *couldn't stomach?* I will tell you the truth. I couldn't stomach the fact that my marriage (my first marriage) was unraveling and I felt powerless to stop the avalanche. We were losing what we once had with each other, becoming strangers under the same roof, and I had no tools to deal with what was happening. And so I did what most people do. I cried, I fought, I withdrew into hostile silences, I punished, I blamed, and I felt very sorry for myself. Yet, I never permitted myself to just *fall apart* in a real way. To drop to the very bottom of my pain and face the truth.

It wasn't anyone's fault. It worked when we were very young, but it couldn't work long term. I wasn't ready for this truth. I wasn't ready to even consider leaving the marriage. I bled instead.

Wonderful doctors in the emergency rooms saved me, stopped the bleeding in time, and I didn't die. But in the end, it was *the emotional healing,* the healing of my heart, *the healing of the pain that had caused the bleeding* that brought this to an end. And the bleedings stopped.

Our emotions have tremendous power. They have the power of life and death.

I spent many years refusing to accept that my first marriage was coming to an end. We had married for life, both of us fighters, survivors, not the ones to quit. I was going to make it work! *If I could just try harder,* I thought, *"work at it"* more, *change myself more,* *"get him to see"* (what a hopeless task!)...*then perhaps.* But it was getting worse. We saw the world very differently, and we were becoming more and more alienated from each other. We were so young when we got married and our differences didn't seem to matter. They intensified with time. A divide we couldn't bridge. Our fights got harder and harder, taking an enormous toll on both of us. From the outside, the marriage continued to look "perfect," but we were each suffocating and dying inside of it. I spent the last summer separated as I went through the intense process of "emotional surgery." Opening this festering wound, cleaning it out and letting it slowly heal. It was the most poignant time in my life and the hardest decision to make.

The "pool of emotions" became my home, the place I lived in every day, dropping to the bottom, *accepting, forgiving,* letting go. The time came when I thought I was *done* with this process. I believed I'd looked at everything I could think of, I had felt all I could, and I had found forgiveness. I had many answers by then. But not *the* answer. I still didn't know if I should end the trial separation and go back home or end the marriage for real and go for divorce. *When was I going to know?!* I was getting impatient. One night, as I was falling asleep, I took myself off the hook. *I will know when I know,* I said to myself. *I am letting go of controlling anything.*

I woke up clear as a bell, knowing that my marriage was over.

When did it slip into my consciousness? How? It happened as soon as I surrendered my need *to have it my way*—to have the answer come to me on *my* timing. Humility opened the door to the Possibility. The possibility to know what I wanted to know with total clarity and the possibility of a different future.

Ending a marriage is never an easy choice. It was the only choice for me.

*   *   *

WHEN YOU ARE faced with a decision that will profoundly change the direction of your life, a decision that will affect the lives of others close to you—your wife or husband you are considering leaving, your children if you have any—a decision that will affect all of your family in the deepest way, so much lies in the balance. So important it is to make the right choice. A choice that is right for you. The one you will not question in the future. A decision that, looking back, you will know was the right thing to do. No matter how difficult and painful it was, it eventually brought healing to everyone it had affected.

When you are making a decision of this magnitude, you need to have *all of yourself* present. *Your thinking and your feeling, your intel-*

lect and your heart. You need to find the *right balance* between your *love* and your *will*.

Your *will* — that strength and power within you *to do what needs to be done*, difficult or not. And your *love*, the part of you that wants to *follow your heart* whether or not it is the right thing to do. *You need to find the balance between them.*

Love and Will are often at odds with each other.

Love may be saying "yes" while your will is saying "no."

"I don't want to leave him, I love him," says your love.

"But I must, it is destroying me," says your will.

Or it could be the opposite. The will may be saying "yes, you are going to stay in that marriage no matter what. You must persevere." And the love, your love for yourself, is saying "no, I can't." Wherever that balance lies for you, you need to find it. This balance is *the core* of your power. Out of it the right action will follow.

To stay or to leave a marriage of twenty some years? Yes or no?

There are no simple answers to complex situations. Our lives are not simple. We are not simple. If you want simple answers, this book is not for you. Close it and put it down. You are not going to find them here.

Freedom is not simple and not always comfortable. There is a responsibility that comes with it. A responsibility to be an adult. To be responsible for our actions. A responsibility to ourselves and to those we love. A responsibility to make the right choices. A responsibility to *not consciously hurt another* with our choices.

The answers we seek come with our understanding of this complexity.

Each one of us is a synergy of so many parts. We each carry the light and we also carry the darkness. We are familiar with our darkness. It is our light that scares us. At times we are filled with the most gracious giving. At other times we can be distant and cold and unavailable. We can be monsters and we can be saints.

We can be everything, and often we are. The more healing we have experienced, the stronger is our choice to act out of our beauty and not out of our negativity.

To look for a simple answer, a "yes" or a "no" to a complex situation, is to not respect yourself. You deserve more than that. Give yourself the space you need. Honor yourself in this way.

Once you've *told yourself the truth*, once *you've let yourself feel all the feelings* you've been holding in check for so long, once you've *accepted and forgiven yourself* and *accepted the facts of your situation* without embellishing them or making them worse than they are, the answers you are looking for will simply be there, and you will just know.

For some it is right to end the relationship, for others it is right to stay. There is no right or wrong answer. It is what's right for *you.*

Don't rush this process. Don't skip the steps. Have the courage to do what it takes so you can be free. Otherwise, no matter what you decide, there will be regret, there will be sorrow, there will be doubt.

The woman in the story made a choice that was right for her. She accepted and forgave herself and she accepted and forgave her husband. And with this, she received a new lease on life and a healing that was miraculous. At the very depth of her being and with the intensity of the moment, she made a choice to live and to be happy.

At that level of choice, magic enters one's life — magic that shows us the Power of the Possible and *our true magnificence.* It takes *courage* to step that far. To let yourself see that *light in yourself.* Not many have that level of courage. Be the one who does. Let your life shine the light on the life of others. If one can do it, so can many. Why not you?

All about Love

There is nothing either good or bad, but thinking makes it so.

—William Shakespeare

A GOOD FRIEND OF MINE, I'll call her Marilyn, stopped by one day for a cup of coffee, and sure enough, before we knew it, we were deeply involved in a conversation, discussing the "right and wrong" ways of being in a relationship. After all, I was writing a book about it, wasn't I?

"So often, when we are absolutely convinced we are right, we are not that right at all," I said.

"Really?" Marilyn raised her eyebrows.

My friend is an open-minded woman. She is always eager to learn, always ready to hear a different perspective. Her relationship of two years had recently ended, and though she was okay with it by then, the wounds had not yet fully healed. The memories of fights with her ex-fiancée were still fresh. She would relive them again and again in her mind wondering if there was something she could have done differently. "Was there another way?" she'd ask herself, arriving each time at the same answer. No. She had been right. She had handled it correctly. She was making sure her needs were met, and no, she wasn't selfish or unreasonable. It was her boyfriend who had been stubborn and childish, while she was simply self-respecting.

"So what you are saying is when we are sure we are right, we are actually wrong?" she asked.

"Yes," I said. "Not wrong as an absolute, but certainly not 'right.'" I knew I needed to explain myself. "Give me an example," I said, "of a situation in your relationship in which there is no question in your mind that you were right. It can be something seemingly minor, it really doesn't matter. What's the first thing that comes to mind?"

Marilyn chuckled. "Oh, that's easy", she said. "How about this one? He moves in with me, and you know, my place is small. I have to go through the kitchen to get to my office. Now both of us are working from home, he and I. And he *would not wash the dishes* after himself! Every time I went through the kitchen or into the kitchen, I would see his dirty dishes in the sink. And it was driving me crazy. I can't stand dirty dishes. It upsets me. I never leave dishes unwashed and out there in the sink. I asked him again and again not to do it. To wash them after he's eaten, so I don't have to look at his mess and be irritated. I asked him nicely. I joked about it. I asked him seriously. I explained to him why I needed it. I got very angry. And still—he would not do it!!!! Now—it was MY place. He moved in with me. Who did he think I was??!! His mother??!!!" She caught herself and stopped. "It's water under the bridge now, but don't you think I was right about it?"

"What did he say to you?" I asked. "Why wouldn't he do it?"

"He said it interrupted his flow. He liked to get back to work immediately after eating and that he would wash everything in the evening. In the mean time, I was not supposed to pay attention to such small things."

She was getting anxious just remembering that time. I put my hand on her knee.

"Look," I said. "I just read about a process that Byron Katie suggested in her book "Loving What Is." I think it's brilliant. Would you like to try it?"

"Sure," Marilyn said. "Sure."

"Tell me again how it made you feel, when he wouldn't do his dishes," I said.

"Oh, I felt angry, I felt like . . . as if he didn't care about me. Like it didn't matter what I needed, it didn't matter at all. And that he did not respect me. If he respected me, he would never treat me this way. Never. I felt he treated me as if I were his mother, not his equal partner." She stopped and took a deep breath. "Yes. That's how I felt every time I passed through that kitchen."

I waited. But she seemed suddenly exhausted. "Anything else?" I asked.

"That pretty much sums it up."

"Okay," I said. "Now tell me something. Think about it and tell me: Was what you felt really true?"

She paused. I could see her face changing. With her eyes closed she was reliving her experience one more time, looking at it from a different angle.

"No," she said finally. "It's not true. I don't think he thought that at all."

I could see she was amazed. Startled, perhaps, by what she had just said. She was looking at her hands, waiting for what I had to say next.

"All right," I said. Let's go back again. When you thought he didn't respect you or care about you, how did that make you feel?"

Marilyn looked up. "How did it make me feel? I was angry. I was so angry I couldn't breathe. I was unhappy. I was irritated, I would look at him at his desk working, and the kitchen was full of his dirty dishes, and I would just be fuming inside."

"Good," I said. "Now we know what you felt, and we know what you thought were his reasons for not washing the dishes. And we also know — it wasn't true. So now — let's turn it around.

You thought he did not respect you, didn't care about you, and treated you as if you were his mother, not his equal partner. Take this — and turn it around. Turn it into an opposite."

Marilyn concentrated. I could see her mind working, turning things around. Suddenly her voice dropped and she almost whispered, "You mean — turn it all around?"

"Yes," I said. "Say it out loud."

What she said then — stunned us both.

"*I* didn't respect him," she said. "*I* thought he was immature. *I* didn't care about what was important for *him*...Oh, my God..." She covered her eyes with her hands. "I treated him as if he were a child, not a man. I did not respect him. I didn't. I was mean. I would diminish him. I would make him so small..." She couldn't talk.

I pulled her towards me and held her as she cried.

"I never saw it before," she whispered. I could see it was hard for her to speak. "I am sorry, Nick. I am so sorry..." She moved away from me, reaching for the Kleenex and put it to her face. "He was so tender, so loving...so young in many ways. And yes, I believed he was too immature, and it bothered me. I was even getting bored. I needed to leave the house and just be by myself to feel good again sometimes. I have always been very independent and responsible. And I didn't think he was. I didn't know how to tell him, so I got angrier and angrier. I knew it couldn't work between us. We were too different. And I didn't want to admit it to myself. So I punished him." She put her hand to her chest. "It is so painful to see it. But I feel like something is releasing right here," she pointed to her heart, where her hand was resting. "I can't believe I never saw it. I was so sure it was him."

I took her hand in mine and held it.

"It hurts so much to see it. But — it's as if we've just lanced a boil."

"And now it can heal," I said. "Now you can let go. Forgive yourself and let go."

Through her tears Marilyn nodded and sighed. "Yes," she said smiling now. "Thank you."

"By the way, Mykaell never washes the dishes either," I said and smiled. "But my first husband did. He washed everything after each meal. I never needed to ask. And he brought me breakfast in bed all the time. And he always brought me roses. In fact, the worse our marriage got, the more flowers I received. I was drowning in roses at one time. He even came to the mediation meeting with my attorney and the financial adviser she had invited (both of them — women) with three bouquets of roses. One for each of us. You should have seen the faces of these women! It didn't save our marriage though. I was miserable and so was he."

"Mykaell doesn't wash the dishes?" Marylyn was incredulous. "And you are okay with it?"

"Absolutely. He will help me with them if I ask, but in general it is not something he does. Don't think I didn't try," I laughed. "I went through the entire process with it. I would get angry, he would promise to wash them, and he would wash them, but then he would forget to wash them the next time, or he would start washing them, but not finish and go do something else. I was pulling out my hair. I was like you were with Nick in a way. And then I stopped myself. I realized — it was not malicious. I realized he really didn't like to wash them. I realized it didn't matter to him whether they were washed or not. If I were to leave them in the sink for days, he would barely notice. His mind is somewhere else, on the things he is passionate about, and order in the kitchen isn't one of them. I realized that it mattered to me, but not to him. And — most important — I realized that he was doing a tremendous amount of other things for me and for us and for our life together all the time. He was my full partner in everything, and that's what mattered, not who did or did not do the dishes. Well, I saw all that and decided to wash the dishes myself!"

Compromise in a Relationship

"Wisdom is learning what to overlook," wrote William James.
Wisdom is also knowing *when* to overlook it.

For purposes of better illustration, let's separate problems in relationships into two categories: *mortal sins* and *venial sins,* Catholic terminology that helps to make the point. Mortal sins, as the definition clearly implies, are just that: the most serious, grievous crimes, ones where a line is crossed, while venial sins are minor offenses, easy to negotiate or overlook.

Every relationship requires clearly defined boundaries of what's accepted and what's not and, of course, these boundaries differ with each couple. Certain things are important to us. Some are critical while other things may not matter that much and so we can let go of them easily. I often hear people say, "You can't have everything you want, so you have to compromise." This is what I call a *half truth.* And like all half truths, if it is not understood as such, it becomes *the blackest lie of all* because it carries a resonance of truth in it but if you don't fully understand it, it can be misleading and even treacherous.

Why?

Compromise in a relationship is a very positive thing but *only if you haven't sacrificed your values for it.* Only if the peace that is achieved by this compromise has been arrived at without resentment. And not as a "give and take" either. Give and take doesn't exist in a good relationship. Only "give and give" does.

You give one hundred percent, and you take zero.

And your loved one gives one hundred percent and takes zero. Everyone gives and no one takes. The thought "am I getting enough?" never enters your mind. You never check the ledger book to see if you are receiving — you know you are. It is woven into the very fabric of your relationship. Because *my greatest joy is* **your** *happiness.* I care more about your happiness than my own.

That's *not* sacrifice. Not when it is a choice, not when it is a preference. Not when the thing that makes me the happiest is your smile — the knowing that I have been able to give you that.

A fantasy? Hardly. It is what happens in every successful relationship. You give to each other totally and wholeheartedly. *You don't abandon yourself — but your focus and your attention are on loving.* It is *what comes naturally.* You don't think about it. It's automatic. It's simply who you are.

So high is the resonance of selfless giving, that more often than not it will pull your partner into it as well. It cannot be otherwise. The only other option for that partner would be to leave. But again, if your resonance is that high, you will not attract into your life someone who can't be there with you. A person who is looking to take advantage of the one who loves him will subconsciously search for (and find) someone who will fit this agenda, someone who believes that love is being hurt, used and abused. *"Some of them want to use you — some of them want to get used by you . . . "* We have always known that. We even write songs about it.

It is up to us to create how we want to be treated. We set the parameters. We make the choices.

Just think about it. Just play with these possibilities. Remember the law of resonance and keep yours high and strong. And if your partner is teeter-tottering in the beginning, he won't be doing it for long.

How often have we seen the same person act completely differently in one relationship than he or she used to in another? How is it that the same man, so selfish and uncaring in the past, is suddenly — and with a different woman — so generous and kind? Could it be that her love had lifted him into this new resonance? Leaving no room for him to be anything but equally loving?

This is what a happy relationship of two adults looks like. You are more concerned with the happiness of the one you love than with your own. Because it is their happiness, their success, their inspiration that bring you the most joy. And it is exactly the same for them. Your passion, your freedom, your reaching for your dream is what matters most to them. So no one feels neglected; no one is overlooked and forgotten. And if each of you wants different things — *you talk about it*. You talk about it until you find a way. You work things out. You don't keep score. Relationship does not require a ledger sheet. If you don't agree on something, you talk about it until each one is heard, until each one feels heard and seen, and then you arrive at what works best. Best for whom? That question should not even come up. The answer should be obvious: *best for us.*

In a healthy relationship *the relationship always comes first.*

Four Principles of Synergy

Let's look at the four principles of synergy developed by David Berenson. They can be very helpful as guidelines for a relationship of any kind, that of business partners, friends, lovers, husband and wife, or a larger family.

We know that synergy means that the whole is greater than the sum of its parts, which means that when we come together, we create a separate entity — *our relationship,* — which is far more, in every way, than what each one of us brings to it combined.

Here are *the four principles of synergy.* If they make sense to you, check them against the relationships you are in. You will see that the ones that work best are the ones where synergy is at play.

For a relationship to have synergy, the following four things must be present:

1. Everyone does his or her part while taking responsibility for the whole.

2. Everyone does what he likes to do.

3. Everyone does what he does well.

4. Each person puts *the relationship first.*

The fourth principle is the most important one.

What is most important in any relationship is the relationship itself.

In the story I told earlier, Marilyn's desire for order in the kitchen and her conviction that she had a right to demand it were far more important than considering Nick's need for what he called his "uninterrupted flow." While for Nick having that flow was much more important than honoring Marilyn's need for a clean, pleasant-looking kitchen. Stuck in their positions, they felt they had a right to them. They felt that what they wanted mattered more than having peace and harmony with each other. Thus a healthy compromise wasn't found, and the relationship suffered.

Have your priorities in the right order, and *make your relationship your number one priority.*

If your priorities are in order, there is a good chance you will get them. If, however, they are not in order, if you don't distinguish between critically important things and things that are easily negotiable, then the success of your relationship will be spotty at best.

How many more examples do we need of families breaking up because either the husband or the wife made their career more important than their marriage? It doesn't mean — forget the career. It is never an either/or, black and white situation. What it means is if it is the marriage that's most important, then we work things out. We take time to talk, to consider each other's point of view, and — what do you know? — somehow we find a way. *Our marriage supports our careers, if it comes first.* Not the other way around. If the career matters most, then the priorities are not in order, and you may very well lose the marriage. And if not technically then in every other way. Too many people are leading parallel lives, having long forgotten why they are still together.

In a personal one-to-one relationship, it is the "us" that has to come first.

What's most important for us, together, comes before me and before you.

If we want different things, if we disagree, if we fight about something, we stop and deal with it. We talk, we fight it out if it comes to that. If we are too angry to hear and see each other, we take a break. We may go to different rooms. We may fume until we calm down. That's okay. Whenever there are two different people, there will be times when they will disagree and fight. That's normal. That's natural. If that does not happen, then one or the other is selling out. But we both know because it's something we've agreed upon before — we will stay with the fight *until we find a resolution.* We won't go to sleep angry, no matter how late it is, no matter how tempting it is to just roll over and stop talking. And no one will leave the house. No one will slam the door and drive off. The other room is okay. The other room is advisable. To cool off. To stop being so bloody sure that you are right. This is the ego's seductive voice. It always lies. Instead of listening to it — stop. Take a short break. *A short break,* not hours of punishing silence. We *will make up* in the end because that's our agreement — *to make sure we make up and not let resentments settle in.* And it will be genuine because we *will let go.* We won't just drop the subject in resignation. This can never work. No. We will talk until we are both okay. Because we know *our relationship always comes first.* Not the job, not the career, not even the children, not me, not you.

Not even the children???!!!! I didn't say that the children were not a priority. But unless the marriage comes first, the children will suffer as well because the marriage will suffer.

The principles of synergy work. They are not negotiable. Try them out, give them a chance, and see for yourself.

The other three principles of synergy are easy.

When everyone does what he is good at and what he likes to do, then everyone is happy and fulfilled. For example, if you like to garden and I like to cook, then that's what we will do, and we will have a beautiful garden and wonderful meals; or if I am good at bookkeeping and maintaining family finances and you love helping the children with homework every night, then we will do just that, and our money will be well maintained and the children taken care of. But if either one of us is sick or out of town or unable to do his or her part for some other reason, then the other partner *will take those duties over* as well because "everyone does his or her part *while taking responsibility for the whole.*" And "the whole" is the relationship. So if one member is out of commission, the other one is there to make sure things run smoothly anyway. That's synergy at work. *You do your part*, no matter what it happens to be, and *you always take responsibility for the whole.*

That also means that if something needs to be done and no one is really good at it or likes to do it, then together we find a way to take care of it. We may hire another person for that particular job or we will each take turns or we will find a compromise.

If it is the relationship that comes first, then who does and who does not wash the dishes is easily negotiated. If you hate it, then I will do it and you will do something else. If we both hate it, we will either have a constant mess in the kitchen or we will decide to stop hating it, stop being childish and become more mature. We may take turns, we may hire someone to come and do it for us if we can afford it. No one has died from washing the dishes yet. Honestly. If you don't believe me, check it out.

In the case of my friend Marilyn and her former fiancée, her anger at him for leaving the mess in the kitchen was obscuring something much more real. It was easier to get angry because there was a pile of dirty dishes in the sink than to deal with the pain of seeing that her relationship was not what she hoped it would be, that the man she was planning to marry was immature, and that she did not respect him. He was not ready to be her full partner in life, his marriage proposal was premature, they were not suited for each other long term, and the relationship was coming to an end.

The Danger of Building Resentments

Once, many years ago, when I was married to my first husband, an old classmate of his came into our life again. He said something to me one day quite unexpectedly, and I never forgot it. It made me angry at the time, so I argued with him and then dismissed it.

"Something is wrong with your relationship with Alex," he said, talking about my marriage.

"What do you mean?" I argued. "There is nothing wrong with us!"

"Oh, yes, there is," he said shaking his head. "It's the way you are with each other. You are *polite.*"

Polite! What's wrong with polite?! I fumed silently. Do you want us to fight? To scream at each other? To be rude???? Of course we are polite! We are both well brought up!

And yet — how right he was in his observation. In fact, he hit the nail right on the head. And it had nothing to do with our having good manners. Happy couples are not polite with each other. They are real. They may fight, they may argue, they may disagree. They are not always kissing and hugging and hanging on each other's words. It is never perfect, but neither is it polite. If your relationship is real, you will still make mistakes, you may still say or do things that will upset your partner, you may forget to pay attention, you may yell at each other or be silent together…and yet your connection will always be there, alive, palpable, unique. And those around you will feel your warmth and your closeness whether it is overt or very private.

"Polite" in a relationship means we are avoiding stepping on land mines. "Polite" means we are trying very hard not to show how isolated we feel. "Polite" is *I have swallowed my anger and rage, and I won't talk to you about what's wrong with us because I have given up.* And it means the same for you. We have both given up. We don't talk about what matters because we've had too many fights where nothing was resolved. "Polite" is our despair. "Polite" is avoiding feeling pain and pretending we are okay.

It's what happens to couples when resentments take root. *"Polite" is the child of their resentments.* I learned it first hand.

*   *   *

RESENTMENT IS THE poison that kills. Resentment is the mortar that holds together the walls of cold hostile silences between two people.

"What's wrong?" he asks.

"Nothing," she says.

He asks again. Again — no answer.

Silence falls. He waits. You can cut the tension with a knife.

"Okay then." An angry shrug, and he slams the door. The screeching sound of tires across the concrete of the driveway and he is gone. She freezes at the kitchen sink, fists clenched, jaws set tight.

Does this sound familiar?

Too familiar, I am afraid.

Why not answer him? Why not say what exactly *is* wrong?

Because *he should know,* she thinks. *He should know very well. He shouldn't even ask!*

It may be true. He does know. He just doesn't want to deal with it. It's better to pretend he has no idea, hoping to get the answer he just got so he can walk away in righteous indignation. Now it's *her* fault.

I asked you, didn't I? I gave you a chance. You said, "Nothing." Fine.

Now they are both pissed. Sick and tired and angry.

He'll punish her by getting out of the house. But she will get back at him. They both know it.

Then, at some point they will drop it. Or maybe it will just go away—until the next time. And the next time, and the next... until it is rooted deep. And it won't go away anymore.

It's an old game. Old and tired. And yet, the same lines are repeated over and over by couples everywhere.

"Leave me alone. I don't want to talk."

"Fine!"

Why not talk? Even if he does know the answer to the question he asks. That's the hook—to hook you into this old dance. Why take the bait? Why not answer the question? And actually deal with something. And what if he really doesn't know the answer? What if he genuinely forgot that he had upset you with something? Men let go of things much faster and much easier than we women do. Why expect that men should psychically figure out what's wrong with us? Why choose to sulk again and again instead of actually telling them what's wrong so it can be resolved?

Resentment is anger, laced with hurt. Unexpressed, unattended anger, mixed with layers upon layers of unanswered hurt. And soon enough the clear blue pool that your relationship once was becomes murky, unpleasant, dark. It should have been drained long ago but it was left unattended. It didn't seem like a big deal at the time.

Not anymore. But now you don't want to even step into this stagnant water. You continue to avoid it, not remembering what exactly is wrong between the two of you. Except it is beginning to feel like everything is wrong.

Beware of your resentments. Like tiny toxic seeds, if left alone, they will sink deep down and will begin their destructive work. They will color your thoughts and feelings, shape your responses, affect everything you do. And they will grow in size, expand, multiply, and soon enough the bigger picture will be blurred, and all you will be able to see is how misunderstood you have been, how unappreciated, and how badly you want to punish this one most important person in your life. The one who used to be *everything* suddenly must be hurt, attacked, destroyed, because "you are right, damn it!" (or so says your ego as it goes thrashing about, smashing everything that's sacred) and you hear yourself say things that should never be said. Awful things, hurtful things, things you must never say even in anger. "The small stuff" becomes huge. You can no longer see the difference. The mortal sins have the same gravity and impact as venial sins. And you are lost. You have lost yourself and most probably are well on the way to losing the relationship as well.

An example of a couple comes to mind.

The husband and wife were talking about the difficulties in their marriage. The wife spoke first. In a flat monotone, she went about describing the endless succession of women her husband had been sleeping with over the years, his promises to stop that were always broken, and how she couldn't take it anymore. "And then he leaves his clothes on the floor all the time," she said in a voice with no inflection. "He never picks up his socks and underwear. He just leaves them lying everywhere on the floor in the bedroom for me to pick up. Who does he think I am, his maid?"

Her voice never changed as she went from one offense to the other. You had to do a double take to make sure you heard correctly. Cheating and not picking up your underwear? Sleeping with other women and leaving socks on the floor? Hmm.

This is more common than you may think.

Shutting yourself down, refusing to feel, numbing yourself with self pity, avoiding, denying, lying to yourself. And then one day — a deadly illness, or — death. Or the death of the marriage.

*   *   *

YES, RELATIONSHIPS CAN be difficult. And difficult they will remain if we choose not to deal with the problems when they are occurring but instead comply, push the hurt down and tell ourselves it is not there. Or slam the door and leave the house, or sulk, but not say what's wrong, punish each other by being silent and hostile. After all, we've seen our parents do that for years or we've seen it in films or read about it in books. We've learned by example and we have also practiced it ourselves. Attacking, defending, withdrawing — it comes naturally, doesn't it? Much more so than creating *a new map* of being together. A much needed map of *having the guts* to stay with the fight and fight it cleanly. And *talk* — talk to each other. Find the character to resist the burning desire to destroy your "opponent" — that one most important person in your life — and actually *try to hear him* and not stop until the conflict is resolved.

I am not trying to oversimplify what is almost always complex. There can be many reasons why people don't talk. Not feeling safe — being frightened of the reaction you'll get is but one of them.

But if things are left unsaid, if feelings are not shared, if misunderstandings are not cleared, resentments will take their place. Like sediment that won't dissolve, your resentments will sink to the bottom of that precious vessel that is your relationship and they will calcify, creating layer upon layer of hardened stuff, the stuff that *will* drive a wedge between you, a wedge that will turn into a wall, separating you more and more.

Remember the Love

Intimacy — or the lack of it — is what makes or breaks a relationship. Not sexual intimacy, which is, of course, incredibly important, but haven't you noticed? Without the other kind of intimacy, sexual intimacy alone has never ever been enough to sustain any relationship.

In fact, by itself it won't even sustain itself. Fiery and fantastic in the beginning, it will fizzle out if there is nothing else to support it. It is that other kind of intimacy that we all long for and so few ever find. Because of the walls we put up, because of the lack of communication, because most of us expect the other to some-how be able to "get" what we want and need, without our actually bothering to tell them.

When things go wrong, when you are in the midst of a bad fight, when seized by the desire to punish and blinded by your need to prove that *you are right*—stop! Just make yourself stop. It is not easy, but it is possible.

Stop. Take a breath. Don't crush and destroy. Don't say the things you will most certainly regret.

Instead, do something different.

In the midst of all this raw energy, make yourself remember something.

Remember the Love.

Yes. Remember the *love*.

That person you are fighting with now is the one you love. If you are able to remember it while in another room breathing heavily in anger, it will shift the energy one hundred eighty de-grees. Most fights are about nothing anyway. Often we can't even remember what started it. *What's more important? The love you share or being right one more time?* Who would you rather wake up with in the morning? The one you love or your precious rightness?

When we remember the love, so much can just fade away. What seemed so important a moment ago, now looks like a trifle. Anger dissipates and is replaced by remorse. Now it is easier to forgive, to let it go, to be able to talk, to work things out.

Don't sweat the small stuff—it's all small stuff.

If love is what's most important, if my being loving towards you is what matters most, then it's easy not to sweat the small stuff.

In the midst of a fight, however, when both people are pos-sessed by the burning need to prove their point, *being right* is what matters most. Not you and your happiness and not my being lov-ing toward you. No. *I have to make you see that I am right!* And it blurs everything else. Small stuff becomes gigantic. It is now given *meaning*—he doesn't wash the dishes because he doesn't care about me, period. And it is given *significance*. Since he doesn't care about me, there is no point in staying together.

Do you see how crazy it can get?

*   *   *

IMAGINE A WILD fire burning out of control. Left alone it is a dan-gerous, destructive, damaging force. We try to stop it by pour-ing water over it. Sometimes it is enough, other times the fire is too strong, and the only way to stop it is to contain it. And so we dig trenches around the area and again we fill them with water. *As the fire reaches the trenches, the water stops it.* And it burns itself out.

The power of the elements is enormous. We see examples of it in the news all the time. Hurricanes, typhoons, tornados, tsunamis, earthquakes, storms, fires.... We see them at a distance, we see them in our own back yard. Attacking, raging, destroying what took us lifetimes to build. And it looks like it is getting worse, doesn't it? But we still don't get it. We are bewildered. Still looking for causes "out there."

The elements of nature are not "out there." They are not just "forces beyond our control." They are also right here, playing out just as powerfully and, at times destructively, in our own personal lives.

Our reality is reflective. We can liken it to a huge looking glass that curves and surrounds us wherever we turn. The signs are everywhere, if we would but pay attention.

We are not separate from nature.

We come home to the one we love to warm our hands by the fires of our relationship.

In the beginning, when we first met, the fires of our passions were all that mattered. The dancing flames burning high, obscuring everything else. Nothing else existed except this passion, this amazing fire of life.

With time, the fire turned into embers — the glowing embers of the deepest, most sensuous red. The fire subsided, but didn't leave. We couldn't cook our food on it before. The tall flames would have burned it up.

Just like passion, no matter how incredible and amazing, if it is not tempered by love, it will burn itself out. It comes in bursts and then it subsides. And then again — the burst, and the calming down. The flames of fire. We love to watch them and to sit by them, but it is the embers with the heat contained in them that will bring sustenance and life.

We have to wait for the embers before we can cook our food.

These glowing embers, the intimacy born out of tending the fires of our passion, tempering them with our loving patience — this is the stuff of magic we seek. And so we will maintain the fire by adding more logs, strengthening, brightening and deepening the embers' glow.

We will tend this fire just as we will tend our relationship. We will not take it for granted. We won't assume that it will always be there because we know *relationship is a choice to love, made every day, consciously.*

It may appear automatic but it really is not.

And we will tell each other about our love. We will tell each other that we love again and again. You can never say it enough times. And we can never hear it enough times either. If you really *hear* it, it is the sweetest music. It is the sound and voice of the heart.

Fire. Such a powerful life-giving force. It needs to be respected, honored and recognized for what it can bring us and what it can take away. Unattended, the fire can die. It can also destroy. Our bursts of anger, our fiery explosive emotions, our dangerous, destructive reactions are the element of fire at work in our lives. You always take fire seriously. You do not play with it. Isn't it one of the first things we teach our children? Why then do we so easily forget?

Remember the love.

Love is the *water* that will contain the fire if it is out of control. Love is what will stop the destruction dead in its tracks. *Let yourself feel it.* Because if you do, then no matter how angry you are and how seductive it might feel to say or do something damaging while in the midst of a bad fight — you won't. *Your love will not let you.* It will surround the fire and it will put it out or contain it until it subsides.

What we call "crimes of passion" won't happen if love is re-membered in time. You won't crush and destroy, consumed by anger and rage, if you but remember the love.

The Voice of the Negative Ego

There is a voice inside our heads, and it never tells us the truth. It plays the same old tapes over and over again. Every time we allow it to speak, it lies to us. Every time we listen and obey it, it brings us destruction, suffering and pain. It is not overly intelligent. Quite the opposite. Our negative ego is dumb. Dumb, but cun-ning, and therefore dangerous. And it is masquerading as our best friend.

When we need to work harder in order to succeed, it tells us we've done enough and need a rest. When we've done a great job, it tells us we could have done it much better. When someone pays us a compliment, it says it is because they want something from us. When a friend gives us constructive criticism, it tells us he is just jealous of our success.

Pay attention to what goes in your head at all times and you'll recognize this voice right away. It always says the same old "stuff." It is incapable of original thought. "They just don't understand me…They just hate my success…She says she loves me but what if she is just after my money?...I am so much more qualified, how come I didn't get the promotion?...Everyone always wants something, and no one ever gives me enough..."

The voice of an enemy inside our heads. It has but one purpose—to bring us down and to destroy everything we have. And yet we listen. Contrary to all common sense, we don't just listen. We follow its advice. We get undone and so do our successes, and soon enough it all tumbles down. A valued friendship—broken, a career—damaged, a relationship—destroyed.

It may only take our ego a minute to destroy what has taken us a lifetime to create.

Othello, blinded by his jealousy, deceived by a calculating enemy passing as a friend, strangles the love of his life, Desdemona, in a fit of jealous, murderous rage.

Why doesn't he listen to her? Why does he trust someone else instead of the one he loves? Has she ever given him reason to doubt her? Why does he choose to believe the fabricated evidence of her betrayal instead of what he knows in his heart? Why not investigate, listen, think? Why doesn't he stop at the last minute?

Because the voice inside his head whispers murder. The voice of the ego, bent on destroying every happiness he has, tells him to kill.

And he does.

And what about us? How much damage do we create by letting our negative egos run our lives? Saying things that should never be said, hurting the ones that matter most, punishing them with our withdrawals and cold silences, then calling it love?

But how do I distinguish what's real from the voice of my negative ego? "Just because I am paranoid doesn't mean they are not after me." Correct. But jokes aside, it is really not that hard to separate what is true from what is a fabrication of the mind. As I said before, that voice that never ever tells us the truth is not smart. It is always the same old story. So start paying attention. Start using your critical thinking. And soon you will be able to recognize the words for what they really are. Then if indeed it the voice of your ego, you can refuse to listen. Instead of embellishing it and letting it take you down the path of destruction one more time, refuse to indulge it. Stop going in that direction. Quite consciously—say no to it.

If a friend breaks an expensive crystal glass at your dinner party, it is not because he is envious of your crystal collection. It was just an accident. Let it go. If someone tells you your presentation was weak and you can do better, it is not because they hate you and are gloating. Maybe indeed it wasn't as stellar as you thought it was. On the other hand, if every time this person tells you how wonderful you are, you just get a sick feeling in your stomach instead of being happy to hear it, trust yourself. Trust your gut and not the voice in your head that says she is really a good friend.

What I am talking about is easy to understand, but not so easy to do because the negative ego, though not smart, is cunning. And many relationships have been damaged and destroyed because people's egos were given free reign.

Lost in paranoid thinking, giving meaning and significance where there is none, we lose what matters most and one morning wake up alone in a big empty bed and wonder what happened. "But I was right," mumbles the voice. "I know I was."

Were you? And even if you were—so what?

Let's Talk about Love

The very word carries within it such immensity of power. It has been abused and misused so often that some refuse to say it. What a sad and painful illustration of our times.

One problem is that we carry so many misconceptions of what

love really is, so many constricting beliefs about it. "Love means suffering," "love means getting hurt," "if you love too much you will only be taken advantage of," "love is difficult," "love kills," "love doesn't work."

Too much suffering has been brought on in the name of love. Too many things were done to us that have crushed us, and we vowed to never again reach for it, never again be that vulnerable, that trusting, that dependent. Our spirit, too often broken. Our hope lost, because we were "loved too much" or "not loved enough."

Some wounds have not yet been healed and new wounds are being inflicted every day. And yet, in spite of all the pain, in the face of our worst fears — we long for love. We reach for it again and again. Always — we reach for love. We need it like the air we breathe. Without love, we will die — if not physically, then emotionally. Without love — there will be no reason not to.

No one teaches us how to love. Learning by example often doesn't work either because, unfortunately, most of the examples we see while growing up only confirm the misconceptions we have heard or held. The one most important thing of all, and yet we have very few role models. Our relationship with love, the one thing that will determine the flow of everything else in our life, and we are expected to figure it out on our own.

Maybe it is not so bad. Maybe we have designed it this way. After all, we learn to ride a bicycle by falling down a few times.

Maybe the exploration of love in all its manifestations is the one reason we are all here. *Maybe the one thing by which we will evaluate our life at the very end of it will be — how good I was at love?*

*   *   *

I OFTEN THINK that in the University of Life I have chosen the study of love as my major, deciding to learn everything and anything I could learn about it through my own experiences, through books, workshops, self-exploration, through intense observation and analysis.

Love in all of its forms is a fascination to me. How much we want it, seek it, talk about it, abuse and misuse it, denounce it, blame everything on it, elevate it, proclaim it. The worst crimes of humanity — have been perpetrated in the name of love — the love of God, the love of an ideal, the love of country, the love of a woman or man... Helen of Troy — "the face that launched a thousand ships." There has been so much destruction and pain, so much confusion, despair, ignorance, hate. And on the other side of it — the soaring of the human spirit, the miracles of healing, the light of hope that will never be extinguished. The greatest sinners have often been transformed with its lightest touch.

How much have I always longed to know this singular force that is life itself. How much I have longed to unravel it and to be touched by this greatest mystery. And in accordance with my choice, my reality complied, providing me with an abundance of experiences, both light and dark, my own and of those around me.

Love. Its reservoirs and wells are always there for us to dip into and to explore. *Love has no end and no beginning, and yet everything begins and ends with love.* Everything in this book is about love. What happens when it goes wrong. What happens when it's stamped out. What happens when it is tended and allowed to soar.

*　　*　　*

I HAVE ENDLESS examples of love gone wrong both from my own experience and the experience of others. The stories are harsh, but not difficult to find.

My first love was my father. Oh, how he loved me, his "little golden girl." I believed it with all my heart. And so did he, I am sure. Was it then the melodrama, the tired old myth of a lonely soul, tragic and misunderstood, that so appealed to his Russian sensibilities? Or was it just callousness and total lack of caring that compelled this highly intelligent man to make me his confidant at the age of five? And so he shared with me one evening when I was in bed getting ready to fall asleep, that tonight was the night he was going to throw himself under a bus. "The pain of living is too much," he told me. He "couldn't bear it anymore."

I was in his study that night on a small fold-out bed in the middle of the room. Why was I sleeping there instead of in my bedroom? The unfamiliar objects around me looked ominous and dark in the flickering light of the street lamp. Paralyzed with fear, afraid to even cry, I lay there shivering, imagining my father wandering the streets, waiting for the bus to come so he could step in front of it. He was the love of my life. No one else in the family mattered. I took for granted the love of my grandparents, the one true and reliable part of my childhood. It came with the air I breathed. Always there, I never gave it much thought. It was different with Father. His love had to be earned and reaffirmed. He was my hero. There was no one else.

Just then my mother came into the room to check for something and saw that I wasn't asleep, saw the tears in my eyes. "What's wrong? Why are you crying?"

"He is going to kill himself. He will throw himself under a bus tonight," I whispered.

I hated her. She was the reason. It was all because of her. But to my surprise, she laughed in indignation.

"Bastard!" she said. "Torturing the child again! Go to sleep. Your father will never kill himself. I wish he would, to put us all out of this misery. Go to sleep, don't listen to him. He will be back home when you wake up in the morning."

And so he was.

I was thirteen years old when I realized I needed to separate myself from his "loving" if I were to stay alive myself. I was twenty-four when I was finally able to do it. It took me decades to

learn how to forgive him, but I did, and I let him be. He was simply — human. A man. Frail and weak and lost. A tormented soul,
perhaps, but human nonetheless.

*   *   *

A VERY CLOSE friend of mine told me once how, as a teenager, he
would come home from school to find his mother with half of her
body leaning out the window of his bedroom. "I'll throw myself
out and end it all!" she would tell him with pathos. I knew the
woman well. I imagine she was probably adjusting her hair as she
was saying it.

How many times did he pull her down as she struggled and
screamed, "Let go of me! I want to die! I can't take it any more!"
Strategically placing herself at his bedroom window at the exact
time he would come back from school.

"She loved me like crazy," my friend said with a shrug. "That's
what it was like for me growing up, however. I think she did this so
I would tell my father. So she could get his attention." He was
shaking his head in disbelief. "She loved me more than anyone.
Even more than my sister. I was always her number one."

"Thank God for small miracles," should have been his sister's mantra, I
thought. But, of course, it wasn't. She was always jealous of her
mother's "love" for her brother and always competing for it with
him. Even after the mother died, the competition continued, taking the form of who was best at maintaining her grave.

My friend was in his forties when he told me about his
mother's constant threats of suicide. He still believed she loved
him very much. "She would just get crazy like that," he used to say,
excusing her behavior. *Not that crazy,* I thought, remembering the
woman. Mean-spirited, duplicitous, and manipulating, she was
sucking the life out of her only son, messing up his marriage, crit-
icizing everything he ever did. He could never do enough for her,
and yet, he never heard a word of praise or appreciation out of her
mouth. Behind his back, she praised him to high heaven. Behind

his back, he was "God's gift to mothers." Eliciting the envy of her friends every way she could. What impact do you think this kind of loving had on her son and his relationship with love?

*   *   *

A GIRLFRIEND I had during my adolescent years prayed every night, as she cried herself to sleep, for her father to stop loving her. This was a case of "it hurts me more than it hurts you" love. Ever heard about this one? Her father beat her methodically and with measured brutality, making sure there were no bruises. "I love you," he used to say as he threw her against the wall. "I love you, and you know that, don't you? Do you know how much pain it causes me to have to teach you this way?"

No wonder we have difficulties with love. These chains of pain span generations.

Making Love Work

Love is action — action, born from the feeling. *It is the actions we take that in response generate particular feelings in the ones we love.*

To be loving is to love the person the way *they* want to be loved, not the way *we* want to love them and not the way we think *they should be loved.*

When you love somebody, it is so natural to want to give to them, isn't it? But just any kind of giving isn't necessarily going to make them feel loved by you. Only if in your giving you have made them *feel truly seen and known* by you, only if you give to them in a way that makes them know that you *honor their needs* and have taken the time to pay attention, will they begin to *feel safe* in your presence. Only then will they want to *trust you* and to open up to you more. Then being loved by you will *bring them pleasure* and there will be a chance for real *intimacy.*

And without the intimacy — not sexual intimacy but the intimacy between two Souls — love will not sustain itself. Love alone will not be enough.

Intimacy: feeling tender, close, vulnerable, trusting. It scares most people much more than love does. But when the two come together and join to create a whole — oh, what magic can be ours.

If we don't care to take the time to understand what it is that makes the one we love happy, what it is that makes them feel loved, then no matter how hard we try, we will end up frustrated, feeling misunderstood and unappreciated because we will be going about it the wrong way.

Love is patience. Love is paying attention to detail. Love is — taking the time.

*   *   *

CONTEMPLATE THIS:

Love me the way I want to be loved, not the way you want to love me.

If you take the time to *know me,* if you take the time and patience to see who I really am and not who you think I should be, then loving me this way becomes organic. Then *giving to me* what I need is what makes you the happiest, and you won't bring me things I don't care about and expect me to like them, and you won't get angry and disappointed if I am myself and not the ideal partner conceived by your imagination. If you love *me,* then getting close to me, understanding what makes me tick and what doesn't is so important to you that you give up your preconceived ideas of what I should be like and instead — really listen. You pay attention. *You take the time.*

Loving me the way I need to be loved is easy, if it's *me* that you love, not the projected version of me.

If I am a woman, then not the projected version of how a woman should be.

If I am a man, then not an imagined, expected image of what a man should be.

If you love *me,* you rejoice in the quirks of my individuality. *You rejoice in my freedom* and I know *you see me,* you are here, you understand. What makes me unique is what makes your heart leap for joy. You do not try to change me into somebody else to fit your expectation. Your love gives me permission to make mistakes. It does not judge me, and it doesn't lie to me either.

And I? What happens to me when you treat me this way?

I relax. I can finally take a breath. I do not have to walk on eggshells to try to please you. I can be myself and not fear losing your love. And I feel safe with you. *Safe.* So critically important. So underestimated at times, and yet so utterly essential. For you see, how can I show you myself and my weaknesses if it is not safe for me to do so? If instead of trying to understand and help me heal, you want to change me one more time?

I feel safe with you, and I learn to *trust you. I become more and more vulnerable.* I open my heart to you and I show you myself. Because, my love, I know you will not hurt me, I know you will not humiliate me. *I am safe.* I see the pleasure it gives you just to see me smile. How much joy it brings you just being with me, seeing me go about my daily life. No one ever loved me this way. Without wanting me to become different, without expecting something in return. No one ever just simply *rejoiced in my presence* quite in this way before.

I look into your eyes and I get lost. I don't want to return. I can live there forever. Your eyes — pools of love, and they caress me. They *know me* with all my foibles and weaknesses. And they tell me it is okay. I am wonderful just the way I am. I do not need to change for you. But I want to. I want to grow, I want to heal myself so I can give you my best self. Because your love has lifted me higher than I've ever been. It has shown me myself the way I never knew me, and I want to bring that gift to you. Myself, my gift. I want to polish it, make it more, for you, for me, for us....

And you, *you respond to me.* You open your arms wide, and *you set me free.* You don't hold me tight, so I suffocate in your love. You set me free so I can fly.

And you are not afraid. Not afraid that I will leave you. You will be sad if I do, and certainly you do not want it. But it is my happiness that comes first for you. Not your fear.

And I do not leave. How could I? And where would I go? I have finally found home. The home I have been searching for for eternity. You are my home, my love. This is where I belong. With you. Right here in your arms.

Knowing Where You Belong

> *Sometimes, if we're very lucky, a hand is laid upon us which has the power, by its very touch, to claim us for its own. And once we are claimed, there is nowhere else to go. We can love another, but not belong to another. Once we know to whom we belong, nothing changes what we know.*
> — Marianne Williamson

We can love another, but not belong to another.

Pause here for a moment. Let this thought sink in.

It is so obvious, isn't it? Most of us in the course of our lives have been in relationships that were not right for us long-term. No matter how much we tried to convince ourselves to the contrary. No matter how in love we might have been at the time.

Some relationships are not to be kept forever. And yet — they may not be our mistakes either. And they are definitely *not our failures if — we have learned from them,* if by being in them we have learned more about ourselves and have changed. These relationships are simply our lessons on the way home. Even if, at times, we choose lessons that are more difficult than they need to be.

Throughout time, some of the most incredible relationships have always been the ones where both people listened to their hearts and trusted themselves. *They knew they belonged with each other* and they had the courage to follow what they knew. It doesn't mean it was always easy, or smooth or perfect. No one promised them it would work. But it did. Because they made it work.

Remember the movie "Notebook?" It is a good example of what I am talking about. If you haven't seen it, rent it. It's beautiful and touching, and it will lift your spirit. I won't describe it here, but I highly recommend it.

> *Soul mates are made, not met.*
>
> — LAZARIS

I don't believe in soul mates. But I do believe in knowing with whom you belong.

Is there a difference?

Yes.

"Soul mates are made, not met."

You do not *find* a soul mate, but you can become that for each other.

So many people spend years in search of a soul mate trying to see if the person they meet fits into their imagined picture of a perfect woman or man. They check them against their list, they look for the right package...and it never works. The soul mate does not come along, does he?

If it is the package that you are after, then that's what you will keep finding. And you will be hurt over and over again and eventually join thousands of other women and men who, like you, have given up hope, certain "that relationships don't work." Because it is easier to indulge in an adolescent fantasy of a fairy tale romance, than to have the courage to trust yourself and your intuition, to see beyond the appearances into the true essence of the person.

Why should it matter how tall or short he is, how old, how thin, how many degrees he has, how much money to his name? Why should it matter what other people would say? Why would you be concerned with what it looks like from the outside? How many more examples of picture perfect marriages that were actually nightmares do you need? The tabloids are full of them. Every week another divorce of a famous couple. But it looked so good! They seemed like such a perfect match. Precisely. Perhaps that's exactly where the problem was.

Let it go. Let go of the need for the beautiful pictures. Our reality — so powerfully reflective — gives us messages again and again. Isn't it time we listen? Isn't it time to live *your own* life, and not the one others expect you to live? If you really want a soul mate, don't miss him when he comes along.

Stop looking for the right wrappings. Pretty or not — they really do not matter. The wrappings are just that — something to look at, and then — to discard. It is the *gift inside* them that counts. The contents, the essence, the gem. How do you *feel* when you are together? What happens to you when it is just the two of you, alone, with no one looking? What happens when you simply take his hand? *Does it belong in yours?* If it does, you will *know*. Do you?

*   *   *

KNOW WHERE YOU belong and honor your knowing.

Make it matter by acting upon it. Don't drop the love when things get tough and you want to run. Refuse to be weak. Fight for your happiness. If you want the magic, then fight for the magic! And it *will* happen. You will heal each other. Heal the pain of the past, heal the loneliness, heal the sorrows . . . and your love will astound you. The Possible will astound you. You never knew it could be so amazing, so filled with light, so close and tender. But it can. It will be. This — and so much more. If you but let yourself *trust yourself.* Slowly, tentatively perhaps, but trust nevertheless. Because deep inside, when you quiet the voices that have no business speaking in the first place (the voices of a child and adolescent in you that can't deal with the adult reality, the voice of your negative ego that only wants to harm you) and let just one voice remain — you *will* hear it. Yes, that one. We all know it. The voice of your gut. It never lies. It always knows instantly and tells us what it knows if we would just stop silencing it and lying to ourselves that we haven't heard it. Let it speak. Hear it and trust it. And then — take the first step.

*   *   *

A POWERFUL EXAMPLE of what I am talking about is William Hurt's character in the movie *Accidental Tourist.* I saw it a long time ago, but I will never forget the scene where a famous travel writer is trying to explain to his ex-wife why he is going back to the woman everyone thought was so "beneath him."

"It's not *the person* that we are with," he says, "it's *who we are when we are with this person* ... This woman," he continues, "I *need* her."

How powerful. How powerful to recognize that and then — *to choose it.*

Choosing to need. Consciously *preferring* to need this one person.

It is not weak. It is the opposite of being needy, something we all detest.

Only a powerful person can make this choice. Knowing you *could* live without her, and yet *choosing not to.*

This might appear contrary to what we have always been taught about self reliance and independence, and yet it has nothing to do with these concepts. We've come upon another paradox. A beautiful paradox of love and choice. Being powerfully self reliant on the one hand, and on the other hand — choosing *to need* the one you love.

Stay with it for a while. Hold both concepts in your mind simultaneously and wait. Open your heart. Open your mind. Don't rush. Give them the time and space to unfold and to mature. And at some point, you will feel the paradox resolving. You will be touched by the light of the Possible. You will feel lighter, with something inside your heart opening up ... making you smile "for no reason at all."

*   *   *

ONCE YOU KNOW *where you belong, nothing can change what you know.*

But the knowing alone is not enough.

With this knowing comes the challenge: to keep the love, to tend the love, to treasure the love. Not to assume it will always be there, not to throw it about, not to beat it up, damage it, destroy it. Finding the one with whom you belong is not a guarantee of happiness forever after.

There are no such guarantees in love.

It is up to us to make it work.

To say *"it will work because we will make it work."* To make this choice. And then — to live by it.

With this knowing comes great responsibility. To you, to me, to us.

Do not take this knowing lightly. Give it weight, give it substance, let it matter. Do not throw away the magic. Do not sell out to your negative ego telling you "you can do better."

Yes, there can be more than one soul mate and more than one person with whom you may belong. But it doesn't happen that often. It doesn't happen every day. "If you're very lucky," if you have found your home, honor it, respect your knowing. And then *fight for your love. Create* your soul mate. Work through your "stuff" with each other. *Make a choice.* Make the relationship the one most important thing in your life. Don't abandon the rest but know this: your relationship, if it is your first priority, *will* support all the other things. It will make everything else flow easier and work better. And do not listen to your friends and their usually well-intentioned but often unqualified advice. Listen to yourself instead. Don't give your power away to anyone. Separate the voices in your head.

Relationships may be our greatest challenge but they can also be our greatest joy — one of the most rewarding, the most fulfilling and most incredible experiences of our lifetimes.

One thing is guaranteed with each and every one of them: all our buttons will be pushed. All our dark spaces will be illuminated and brought up for review. And not just that. We will no longer be able to hide who we truly are. Our light, our beauty, our magnificence will shine as well. We will be seen.

*   *   *

LOVE IS A mystery. The firebird we want to catch. The phoenix that rises from the ashes refusing to die. You can never capture her. She cannot live in captivity. But she can come and sit by your fire. And she may never leave, if you allow her to spread her wings. If you allow her her freedom and her mystery.

There will always be things we will not know about the one we love. The deeper we go — the more there will be to discover.

And isn't it wonderful?! Would you ever want to be *done*? To have learned all there ever was to learn about each other?

Love will never disappoint us in this way. Ours is not to become complacent. Ours is to allow for the unexpected, to let ourselves be surprised.

It is in love's mystery that we find its magic. It can be touched, but never fully uncovered. Alluring, enthralling, captivating... it beckons us, promising untold riches. Frightening us with its immensity of power.

To give one person the power to be your whole world . . .

Most will not do it. Most will never go there.

It is a tall order. It is not something we *have to* do. It is not an imperative for our spiritual growth. It is just a path. One path. Fraught with pitfalls and dangerous turns. It doesn't come without risks. It gives us no promises and makes but one demand.

The only demand love makes — is that we love.

Till Death Do You Part

Angels can fly because they take themselves lightly.
— G. K. CHESTERTON

Angels also fly because they take their freedom seriously.
— ANDREA

WHEN JULIA MARRIED PETER, she married him for life. It was a civil ceremony. Peter did not want a church wedding. And she had agreed, of course. It didn't matter. As long as they were getting married, as long as it was finally happening. Her dream of three years coming true at last — she would have agreed to anything just to be his wife. Just to finally be his wife. At twenty-one, she felt mature and wise, standing beside Peter repeating her marriage vows after the judge.

She had promised herself not to cry, but it was not easy, so beautiful were the words and how they were making her feel. She could barely breathe, and yet she was able to speak somehow, looking straight at Peter, repeating her vows in a voice she didn't recognize as her own, feeling her old life float away on each word of the promise. She couldn't feel her body, just her eyes, ready to overflow any minute, and her hands pressing the wedding bouquet to her chest tightly. She had made the bouquet herself, having picked up the flowers the night before from the florist next to her building. White roses, white tulips, and the fragrant violet lilacs that she loved so much. A simple bouquet that went well with her little white dress, short and sleeveless, so flattering against her fresh summer tan. She had no veil and no bridesmaids. Just her parents and Peter's mother, plus a few of their closest friends. That's the way Peter wanted it and it was all right with her. A civil ceremony, and then — off to the Caribbean Islands. A husband and wife, away from everyone else.

"To have and to hold, for better and for worse," she repeated, echoing Peter's voice.

"In sickness and in health . . ."

Something was happening to her that was so powerful it was making her dizzy. She knew she was being changed in a profound, irreversible way, becoming someone new. An adult woman. A wife. Peter's wife.

She would be true to him. Stand by his side "for better or for worse" just like she promised. The two of them — always together, as long as she lived.

How amazing — the words of the vows. She felt they were sinking into the very core of her being, imprinting themselves onto her Soul to sustain her for the rest of her life. Even her body felt brighter and brighter, exalted in her desire to give herself away to the man she loved.

She would be a good wife to him. She would never betray him. Never. She would be a good wife because that's what she wanted more than anything. Waited for it, imagined it, dreamed about it. *Oh, thank you God,* she thought squeezing Peter's hand. She, who wasn't ever quite sure about the existence of God, suddenly found herself turning her eyes upwards towards the sky, where God would be, thanking him for this miracle.

"Forever,"she heard the judge say, and she repeated "Forever . . . till death do us part."

Every word — an oath. Every word — a promise. A sacred promise, sanctified by God.

She was but twenty one, yet the clarity was luminous. She was giving herself away to Peter. All of herself. Nothing less would do. The intention so pure of purpose, so uncomplicated in its innocence. She was alive like she had never been in her entire life.

Lost in the reverie of the moment, filled with wordless gratitude, it was hard to hold back the tears, and she tilted her head back just a little, willing them back into her eye sockets. She could feel Peter's eyes upon her, and she looked up to see his beautiful face.

"I do," she said, and he put the ring on her finger. "I will be your wife forever," she said to herself. "I promise." And the promise was sealed.

They were married. Never to be apart. To stay together, husband and wife, from now on and for eternity...to go off into the sunset together...to run on the beach...to play with the golden retriever they would buy...to raise beautiful children...

Alas, it was not a fairy tale. It only looked like one.

*   *   *

JULIA'S MARRIAGE TO Peter worked well enough for a few years.

But then it didn't.

Still, they had stayed married, raising their two children, a daughter and a son. Finally, at forty-five, they divorced. After twenty-four years of marriage, with their children grown and on their own, Julia had finally mustered the strength to leave Peter.

"It was the most difficult decision of my life," she told me shaking her head. We were sitting across from each other in my living room. She had asked for a cup of coffee but hadn't touched it since I placed it in front of her half an hour ago. "I never believed I would be able to do it. It was unimaginable — to have a life without him. And not because I was still in love. That ended years ago. We grew apart. We changed. Too many things happened to us, bad things. Too much had gone wrong. I was desperately unhappy, and so was he. He treated me terribly, he drank, he was abusive. I was beginning to hate the very sight of him ... Everything was pointing to divorce and yet — I simply *could not leave him*. I just couldn't make myself do it."

She leaned back and reached for her coffee. "We were suffocating," she continued. "We were miserable, both of us. We did not agree on anything. We became almost like strangers. Sex with him had turned into an obligation, something I couldn't stand, and yet he demanded it like it was owed to him. It was a nightmare in many ways. I knew that had I stayed, I would have developed some kind of illness — and would have died in a few years. But I couldn't leave." She stretched her legs and pulled on her skirt, then looked at me and shrugged.

"I can't explain it. Even now, ten years later, I still feel him around me sometimes. And we haven't even spoken in years."

"Tell me more," I said. "Why was it so difficult to leave him?"

A shadow fell across her face. She removed a loose strand of hair exposing some grey underneath and looked at me directly. "I don't know," she said. " I have been puzzled by it all these years. It is as if I couldn't shake him off then, and at times I think I still can't shake him off now. Life without Peter ... I just couldn't imagine it. Then I had a dream one night. It woke me up. I saw myself dying. I was in bed in our bedroom. I was exhausted, bitter, angry at the world and at everything, and I knew I was dying. Brain tumor, I think."

"That's when you decided to leave?"

"The dream woke me up from the stupor I had been in for years. I don't know if the dream was prophetic or not. It didn't matter. I looked at my life and decided I was not going to die over a failed marriage. I suddenly had this absolute clarity."

She closed her eyes for a moment. "Still it was incredibly difficult to leave him. And he would never have left on his own. He thought we should just go on like that. He used to bring me roses all the time and tell me that he loved me. And then he treated me like I was garbage in the next instant. It was crazy-making. I wanted to throw the roses in his face."

"Tell me about your wedding ceremony," I asked. "How did you feel when you were saying your vows?"

She shook her head. "Oh my God," she was suddenly smiling. "You should have seen me there. It was the happiest day. I was so young. And so in love. I gave myself to him body and soul." She stopped, suddenly serious. "Yes," she repeated. "Body and Soul."

No wonder it was unimaginable to divorce him, I thought. "Body and Soul" was more literal than she knew.

The Sacredness of a Vow

A vow is more than a promise. It is a *sacred* promise, made sacred by the meaning we give it and by what it signifies. *A vow is a promise given in the intensity of the moment, with extraordinary depth of feeling and singularity of will.* It is a promise witnessed and sanctified. Even when there are no actual witnesses present, we become our own witness — our subconscious mind, our Soul, God — are all present. We are never alone when we make a vow, and there is a part of us that knows it. A promise made as a vow becomes an oath, an oath that affects us at our very core.

There may be people who take vows lightly, but most do not. "As God is my witness, *I will never go hungry again,*" says Scarlett O'Hara in *Gone with the Wind* making a vow to herself. Anyone who remembers the film remembers the force and the intensity of these words. Scarlet is alone when she speaks them, yet on every level of her being the promise is heard and noted. It is an oath, a sacred vow, a pact she made with herself, and it *will* be carried through.

*   *   *

IF YOU ARE among the people who have gone through the experience of divorce, you know very well the pain and trauma of ending a marriage. It is somehow different from the pain of ending any other relationship. Something happens to us when we get married and then divorce, something I have thought about for a long time.

The choice to get divorced is a choice to break a promise. And not just any kind of promise, but a sacred vow. When we get divorced, we are not only choosing to no longer be together and live our lives separately, we are consciously choosing to break the promise we made to each other "body and soul." *The promise that was never to be broken.*

Breaking an oath is not as simple as changing one's mind. No matter how determined we are, nor how necessary it may appear, breaking a vow literally rips the psyche because we are breaking a sacred contract. *We should have never made a contract in this way to begin with,* but we did. Following tradition, we did it with an innocence of heart and the best intentions, as Julia did, not realizing the price we would have to pay if we were ever to break it.

Traditions may all be well and good but they can also be dangerous, especially if they go unexamined. I believe *the tradition of getting married by making sacred vows* to each other and thus turning the marriage into an *emotional* and *psychic contract* (not a legal one only) belongs to another era. Not to our modern times in which half of these contracts are almost guaranteed to break. Today, divorce has become expected, almost matter-of-fact. We have become quite cynical about it. So much so that often guests at our wedding ceremonies listen to us say our vows while making bets on how long we will stay together.

And even we are not that sure. Sometimes we stand before the altar *promising each other eternity,* while having taken precautions in advance in case things don't work out. Unlike Julia at twenty-one in the 1960s, we are not so naïve. We were not born yesterday. We know that people change, we understand free will (which includes our right to mess up as well). We know that divorce is our safety net—just in case. When it comes to the way we get married, we allow a number of contradictions to exist simultaneously, creating nothing less than a conflict of consciousness. These contradictions are so much a part of our life that we accept them instead of questioning them. But we pay a very high price for our complacency.

I am talking about the inherent contradiction of *taking the vows of marriage* while simultaneously *making pre-nuptial agreements prior to taking the vows*, agreements that if they do not presuppose divorce, certainly allow for its possibility. I am talking about the *existence of the institution of divorce* itself. Perhaps we have reached a point where we can actually notice the glaring inconsistency we have created and do something about it.

So what am I suggesting? To *not* get married at all? Or to get married and to *never* divorce? To throw away the pre-nuptials?

No, no and no. Of course not. It is a blessing to have the ability to indeed end the marriage that did not work out. And it is very important to be able to have the pre-nuptial agreement if we so choose because for reasons that are both many and complex, a number of marriages fail.

What I am talking about are *the marriage vows*. We make promises fully aware that there exists a possibility that we will break them. And whether or not—in the exhilaration of the moment—we deny this possibility, it is still a fact. And then, if and when the time comes, and we do try to break the sacred vows we've made to our Souls and to God, we discover that it is not a simple matter. We don't let ourselves off the hook so easily when it comes to this level of promise. We have always been our own harshest and most punishing judges. *It is never God, never the Goddess, never the Divine that judges and punishes with such severity* but always us, each one of us, doing it in our own way. As a result, ending a marriage in the only way that really counts—*the emotional and psychic way*—is exceptionally difficult.

Some are so cut off from themselves and their feelings, so separate in their loneliness, that they may not notice the ripping of the fabric of their being that takes place as they break their sacred oath.

Too used to the ever present hurt and isolation they live with every day, they may shove down the pain caused by breaking off their vows, denying its existence, pretending it's not there, even believing it at times. "I am okay," they say (to themselves, to others). "I am better off now." And it simply becomes one more layer, "one more brick in the wall" of pain they have built to protect themselves from feeling.

But those who are more sensitive will experience what Julia has experienced — the unimaginable difficulty, the utter impossibility of acting on her desire to leave the marriage, as if some invisible cords had tied her and her husband together — the cords that are harder to break than steel cables.

When a promise is made with the intensity of *a vow, it carries with it a finality that cancels out other possibilities.* You've taken a vow, you've crossed the line, and now your life together is not just a freely made choice. It is *a psychic contract.*

There is a particular phenomenon, a severing of a part of oneself, that happens with any psychic contract, be it a *contract of love* or a *contract of pain.*

With a vow of "forever," no matter how lovingly, willingly and joyfully you give yourself away, a part of you is psychically severed in that instant. That precious part of you now belongs to your husband or wife — to remain his or hers for the rest of your life. And as they accept your promise, they lose a part of themselves as well. They, too, are signing this contract, cutting a piece of themselves off.

And neither one is free any longer to continue to choose or not to choose to be together. A psychic contract, stronger than if it had been signed in blood, will hold them to the pledge they made to each other *unaffected by circumstances or time.*

*   *   *

Beware of the promises you make. Do not make ones you may not keep.

Remember: freedom is our ability to *enhance or diminish our lives.*

That means that at any time, anyone can choose to enhance his or her life or to diminish it. Too many things can go wrong in the course of living together. If, for example, your marriage becomes abusive, you may choose to end it. It is your right — not to stop loving, perhaps, but to leave the abusive and unsafe situation.

But you have taken the vows and you promised forever, till death do you part. And there were *no clauses in the marriage vows* allowing for breaking them.

And now, years later, you find yourself paralyzed. Agonizing about the decision that is so obvious to others. Going back and forth in your mind. Hoping against hope, sometimes even putting your life and the life of your children in danger. Why do you hesitate? Why is it so difficult to do?

Because the breaking of a sacred promise is unimaginable. Because in the eyes of your psyche you are committing a crime. It is easier to suffer the pain of a bad marriage than to be a traitor. Though in truth the *betrayal has already happened*. It happened long ago with *the promise* you made — *betraying and abandoning yourself* by giving yourself away even though you thought you did the right thing and did it willingly, joyously, euphorically.

The internal severing also happened to the one you married. If you were able to lift out of the present moment and travel back in time, you'd find both of you (your two younger selves) still there at that altar, a prisoner and a warden, frozen in time. They haven't lived your lives. Haven't known the pain and the losses you've suffered. They are still there where you have left them, unable to move, insisting that you stay together forever just like you promised. *That's the internal conflict.* Their pain, their bewilderment, their pull to keep the promise you made. That's why it feels so unimaginable to you here. And you use exactly the right words for it, of course. "I felt torn apart," Julia said, as her subconscious mind slipped the message in. Because she was. More literally than she knew.

The Power of the Subconscious Mind

The subconscious mind of a person is a huge depository of every bit of information that has ever come his or her way. It can be likened to a giant library that holds an infinite number of index cards cataloging the contents of every book, all of them about you. Or you can imagine it as large warehouse with endless storage rooms filled to overflowing. All holding various pieces and bits of information about you. Or better yet, our subconscious mind is like a super powerful computer with an infinite amount of software. It stores everything we have ever seen, heard, thought, felt or experienced. It records every decision, promise and choice we've made ad infinitum.

Except it *does not* just *passively* store it. *It is in charge of maintaining it according to the instructions we've given it.*

If, for example, at the age of seven you lost in the school swimming competition and decided out of a child's embarrassment and anger to never again try so hard to win at anything in any competition because "it was too damn humiliating to lose," and if you made this decision right there and then, filled with the pain and shame of your failure, made it with intensity of feeling and with powerful intent — your subconscious took notice and made it *a rule*. You might have long forgotten about it, but somehow, whenever a chance to compete comes up — a promotion at work, the attention of a woman or anything else — you find yourself withdrawing, capitulating, stepping back, doing nothing. You find yourself following the silent direction of your subconscious mind that has been maintaining the rule you had made at the age of seven with unflinching determination.

The power of the subconscious mind is that immense. And its job is quite simple — to record and remember everything and to maintain consistency at all cost. The subconscious mind does not evaluate or judge. It does not decide what's good for us and what isn't. Just like a program in the computer, once installed, operates on its own. But while we can uninstall a program in the computer, it is not so easy to reprogram the subconscious mind. From time to time I teach a class on reprogramming the subconscious mind. You can find information about it on my website *www.powerofthe possible.com*

It bears repeating. *Your subconscious mind wants but one thing — consistency.* And it will make sure everything in your life is consistent with the original instructions.

In the eyes of your subconscious, once you get married "till death do you part" you do exactly that. But then, when time passes and you end the marriage — parting ways not because of a death, but out of your own free will — it creates a contradiction. First, you make a vow and then you break it, giving two conflicting messages at two different times. One message says "I will be with this person forever" and the other one says "I didn't really mean it" or "I have changed my mind."

This is not a benign conflict, and it will affect us on many levels, for the subconscious mind plays no games and is unable to pick and choose between opposing commands. It will follow the original command every time, especially since it had a greater dimension of intensity. And it will dismiss the new command as superfluous.

In most cases, the vow to stay together forever had much more power and juice, and that's what the subconscious mind will insist on maintaining.

No wonder it causes so much torment and doubt to end a marriage, even if it has been dead for years. And we are puzzled, confused, bewildered by our inability to act on our decision to have a divorce and at the pain and suffering it causes.

"I will be your wife forever," says the young bride, filled with the exhilaration of the moment, fully intending to keep the promise. And her subconscious mind hears every word and takes it literally. It does not edit. It does not revise. It follows the instruction by the book.

But what if she changes her mind? Can't the subconscious follow the new program then? It may. But it will take powerful conscious work to undo the old one first. It will take making a new choice at the same level of intensity that the original one was made. And it will take adhering to it unflinchingly.

Because if you doubt it, if you go back and forth in your mind, the clarity and the determination will be missing. The new choice will have no power of will and no intensity and the subconscious mind is keenly aware of that. So it will pay no attention, of course. As far as it is concerned, you are not really serious. *You are still married according to the vows you took. And it is still "forever" in its book.*

But you have gone through divorce and now have the papers with the stamp of a judge to prove that your marriage is over. "No matter," says the subconscious, undisturbed by this fact, continuing to follow the original instruction. It does not adapt to change that easily. "Forever" means forever, whichever way you look at it. And the more serious you were about your promise, the more you will be torn inside. *You may be legally divorced, but not as far as your subconscious mind is concerned. Somewhere deep inside you will remain each other's husband and wife, connected and tied in ways no legal document has the power to override.*

*   *   *

YES, THE SUBCONSCIOUS mind is that powerful. And it is very important to understand its mechanism if we are to lift out of our subconscious conditioning and begin to create the life we want more consciously. Otherwise it is the subconscious that is behind so much of what does or does not happen in our lives. And we will follow its program whether we understand how it works or not. Most people don't know the mechanics of the car they drive and what exactly makes it get into the driving mode and take off, once you turn the ignition, shift into gear and step on the gas. But they know that they can rely on it to do just that because it has been built this way and will operate accordingly. Similarly with our subconscious mind, we put in the programs and then it operates our lives accordingly. If it believes that you are still married, it will create circumstances, feelings, situations and events to support that and to dismantle anything that stands in the way, bringing additional weight to a divorce decision and keeping the two of you connected long after the divorce has taken place. Your ex-husband or wife may be hundreds of miles away, divorced from you for a long time, *but that's just on paper.* Something else is going on deep inside of you. Subconsciously, he is still your husband and you are still his wife. Even if both of you are now married to other people.

Crazy? Yes, it is. Crazy and crazy-making. But if we don't make the vows of "forever," we can avoid this ordeal. So much pain and loss already comes with the break up of a marriage. Let's not add to it this crisis of the subconscious mind.

The good news is that even though the subconscious mind is extremely powerful, *the real power lies with the conscious mind.*

Choice is always conscious. And there is nothing more powerful than that. *Conscious choice,* conscious and powerful *intention,* and our *belief* that we can free ourselves from any conditioning will determine how successful we will be in undoing the vows we took when we got married if we choose to end the marriage for real and not on paper alone.

The Sacred Covenant of Choice

Don't lock me into wedlock, I want / marriage, an / encounter —
— DENISE LEVERTOV

The stronger our love is, the greater our need *to honor* each other by making *no demands for promises* and by *not making promises* ourselves.

A better way, a truer way to get married — a much more powerful and honest way — is to enter this sacred covenant based not on promise, but on *choice*. The choice you fully intend to continue making for the rest of your life — a freely made choice *not bound by the finality of promise.*

Pause and think for a moment about these two concepts: promise and choice.

Can you feel the difference?

One *holds* us to something we believed to be true sometime in the past, as if we were stagnant and unchanging rather than constantly evolving beings, while the other — a daily intentional encounter — *reaffirms our freedom* even as we grow and change over the years. Isn't it better to always act out of our freedom? To continue to make the choice to love and to stay together *because that's what we want* more than anything? And *not* because years ago we made a vow to do so?

"But what if my marriage is working and I am happy," you ask, "and my vows do not differ from my choices?"

That's wonderful! There is no conflict. But you are still choosing to love every day, even if you are not aware of it consciously. You are probably called "lucky" by your friends. And you are! Although your happiness has to do with much more than luck.

So often what we call "luck" and "chance" is actually *magic* (changing your reality according to your will) and *choice*. But that's too frightening for most people. The freedom inherent in the very concept of choice is what is frightening. It is too open ended. Too abstract. The fluidity of freedom and choice does not feel safe. A promise, on the other hand, feels much more secure, in spite of all the divorces around us that demonstrate every day that a promise does not guarantee anything at all.

Still we cling to it. The very idea of choice with its freedom makes us uncomfortable. It means you or your spouse can rechoose at any time, something we want to avoid at all costs. *We want to secure the choice of the one we are marrying by turning choice into a promise.* But think about it. Wouldn't you rather your spouse was actively choosing you and only you for the rest of his or her life instead of staying with you bound by a promise? Wouldn't you want the same for yourself?

Security Versus Freedom: Resolving the Paradox

Security and freedom are often at odds with each other. On the one hand — the security of a promise, on another — the freedom of a choice. It is a paradox, the fact that we want both — one of so many paradoxes in our lives presented to us with regularity and at pivotal times, giving us the opportunity to reflect, to grow, to become more evolved as human beings.

A paradox by its nature cannot be solved. If it could, it would not be a paradox. But while it can't be solved, it can be *resolved.* And those who have successfully resolved the paradoxes that they came upon have discovered the tremendous power contained within them.

To re-solve this paradox, simply sit with it without trying to do anything about it. Just sit and feel both the *fear of no security* and the *excitement of having free choice.* There is not going to be a solution to this, so just be with it for a while. Allow the feelings that come to wash over you without trying to find the answer. It is a mystery and, as such, has the power that will expand and re-arrange you in ways you cannot control. It may be a good idea to put the book down right now and to stay with these two seemingly contradictory concepts and with the fact that you want to have both. Don't rush anything. Be patient with yourself. And suddenly it will be as if a veil has been lifted while you were looking the other way, and you will be able to see more clearly. The answers you were seeking will now be inside you, even if you don't quite have the words for them yet.

When we accept our powerlessness to solve the paradox, we will be changed by its power. You go *through* the paradox, and you come out on the other side ready to receive its gift, its wisdom and understandings. The paradox that was once a conundrum fades away.

The idea of bringing freedom and choice into the way you get married can now be exciting instead of frightening. You can choose to trust yourself and the one you are about to marry. And when you stand before the altar, before the minister or the judge, the words you say to each other carry the power of a *clear and willed intention — an empowered choice* of two adults who love and honor each other and themselves. Two adults entering into this sacred union with their eyes open, their hearts filled with love, and their feet planted firmly into the ground of their commitment.

Between freedom and lack of freedom — *always choose freedom.* There is no concept more sacred. "Give me liberty or give me death." For as long as we have been walking this earth, humans have fought and died for freedom. Some never having touched it, never even having glimpsed it. And still they dreamt. Still they fought and risked everything they had *just for a possibility,* willing to die just to have a chance. And what of us? Born in freedom, to us it is like the air we breathe — easy to take for granted. Yet it is always a mistake to take anything in life for granted. *Especially freedom.* Otherwise, you can lose your freedom without even noticing it, relinquishing it little by little, step by step.

Yesterday's freedom can become today's prison.

Yesterday's joyous promise can become today's heavy burden.

That's why it is so important to pay attention, to re-examine and reassess our freedom on a daily basis. *Consciously choosing everything in our lives, instead of automatically conforming to the status quo.*

When it comes to the way we get married, let's not mistakenly give our freedom away or take it from another with our marriage vows — even though in the immensity of our love it may appear that we are not doing so. Let's instead, have our marriage be a mystical, sacred temple, built on the foundation of both our love and our free choice. That should be enough. That will allow for all the rest.

Let's have our marriage be a sacred covenant, not a psychic contract. Not *giving ourselves away*, but in the intensity of the moment, awake, aware and present declaring our choice and *fully intending to always be making this choice*. Can you feel the power of that? Can you feel the difference?

Commitment as a Choice

A commitment made through choice is different than a promise, and this difference is fundamental.

Think about a mother's love for her child. A mother doesn't promise her baby daughter that she will love her, and the daughter, were she able to speak, doesn't ask for a similar promise from her mother. Nor does she ask for a commitment. The child knows if she is loved and if the commitment is there. She knows it intuitively and is never wrong. She feels the love and the commitment or the lack of them. A mother's love and her total commitment to her child are given freely from the bottom of the mother's heart. And if (sadly) they are not given, no demand can make them come.

In a happy marriage *we make the choice to love every day*. We wake up in the morning and a choice presents itself. Will I be loving and kind, or will I be grouchy and indifferent? Will I make him or her feel loved or ignore him and get busy and self absorbed? Small things? Hardly. These small things color the way we interact with each other and affect the overall tone and texture of relationships. Sure, one morning may not matter. Except everything matters. *"Love pays attention to detail."* We cannot take love for granted. If you leave a beautiful plant in a dark room and forget to water it, it will shrivel and die, won't it? But it was so fresh, so alive when you bought it! I was just so busy, I was going to get to it later.

It only needed light and water. It only needed your attention. And you know all too well not to abandon the tender blooms and expect them to keep blooming in the dark. You know that if you care for them lovingly, they will bring you new blooms and will be warming your heart with their beauty for a long time.

Make your marriage a temple where love, honor, freedom and respect dwell side by side. Where *you remember the love* and *rejoice in each other's presence.* Where you practice *kindness* and *patience* tempered by *trust* and *humility, knowing that while things were a particular way before, they may be different next time.* They may be better; they may be worse. Don't assume anything. Don't abuse or ignore the love and expect it *to carry you* because they say "love will carry you through" and besides, "I was promised forever." Don't ask this of love, ever. And instead *carry the love* in your heart always, so it will *see you through* everything.

Make the choice that is unencumbered by promise.

Make it freely in the exuberance of love with the commitment of heart and mind, Spirit and Soul. Take the time, sit down in advance, focus, think, look inside. Then write down exactly what you are choosing to create in this union you are about to enter. And then say it. Say it out loud, the same way you would, had you been making vows, except now there will be freedom in your choices, for that's their very nature, unlike the finality of promise. Speak your choices and intentions for your life together and have it be witnessed and sanctified, without severing a part of yourself, without the psychic contracts, but with the powerful intensity of will.

Mykaell's Marriage Proposal

I was among those who got married "body and Soul" and then (years later) got divorced and had a difficult time deciding to get married again.

And how else could it be? How could I get married again if I was still "married"? A force much more powerful than the stamp of a judge stood in the way of my freedom, holding me to the promise of "forever" that I'd made ages ago. Time and physical reality have no meaning when it comes to that level of promise. It took me a long time to understand this. I thought I had all but left my past behind, but then the time came, and a new exciting future called promising untold happiness. That's when the wall harder than stone rose before me blocking my way, demanding I pay attention.

When did it happen? Seven years after my legal divorce from my first marriage.

Here is my story.

It was a wonderful, happy time of my life. I was in love again, and I had finally said yes to Mykaell's marriage proposal. My boyfriend of almost seven years, the love of my life, the man whose love took my breath away, transporting me to states of happiness I never dreamt possible. He was my home, he was my life, he was quite simply — everything. And by being that, he made everything else in my life, everything that truly mattered — matter more. It was not an "ideal" relationship, nor was it a "perfect" one. But it was close enough for me. Even when things were difficult between us, it was easy. We belonged with each other, and we were committed to working through everything that stood in our way. With all the ups and downs of a real relationship, ours breathed and expanded with each passing year, turning into something extraordinary. A gift. A miracle. The best thing ever.

And yet I did not want to marry Mykaell. I did not want to get married, period. I was not against marriage *per se*. Not at all. I believed I wanted to get married again one day, and certainly to Mykaell. Just... not now. We talked about getting married from time to time, but never seriously. Somehow I managed to stay away from the subject or change it soon enough. Something would happen to me at the very mention of getting married again — a reaction I could not explain. It was the same reaction every time — tension in my stomach, a wave of anxiety, and an urgent need to change the subject as if an impenetrable wall would rise before me blocking my way, not letting me pass. "You cannot go there," was the message. "Not you. Not now. Not ever."

I was an open book to Mykaell. One look at me and he knew exactly what was going on. I did not need to explain. He never pushed me to do anything. He knew I loved him, and that's all that mattered. And if I needed time — then I needed time. We had been inseparable since we met seven years before, and happily living together for the last three. "What else could I possibly need?" I would say to myself. "Why did I even need to get married?"

Still, I was confused by my resistance. It was beyond logic and reason and certainly contrary to my emotions. We were getting happier and happier with each day. Why then was I hesitating?

I decided to ask for help. One night, prior to falling asleep, I asked to be shown the reason for my resistance. "If it is the scars from my first marriage, please lift them. And if it is my intuition, and I should not be getting married right now, please show me the reason." I was accustomed to asking for help in this way, and, of course, I always received it. I asked and I fell asleep. And then I forgot about it.

A couple of days later with a sudden jolt, the memory of my request dropped into my consciousness. Immediately, I tested the thought of getting married by imagining it, feeling it, trying it on. To my amazement, the familiar wall I had become so used to by then was gone — gone so completely I had a hard time believing it. Again and again I tried to find it, but I couldn't. The more I imagined myself married, the happier I was beginning to feel. The harder I looked for the wall, the more excitement I felt about not having it. I felt the joy and thrill and the expectation of wonderful things to come. I felt a surge of gratitude so complete it brought tears to my eyes. "Thank you," I whispered looking upwards. "Thank you, thank you, thank you."

I was free! Free to get married if I wanted to, which I was happy to discover I did. My strange conundrum was over and nothing was holding me back anymore. I smiled anticipating seeing Mykaell that night. It was time for the wedding plans.

But then something else happened. Something I didn't expect.

*   *   *

IT WAS A beautiful summer evening, warm and wonderful, so rare for the cool climate of San Francisco. From our favorite table at a North Beach restaurant we were watching the crowds outside the window. It seemed the entire city had spilled into the streets, refusing to stay indoors, as if San Francisco itself—tired of the long and cold summer—took a deep breath and relaxed, releasing people into the night, filling the outdoor cafés with music and laughter. Dreamlike, suspended in time, I watched the night unfold in front of me like a movie—a movie I was part of as well, full of romance and magic, with a crescent moon over the Transamerica pyramid hanging motionless like a picture, lighting the sky with thousands of stars, and couples walking hand in hand bathed in the halos of light. There was Joe Cocker's voice, raspy and strong, singing about love from someone's boom box and young girls whispering on the side walks. Smiles brightened people's faces as they walked on by, and at "City Lights" book store down the street, an evening of poetry was in full swing. It was a night like no other. A perfect night. Divinely choreographed just for us.

I remember the twinkling lights of the café across the street and the heady smell of jasmine from the garden below the terrace. I remember feeling beautiful and young, serene and exhilarated, ready to burst into laughter and yet filled with peace—all at once.

"Let's get married in Venice," one of us said. And that was perfect, too. We knew it as soon as we said it. Venice belonged to lovers. And so it belonged to us as well. We couldn't get married anywhere else.

The waiter brought our order, set the dishes before us and left.

I smiled and touched Mykaell's hand. Something always happened inside me every time I touched his hand. A wave of safety, of peace, a knowing of home. I couldn't stop smiling. Everything was making me giggle that night. I reached for a glass of water, took a sip, swallowed — and felt a sharp pain in my throat.

A sore throat in the middle of summer coming suddenly out of nowhere? But it wasn't just that. I was getting hot, beginning to sweat under my light clothes. I touched my cheek. My face was burning. "I think I am coming down with something," I said. "I don't feel that great."

We cut the dinner short, of course, and I was in bed as soon as I got home. Before midnight I was burning, and my fever ran high. I was worse in the morning. My temperature remained high, and my throat closed completely, making it very painful to speak. I couldn't get out of bed. *Everything was so wonderful last night,* I thought, *why did I have to get sick so suddenly? And right in the midst of talking about the wedding....*

As soon as this thought crossed my mind, I was struck with this coincidence. Coincidence? I knew there was no such thing. Was I trying to tell myself something? Was my body sending me a message? A loud message? A shout? Making certain I wouldn't miss it? Too sick to go into the depth of it, I was suddenly certain it had to be about my getting married. Once again, I checked for the familiar wall, and once again found it gone. I felt no blockage about getting married to Mykaell. Not as far as I could tell. Why then was my body falling apart on me in such a demonstrative fashion?

I was too exhausted and too sick to go into a real meditation, something I usually do when I am looking for answers. Sometimes in meditations of the past the answers would come as metaphors, other times a precise thought would formulate in my mind, the thought that was clearly put there in response to my seeking, giving me the needed answer. I reached for the tea that Mykaell had left on my bedside table, but it was too painful to swallow. My sore throat had gotten worse, and so did my fever. "I will meditate the best I can," I decided, though all I wanted to do was curl up and sleep.

I closed my eyes. "What's going on with me? Why am I suddenly so ill and why—my throat?" I asked and relaxed into the silence. Before long, I was drifting somewhere, half in trance yet still aware of where I was. Then everything became blurry, and I entered a state of deep meditation, dreamlike and yet awake, in my room, and yet even more powerfully—somewhere else. In a forest, and then at a beach. It was night time. I was alone, and I knew it was very important for me to be there. I looked around. Nothing but miles and miles of sand, stretching in each direction. A quiet, peaceful sea. Low tide. "Look at the ground," a voice in my head said, and I did. In a small mound of sand by my left foot something was glistening in the dark—something metallic and shiny I needed to pick up, but I was reluctant for some reason. It held the answer to my question. I was certain of that....

I noticed my hesitation. Suddenly, I did not want to know. I took a deep breath, bent down and pulled the shiny object out of the sand.

I would have recognized it anywhere, though I hadn't seen it in years, nor had I held it or thought about it in a long, long, long time. Yet there it was, returned to me from the distant past and now sitting squarely in the center of my palm. Its elaborate design, once cut so sharply into the soft gold, had lost its luster long ago, and the tiny grooves looked dull, aged by the passage of years.

A strange tenderness filled my heart. I touched the tiny circular object with my index finger cleaning the sand out of its grooves, then closed my fingers around it and lowered my arm. "I thought it was over," I heard my voice, and felt my heart stop. "Not yet," another voice inside my head said. "Not yet."

I began to sob. I didn't know I still had tears left in me for the failure of my marriage to Alex. I thought I had cried all of them out and then cried some more. I thought I was done with it, the pain, the loss, the acceptance of the needed end. Yet there I stood, alone on this deserted beach, clutching my old wedding ring in my hand.

I was in meditation, and I cried real tears. "When will this sorrow be over??" I asked. When is it finally *done* and is there even such a thing? Is the old pain ever over for good, or will it keep tripping me up, rearing its head when I least expect it, pulling me back into its murky pool every time I am sure I have left it behind? And who was I crying for anyway? Certainly not for Alex. Not anymore. This much I knew. What was it then that was twisting me inside, pulling on my heart, making it hard to breathe? Whose heart, still broken, still in pain, was calling to me through time asking for the release and for healing?

Growing Spiritually in a Spiral Motion

Imagine a person's lifetime from birth to death as an upward rising spiral. It is a good way to imagine it, for this is how we human beings grow spiritually. By sweeps and surges of spiraling upward motion — and by downward spiraling setbacks that happen along the way. Turning with each ring of the coil, going at our own speed, we take a few steps forward, then take a couple steps back, then continue forward for a while, then take a step back again. Ideally, we keep growing, keep moving forward, but always in a spiral. It is high time we give up on our attachment to the idea of a "straight line," for in reality it rarely actually applies. Even the most elaborately engineered missile fired and sent to its precisely calculated destination by the most sophisticated technology does not reach it by moving straight on. It must veer off course in tiny increments all the time, self-correcting as it goes forward if it is to reach its target. Scientists have known this for a long time, and it is true of everything in our world, in spite of our resistance and our love affair with the straight line.

Let's imagine a vertical spiral (to represent the way we grow) and let's draw a straight line cutting through it somewhere also vertically to represent our pain. See how the line you drew touches one particular spot on each coil of the spiral? Now imagine yourself climbing along the coils, moving upwards at your own speed. At some point you will reach a spot where the straight line you had drawn touches the coil, won't you? And then you will pass it, moving on, continuing along the spiral and having left that spot behind. Until — now on the next coil already — you will come to yet another place where the straight line is cutting through. You will pass that one as well and continue on. And the same thing will happen with each ring of the spiral as you continue on your way up.

I use this illustration because it is a very good analogy for understanding what happens to us as we grow and heal from old pain. For the most part, we do not feel the pain all the time. Rather — we stumble upon it now and then, seemingly out of the blue, and then we move on, leaving the feeling behind.

And similarly, when it comes to healing it, we do not heal everything all at once either. We heal as much as we are able to, as much as we can handle at the time, and then we move on until the moment comes when the line of pain again intersects the coil — our life path — and we are ready to heal at a deeper level.

At times, we go through life barely remembering the past, believing that we've moved passed it, that it doesn't matter any more, and that we are *done*. It is finally over, until suddenly — often when we least expect it — something happens to us. A memory gets triggered by a scene in a movie, or by a song, or by a story in the book. We pass by a place from our past or see that person we thought we'd left behind ... and we are undone. We fall apart, we can't breathe. Suddenly we are back where we were so long ago as if all of it had just happened yesterday.

"Why?" we wonder, "Why now? And why again? I thought I didn't even care about that person any more. I thought what had happened then didn't matter one bit now." And we may be right in a way. It doesn't matter anymore except for one thing. *We are now ready to look deeper,* and to have a greater degree of healing. There is still more to be gained from the lessons the past holds for us, and that's why we give ourselves the opportunity to look at it again. And then again. And then — again. Until it is *really* over. Until we no longer come across the places in the spiral of our growth where the line of pain is cutting through.

That's what happened to me as I was getting ready to get married again. I had simply stumbled onto such a place — stumbled upon it at the exact right time, so that I could be finished with the "unfinished business" of my past and step into my future with a deeper degree of freedom.

Letting Go of the Past

Our past is only "past" once we transcend the experience and thus let go of it completely. You will know if you are there because the events of the past will begin to look as if they happened to someone else — as if someone told you about them, or you had read about them in a book about yourself, or about someone else you know well, or as if they took place in another lifetime altogether. Until that happens, you are not fully free. There is still more to be gained from the past, and more gifts to be gathered.

Yes, gifts. The old pain is there to give us a chance to take another look at what happened and the role we played in it. We've paid a very high price for the lessons we've learned and still can learn. Let's not lose them in the haste of rushing to leave it all behind.

Perhaps the treasure the past holds is a *recognition of how deeply you can love,* something you've never really owned up to before; or a *discovery of how much you* actually *value and respect yourself;* or of *how strong your boundaries are.* Maybe for you the gift lies in *being finally able to accept yourself* or in coming to *a deeper level of forgiveness.* Maybe you needed to *see your own courage* or *how much you can really rely on your intuition.* Perhaps you've never actually looked at *how clear you are about what really matters.* Or maybe you've left a part of yourself behind and with it a piece of your Soul, and *there are vows you once took that are holding you hostage, which need to be undone once and for all.*

The gifts are different for each of us, but they need to be retrieved, and until we do this, our past will call us back from time to time to bring it to our attention. Events and circumstances will be presented to us at critical times showing us what we might have missed in the lessons learned, so we can gain new depth and a more profound understanding.

We grow at different cadences, and we are only *done* when we are done and not a minute before. Patience, together with humility, is what brings us closer to the freedom from pain.

Yes, *patience, the love of self, and humility.*

This pain may be over completely one day, and there will be no more spots on the spiral to trip us up, but not until it is really over. That's why we have arranged it this way. Peeling the levels of pain off one by one. We couldn't do it all at once. It would be too much. That's why we have given ourselves years of living in which to grow and to heal. That's why we actually have time. So we can use it to heal ourselves, and to learn what we came to learn.

We could never heap all we wanted to learn in a lifetime into a tight "lump sum" experience. Thus time becomes an ally, not something to run against.

After "the wall" of my resistance to getting married again was so magically removed, I concluded that the pain of the failure of my first marriage had finally healed. I thought "the wall" was the last thing in my way since I believed I had seen and done everything I knew to do. I believed I had looked at all the reasons for what had happened between me and Alex, and that I had felt all my feelings about it. I had worked through all of it, and I did it consciously and conscientiously. I had been able to truly forgive myself, and I had genuinely forgiven Alex. I carried no resentments and no ill feelings toward anyone even peripherally involved in my divorce. And I knew I had genuinely let go of my first marriage.

And yet, I had forgotten something very important. In my zest to be free of my past, I had left someone very important behind. The younger part of me, the one who in the exuberance and innocence of youth had given herself away "body and Soul" to the man she had married, having fallen head over heels in love with him when she was barely eighteen-years-old, and then married him with her entire being, never to be apart, husband and wife forever. The me who married Alex "for life" and in doing so, lost a part of herself to her marriage contract because it became "written in blood." Stuck in time, she had never lived the years that followed, never experienced the unhappiness of the marriage, never understood the divorce, and refused to accept another marriage. It was she who was calling on me now across time and space demanding an explanation.

My old wedding ring clutched in my palm, I wiped away my tears with the back of my hand. I heard a rustle of clothes behind my back and turned to face — myself.

She hadn't aged a day, and her hair was short, just the way I used to wear it so many years back. She looked like she always did in old photographs of that time, the ones I had packed in a box years ago and hadn't looked at since. Only her eyes were different, without the usual glow that everyone always had commented on. It was as if a veil had been drawn across her face a long time ago, shading her from incoming light. A lonely figure against the night sky, she stood a few steps away looking at me with reproach. She had my old wedding photograph in her hand, and she offered it to me without a word.

"You can't get married again," she spoke and looked down. "You are married already. Don't you know that?" I didn't think I could move. I felt my feet sinking deeper into the cold sand, sending shivers through my body. I swallowed and reached for her, pulling her close. She did not resist, but her body felt limp and tired in my arms. She found my hand and put her head on my shoulder. I wanted to stroke her hair, to hold her and never let go. I wanted to say something, something that would take away her sorrow, erase all the years of loneliness. I felt a movement inside my chest, a tenderness, a love. It left no room for words. Anything I would say would sound false. "Come," I finally whispered, "Let's go walk on the beach. We need to talk."

I had forgotten my younger self, left her behind, though I should have known better. I had neglected to do what had to be done in spite of having the needed understanding of it. What I had needed to do but had not done, was *bring her back* into me and *undo the old marriage vows.*

It hadn't occurred to me that undoing the marriage vows would be so important. I was too anxious to move on. And so my Soul rose before me making her presence known, as my body burned with the high fever, and my throat closed, taking away my voice.

*   *   *

OUR SOUL'S LOVE for us is immeasurable, *but its interest is always in the bigger picture.* And the bigger picture is but one: *we must grow* spiritually. If it takes extreme circumstances to get our attention, then that's what the Soul will bring on. If we respond to her "whispers" then there will be no "shouts." But the Soul *will* get our attention at any cost. In my case, all I had was a high fever and a bad sore throat. It was different for Mykaell, my husband-to-be, who started having a series of car accidents as soon as I said yes to the marriage proposal.

Remember we talked about the subconscious mind maintaining consistency at all cost? For most of us the old wiring has it that "life is hard, and things don't really work out the way we want them to." Consequently—when, contrary to the old programming, things suddenly start working out famously, the subconscious immediately looks for (and usually finds) ways to turn it around.

It took three car crashes and one head-on collision for Mykaell to actually notice the very low probability of these accidents being mere coincidences and to do something about it. He, too, had known better, and he, too, just didn't want to pay attention. It was much more fun to think about the wedding than to hear his Soul's voice and look at what needed to be cleared out from his past conditioning. Only after the driver of a huge passing truck took the door off of Mykaell's car just as he was opening it to get out, did he finally decide he had had enough. It was time to put this madness to an end. And so he sat down and unwound the program in his subconscious mind that said "he could not have what he most wanted." After that the accidents simply — stopped.

Back to my story.

With my throat sore and my fever running high, I was confined to bed in one reality, yet involved and active in another at the same time. There, in the deep trance of my meditation, I was walking with my younger self on the night beach talking to her about the life she'd missed, explaining my reasons for divorce, helping her to understand it the best I could. I told her about the years that passed and things that happened in her absence. And then I asked for her forgiveness, for I had let her down. I did not stay married forever, as I had promised to do in my marriage vows. I had ended the marriage and gotten a divorce instead.

She listened quietly, trying to take it all in. It didn't really matter whose fault it was that my marriage came to an end. It is rarely ever that black and white. Both people are always responsible. In fact, if I was going to set myself free from that marriage, undo the old vows, and cancel the old contract and its consequent subconscious programming once and for all, who was right or who was most to blame mattered least of all.

In the end, the only thing that mattered was to release both Alex and myself from the old psychic contract, and to do that without hate or anger, but with dignity and respect for both of us. Only this could free me from the past.

The Ritual of Undoing the Vows

The marriage ceremony is always a sacred ritual, regardless of whether we get married in a temple or church, at the City Hall, or on the beach. The Soul is always present, and the subconscious mind is always taking note. That's why the vows made in this way have such a powerful impact. And that's why the most effective way to undo them is through *another ritual*. A ritual of a different kind, but just as powerful. This time — *undoing the old contract and releasing both people from their vows.*

It doesn't matter whether we create the ritual in our physical reality or in a meditative state. What matters is the *clarity of our intention* and the *intensity of our feeling.* Our emotional body cannot distinguish between what happens in our imagination or in our physical world. That's why we cry our hearts out while watching a movie or reading a book.

Imagination is one of the most powerful gifts we have. Spoken in images and pictures, it is the language of the Soul, a language our subconscious mind understands perfectly.

Suddenly, I could see it all clearly. Not only did I need to create a ritual of ending my first marriage, *a sacred ritual of undoing the marriage vows,* but I had to do it with the same level of power and intensity of emotion I had when, as a young girl, I married the boy of my dreams. This was the best way to communicate my new choice to my Soul and to my subconscious mind and to have it register on every level of my being, sending a powerful message to the Universe and setting both Alex and myself free to live our separate lives. That's what I was saying to myself by getting sick in such a conspicuous way. That's what was being revealed to me through my body.

All of it made perfect sense all of a sudden — my body's mysterious response to the prospect of my new marriage, my old wedding ring waiting for me in the mound of sand, my younger self's eyes filled with reproach and sadness.

I knew what I had to do. "We will create a ritual," I turned to my younger self, excited and clear in my determination and will. "A ritual to symbolize the ending of my first marriage. We will do it now, on this night beach, and we will bring Alex to do it with us."

No sooner did I say this, than she started gathering driftwood scattered everywhere along the beach. Old branches, pieces of bark from the pines in the high dunes, old scraps of paper. I joined her right away. I knew what she was doing, for we were suddenly in complete accord. We gathered the driftwood and started a bonfire, waiting for it to get high and strong as we stood side by side watching the bright flames lick the black air of night and throw shadows on the empty beach behind them.

Holding my old wedding ring in my outstretched hand, I was ready to begin the ritual. Yet something was holding me back, and I felt my younger self squeeze my hand and take a step back from the fire. I could feel her trembling, standing behind me now. "Trust me," I whispered. "We will be all right. It must be done." But something was happening to me as well.

Just a second before, I was sure I knew what I was doing, yet suddenly I, too, was caught in a wave of dread. I was committing a crime, breaking the law for which the punishment was death. That's what the voices in my head were saying, the voices I thought I'd left behind ages ago.

I let them speak for a while, the old, tired voices of my conditioning. *They needed to be heard and expressed so that I could make peace* with them and *let them go.* I had *denied* them all the years since my divorce, and so they got louder and louder. Telling me I did not deserve to be so happy, telling me it wouldn't work out again, and that I would only be hurt. Telling me I couldn't do it right the first time, what made me think I could do better now? The voices of self-judgment, the voices of fear. I let them speak — speak until there was nothing left to say. Until they were finished, spent.

I put my hand to my stomach. I was hurting right there, in the center, as if I had swallowed a heavy stone. I was on the verge of truly ending this entire chapter of my past and stepping into a new life. I should have been excited. I should have been full of anticipation and hope.

What I felt instead was *dread.*

Dread is an emotion *beyond fear.* It is a higher octave of fear, and it shows up in its extreme at times of transcendent shifts *when we die to the old way of being and are born into the new.* At times like that, the change that happens to us is so profound, it feels like stepping into the void. Will I fly or will I crash? At least I knew how to function in my old life. I might have been crippled, but I learned how to walk with my limp.

When the change that happens to us is that powerful, it reaches deep into our Soul, and we absolutely know *nothing will ever be the same.* We know it in the very core of our being. And we feel *dread: the ultimate fear of "non-being"* — a fear so intense and often so incomprehensible, it feels totally paralyzing. We could have just reached the top of success. We should be thrilled, overjoyed, ecstatic...yet we find ourselves terrified. That's dread. And actually it is a good sign. *Dread is there to show us that the past is dying, and we are about to be set free from our prison.*

It doesn't have to last forever, though it may feel like it will never end. It will dissipate and be gone soon. And if we understand it, accept it, and have compassion for ourselves, we can more quickly go through it and come out on the other side.

The way out of fear is through it. I straightened my back digging my feet deeper into the sand, then took a deep breath and pulled back my shoulders. "I am ready," I said and turned to the fire, feeling its heat on my face, breathing it in, welcoming it into every pore of my skin.

I began to speak slowly, focusing on each word, releasing my intention to the night air, to the light of the moon, to the earth beneath my feet. "I choose happiness," I said and felt the power of this choice run through my body like an electric current, lifting me into an exalted, elevated state. "I choose freedom and happiness. It is my right. I deserve it, I choose it, and I *will* create it. I choose to release myself from my wedding vows to Alex. I choose to have the vows be undone. I choose to set both of us free."

A wave of sadness, bittersweet and beautiful, filled my heart, as pictures of my life with Alex began to play before me emerging from my consciousness in no particular order. Happy pictures and sad pictures, moments of love and moments of pain. Memories shifting and changing before my eyes, floating towards the fire to be consumed by it, one by one.

My younger self beside me, I raised my hand holding the wedding ring between my fingers. "I bless you and I let you go," I said and tossed it into the flames. In an instant it was gone, disappearing behind the wall of fire without a trace. My old wedding photograph was next. I released it to the blazing flames watching it curl and then be gone in a flash. Responding to my intention, the fire consumed my offerings, sending a cloud of hazy smoke into the dark night sky. I felt a movement at the back of my heart, between my shoulder blades, as if a tiny door was swung open letting in the cool night breeze. I took a step back and adjusted my clothes. I was ready for the next step.

I called on Alex by speaking his name, imagining him right in front of us on the opposite side of the fire. Immediately, he was there, uncertain why he had been called, but sensing that it was important. I could see it in his eyes. They shone with the intensity of the moment, impatient for the explanation, yet guarded and veiled as always.

In the protection of the night, embraced by the sacredness of the moment, I could speak to him freely and with an open heart. All I could feel was compassion for both of us and gratitude for the lessons learned. And so I thanked him for the love we had shared and for all the good times we had had together. I thanked him for our son, Arthur. My love for him had opened me to the dimensions and depths of heart I could have never conceived of or known. I thanked him for all the *growth* I had gained through our life together and for the richness of our experience.

"I have released my old wedding ring to the fire," I said, "and I have released the photo of our marriage to signify its end. The fire accepted my offerings and consumed them. Our contract is now dissolved, and our vows undone on all levels. I wanted you to know this. Thank you for responding to my call."

He smiled, raising his hand in farewell as his eyes changed, filling with gratitude and relief. His lips moved slightly. "Thank you," I heard. "Be well."

"You, too," I whispered. "You, too."

He turned away and was gone in an instant. Just faded into the night without a word. I turned to face my young self once again. One thing remained to be done. We both knew it.

"Come," I said. "We've been apart too long. Come back to me now." I opened my arms. "Come home." She took a few steps towards me and was now standing so close, the tips of our noses touched. Her breath hot on my face, I could sense her anticipation. "On the count of three," I said. She nodded, smiling. I counted and closed my eyes feeling her melt into my body, merging with me completely.

I was whole again. Standing alone in front of the fire.

*   *   *

I OPENED MY eyes. Back in my bedroom, it felt like I had been gone for a very long time. I looked at the clock. How long was I in the meditation? Three o'clock, it said. Just forty minutes. It couldn't be. I reached for a glass of water, drank some and lay down again. I was very weak, and all I could do was remain in bed. Suddenly, nothing felt better than falling asleep. I unplugged the phone, rolled to my side and closed my eyes.

The front door slammed waking me up again. Five o'clock. I'd been sleeping for two hours. Mykaell entered the bedroom, smiled and put his hand on my forehead. "You are much better," he said, kissing me. "The fever is gone." I sat up. Could it be?! Is it?! But there was no need to take my temperature. The fever was gone, and so was the sore throat. As mysteriously as they had come, both were gone, leaving no trace.

"I am completely well," I said. It was astonishing. Only two hours ago, I could barely sit up.

"That's wonderful," Mykaell said. "Did you take anything?"

I shook my head. "I did something better," I said. "Something no pill could ever do."

Suddenly, I couldn't wait to get up. I wanted to go out, do something exciting, celebrate my magic. We had cut yesterday's dinner short, but there was no reason not to pick up tonight where we had left off.

Our Sacred Ceremony

We got married in Venice in a sacred ceremony that we had written ourselves. The only people present were nine of our closest friends (one of them — the officiating minister) and my son, Arthur. It rained on the day of our wedding, which Italians believe is a good omen, and we had to go to plan B and move the ceremony into a private room instead of having it outside in the magnificent garden by the lagoon.

Purple and white orchids decorated the room, spilling from

tall Murano glass vases on the tables by the windows. Pink and violet peonies arranged in elegant bunches along the walls filled the room with their sweet perfume. Across the lagoon, stood the palazzos of Venice — the most spectacular sight on earth — silent sentinels, witnessing and blessing our union.

We made no vows to each other. Instead, we entered into the sacred covenant of our marriage with the twenty-three *choices and intentions* we had written together. We still review them every year to see if we want to add a new one, or if one of the choices we made has become redundant. But they remain as fresh and alive as on the day we spoke them in Venice on that magical afternoon in May when we closed one door and stepped through another to never ever be the same.

I will share our choices with you, and if any of them appeal to you, and you are about to get married, feel free to make them yours as well, or you may use them as a template to create your own.

1. I choose to be your wife (husband) and for our marriage to be a complexity where I am one with you and at the same time remain myself, never loosing my individuality, always becoming more.

2. I choose to grow so that I can always bring more of my Truer Self to you and to us.

3. I choose to always function in synergy with you, putting us before me and before you.

4. I choose to take responsibility for our marriage and for making it a true partnership.

5. I choose to always see your light and to rejoice in your presence.

6. I choose to support and encourage your passion for life and for doing what sparkles and inspires your imagination.

7. I choose to never take you for granted and to become complacent in our relationship.

8. I choose to not hold you or myself to the standards of perfection.

9. In time of conflict, I choose to seek and find resolution through wisdom, intimacy and character.

10. In time of conflict, I choose to have the character not to follow the path of righteousness and judgment.

11. In time of conflict, I choose to remember my love for you.

12. I choose to become more and more forgiving of myself and of you.

13. I choose to have open and honest communication.

14. I choose to have our marriage be a safe place where I share my joys and sorrows with vulnerability and trust.

15. I choose to be always worthy of your trust.

16. I choose our marriage to be an expression of our ever growing intimacy with each other.

17. I choose for our marriage to be a declaration moment-to-moment of my freedom and an inspiration to seek greater freedom.

18. I choose to support your freedom and never try to possess you.

19. I choose to honor and respect your freedom and to challenge you to seek greater freedom.

20. I choose the thrill of life, the fun of life, the adventure of life to be my motivation in creating our future.

21. I choose in times of rejoicing and in times of difficulty to always carry our love.

22. I choose to co-create our life together from the place of dominion and ever expanding magic.

23. I choose our future to be filled with magic, miracles, happiness and joy.

Synchronicities

I could have ended this chapter here, but I couldn't help noticing a number of synchronicities happening around me as I was writing it. It is as if the Universe has been conspiring to give me new examples to confirm my own thoughts. I call these synchronicities "cosmic winks." Here is one.

Just the other day, I read in a magazine about a celebrity couple getting married on a tropical island. They met less than a year ago, while both married to other people. It was "love at first sight" they both said, knowing "they were meant to be together." They promptly left their spouses to get married to each other. In the photographs of the wedding, they look radiantly happy as they exchange marriage vows they had written themselves. They plan to stay together forever. That's the promise they made to each other in a powerful ritual on the beach.

"I promise to love you forever," read the groom. "I promise forever to protect you with my very life."

I hope their marriage lasts forever, just like they promised, and I hope their love remains as strong and alive as on the day of their wedding. From the bottom of my heart I wish them the best, and hope they stay true to their promises.

But what if they don't?

One of them, only a couple of years ago, had another much publicized wedding to somebody else. And the other had adopted a child with the former spouse just weeks before meeting his new love.

Sometimes it is a sign of mastery to change major life circumstances after thinking about it for only fifteen minutes, and a sign of weakness to do anything less.
— MARIANNE WILLIAMSON

I agree. Reading it sent goose bumps down my spine. Except few of us are such masters. Few have the mastery required to *trust their own knowing* and then to follow it courageously. And only too often new marriages spring up *not* because of this knowing, but simply because of the magic of falling in love again while other hearts are left bleeding in their wake.

And still we promise "forever" — romantics to the end, making and breaking promises, and with them — the hearts. And someone else is left to pick up the pieces.

Oh, the thrill of *falling in love!*

How it differs from the solid strength and the adult power of *standing in love and living in love* and from the *courage* it takes to do it.

*   *   *

WHILE WRITING THIS chapter I met Ann Marie at a party at my friends' house. She led the conversation during dinner, telling everyone of her happiness with her husband.

"I would never have married a divorced man," she said suddenly. "Never." This got my attention, of course.

"Why?" I asked. "Why not?"

"You can only make that commitment once, that's why," she said.

This statement raised a few eyebrows. Suddenly, all conversation at the table stopped, and everyone's attention was on Ann Marie. Unfazed, she sipped her wine slowly. I was fascinated.

"But what if the wife left *him?*" I asked, watching her face intently.

"Or if he is widowed?" added someone else.

"Still," Ann Marie answered with a shrug. "It doesn't matter. I can't explain it. I just would never do it, that's all."

I could see how strong her feelings were on the subject, and I also saw that she was telling the truth. It was clear to me that she was simply following her intuition. She couldn't explain why she felt this way even to herself, yet she was absolutely firm. For the first time, I had come across someone actually expressing the intuitive knowing of what happens when we take the marriage vows. She didn't know why she was feeling what she was feeling, but she was right on target. She did not want to marry a man who already *was* another woman's husband. Not had been, still was even if he was widowed or divorced on paper.

"You can only make that promise once," she said again, as if responding to my thoughts, confirming to me her understanding of the power inherent in a sacred promise — the power neither death nor divorce can override.

And then she said something else, changing the subject, but bringing my attention to yet another thing I was going to write about.

"I never wanted to get married at all," she said. "Not until I met my husband."

"Why not?" I asked again. This was definitely an interesting woman.

"I used to think marriage was a trap, that's why."

"Do you still think that?" I asked.

"No," she said in her direct way. "No. Not at all. Now I think marriage is wonderful."

Most of us have been there. We've felt that same fear only too many times. "If you get married, you can kiss your freedom good bye." And, of course, most of us have risked losing that "freedom" anyway. Remember My Fair Lady, the famous play and movie? "Let a woman in you life..." sings Professor Higgins, lamenting the woes of being married, "...she'll reorganize your home..." and God only knows what else she will do to take from you your way of life. Yet even Professor Higgins, a confirmed old bachelor, throws his hands in the air and takes the plunge.

"Women! Can't live with them. Can't kill them," says a gangster character played by Bill Murray in a movie *Mad Dog and Glory*. And we laugh and turn this line into a quotation because we can all relate to it, regardless of our gender. It touches on a common thought — that once we get married, our precious freedom is gone forever.

But is it really so? Ask anyone who is happily married if they want out. You know what they will say, don't you?

What if the real reason for the longevity of this myth is our intuitive knowing (just like in Ann Marie's case) of what happens to us once we've promised "to be there forever" — promised it on the deepest level, in the presence of our Soul and God? We know there is a chance we may not keep this promise, and we also know, though maybe not consciously, that this promise may indeed imprison us, becoming "a trap" were we to decide to break it. That's what scares us and makes the fear legitimate. We are afraid of being held to a promise that we *may* not be able to keep.

*   *   *

GIVING A LOT of thought to what I wanted my marriage to be like, the meaning of commitment and of promise were very much on my mind as I was writing our marriage ceremony. I am always touched by how amazing our reality can be if we but pay attention. The whispers and the signs are always there, often showing up in a form of synchronicities. And so we went to see the movie *Keeping Faith*, which by "coincidence" had just started playing at a theatre close by.

A young Catholic priest Brian (played by Ed Norton) has fallen in love with a woman and is gripped by internal conflict. If he were to pursue his passion, he would have to stop being a priest and break his vow of celibacy, a vow he had made to God.

How does one handle such turmoil? In his pain, Brian seeks advice from the older priest and hears this: *"You cannot make a real commitment, be it marriage or faith, unless you accept that it is a choice that you keep making again and again, every day."* Thus giving Brian permission to pause, to reflect, and to either reconfirm his previous choice or to make a new one.

We human beings are not perfect. We can't be perfect, we never will be, and we might as well give up on the whole idea. We live and grow and change, sometimes through leaps and bounds, and other times through hard falls. We make mistakes, we clean up our messes, we ask forgiveness and we forgive. There will always be times in our lives when we will question things that, at other times, we believe to be beyond doubt. There will be times when we will find ourselves in crisis, and we will question ourselves and our lives and take a fresh look at our commitments.

That's normal. That's the only way it can be. It is our very nature, and it is the nature of any commitment. *Commitment is not written in stone and cannot be guaranteed.* Commitment is only real if it is allowed to breathe, which is impossible if it is suffocated by promise.

Commitment is more than a promise can ever be because it is inseparable from choice. And both *can only be made freely and can never be forced.*

Nothing is more powerful than choice. And no matter how seductive and safe it may appear to have someone promise us to be there forever, it's time we give up on this false security. We do not need this promise, and it won't guarantee us what we are after anyway.

Let us learn instead how to trust ourselves better, and how to know if we can trust the one we are about to marry.

And let's give the old tradition of getting married by my making vows a well deserved retirement. It truly does belong in the past, when marriage had very little or nothing to do with love and was all about property and ownership and business. We live in a different time, and our world is changing faster than we can imagine. And if we choose to get married, let's have our marriage be born of *freedom,* and let it be the celebration of our *love* and of our commitment to it and to each other, so we can let go of the myth that marriage is a trap all together.

A happy marriage is never a trap. It is actually the opposite. A happy marriage brings with it levels of *freedom and peace* that we can't even imagine while being on the other side. That peace and that freedom lie beyond the bridge of commitment and can only be found by crossing it. *If the marriage works,* if the marriage is a happy one *it is a way to greater freedom, not the opposite,* as most would have us believe.

Just think about it.

Freedom is being free from conditioning and acting out of our own free will.

As long as we keep deliberating, as long as we keep going back and forth, as long as it is "to be or not to be?" — we are not really that free, are we? We are in the grips of indecisiveness. Anyone who has been there knows this well. We are confused, uncertain, even frustrated.

And whose voices are these playing in our head, anyway? Voices of friends and acquaintances who believe that love doesn't work because it hadn't worked for them? Is that who we are having silent dialogues with? Following advice of people ill qualified to give it? Or are we having silent conversations with our ego disguised (as usual) as a friend?

This is not how freedom feels. Freedom is an empowered, inspired state of being. Freedom is responding to your own voice, not to the voice of the consensus. And there is nothing confusing about it.

The confusion dies once we have made a decision (as is the

case with any decision, whatever it happens to be). Now we have in essence closed the door that until that moment we've kept slightly open just in case. We've closed the door to the so-called freedom and stepped into *the real freedom that is inherent to any choice.* Any indecision keeps us in limbo and there is nothing that feels free about being in limbo. And strangely, and to our surprise, once we've made the choice, *all the energy that was being expended towards the indecision has now been freed.* We can exhale again. We can focus on other areas of our life, and we can create a new life together.

That's what happens with commitment and choice. Our fear of losing freedom by getting married dissipates and is gone. And the only freedom we lose is the so-called freedom of "I want to do whatever I want, and if I get married I won't be able to," and there is very little that's free about this attitude. It is an attitude of reaction. A reaction of an adolescent who is rebelling against authority.

We don't react when we are free. In freedom — we act.

We may pause and reflect before acting, but that's a different matter. When we act out of our freedom, we act out of our own power and out of our own authority. Then being responsible for our actions does not scare us at all, but feels exciting and liberating instead.

There is no freedom without responsibility. Freedom without responsibility is anarchy, and we know from the lessons of history what that is like.

As long as we remember *to put our relationship first,* always first, *before each one of us, and before our work and career,* as long as we remember *not to promise forever,* but instead — *choose to love each other every day,* as long as we choose to be happy over our "right" to get our own way, we have a real chance to make our marriage work.

Say: it *will* work, *because I will make it work!*

Add this choice to the other choices you make every day. And then expect it and accept nothing less.

I know it is easier said than done. I know it is not that simple. But nothing that's worth while is simple. Learning to live with another person and to not impose our will upon them is a challenge for everyone. Learning to love them and not to possess them, to be understanding instead of demanding to be understood, giving up our "right" to tell them how they should be. These are a challenge. And so is learning to honor their freedom and being there for them every day.

But what a wonderful, grand challenge it is! A challenge well worth giving up our false freedom for, so we can *Stand in love and Live in love,* and fall in love with each other anew again and again.

When Love Is Not Enough

The minute I heard my first love story I started looking
for you,
not knowing how blind I was.
Lovers don't finally meet somewhere. — They're in each
other all along.

—RUMI

LOVE IS ALL THERE IS, WE SAY. We say it often, sometimes without really understanding what we are saying, yet sensing the truth of it. The river of love runs through everything in our lives, changing everything it touches. It is for us to learn how to navigate it, how to not drown in it, but to negotiate each dangerous rapid and each treacherous turn, as it takes us through life promising only one thing: nothing will ever be the same, and everything will come up for review. How often have we lost to the river, trying to beat her to submission, she who will always be free? How often have we insisted on swimming upstream rather than flowing with her current? How often, having "almost drowned," have we sworn off love, giving up on life's greatest gift and most powerful challenge?

Some of us are better at love than others, but all of us are attending the same school. We are learning how to become winners at love, for if you are a winner at love, you are a winner at life as well.

Everything in our life reflects our relationship with love—

who we are, everything that has ever happened to us, and what we have become as a result of it.

Love is all there is, we say. How is it then that it is not enough to sustain a relationship or a marriage? How come, if love is all there is, it is still not enough?

Let me tell you one last story. A love story with an unhappy ending.

Two lovers got into a fight over a small thing. She wanted his help with washing up after dinner, while he was tired and didn't see why it couldn't wait till tomorrow. Each certain that they were right, they allowed the fight to escalate and to get out of control. One was attacking, and the other one defending himself, and neither one of them heard the other. So caught up were they in their fight that they forgot about their love for each other in the midst of it. They just kept on fighting and hurting each other, blinded by their need to prove their point. And the fight got worse, and the desire to punish took over, blocking all reason and shutting off the love, and things were said that should have never been said, not unless you really mean them ... and just like that — in the heat of the moment, to their utter shock and disbelief — the relationship was over.

Perhaps you already know this story. Perhaps you have been a principle character in one just like it, or maybe it happened to someone you know well, and just like them you could not believe it was over. That one stupid fight was all it took — one fight that went too far was all it took to kill the relationship.

It is a very old story, and most of us have heard it, and yet every time it happens people are shocked, refusing to believe it, certain that there must have been more to the story and that the fight that put an end to the relationship was simply the last straw. They are usually right. There is always more to the story. And though the circumstances are different in each case, some elements are common to all of them: the pride that blinds and blocks all sense of adult responsibility, the ego out of control, and the desire to punish that takes over, fueled by the insatiable *need to be right* one more time.

Thousands of similar fights are happening right now everywhere around the world — in the streets of New York, in homes in Iowa, behind the closed doors of Paris apartments, in San Francisco and in Boulder, Colorado, in the flats of London and in the alleys of Tel Aviv. Everywhere you look, if you were allowed to watch it, people of various ages are desperately fighting each other for their "right" to be right. Consumed by anger, lost in their rage, they are saying terrible things, punishing and hurting each other, destroying their relationships, the one thing that matters most and that has taken them a life time to build.

There is a *need* that most of us have developed. A need that has become insatiable. And it is driving us apart, creating the opposite of what we are after. It is at the root of most if not all of the problems in every arena of human life, and it has no chance of ever being satiated. Not as long as we go about it the way we have been. It is what causes our loneliness and our isolation; it is behind our inability to be intimate and real with each other; it is what makes us feel cut off, separate and always alone. This need, simply put, is *the need to be understood*. We want to prove our point. And we want *them* to get it.

And yet, we are not here on earth to be understood. *We are here to be understanding.*

Shocking as it may appear to some, it is the truth.

We are not entitled to being understood, and we do not have a "right" to demand or insist or even expect it from others. It is neither our God-given right nor our privilege as human beings. We are here to love, to learn how to love and to become good at it. This is our greatest challenge and also our greatest reward. To be loving to others, to be kind and to be understanding. To be compassionate of heart and generous of spirit. Because when we are—the need to be understood simply does not exist. It belongs on another plane of reality all together.

Let me tell you about the movie I just saw, *The Break Up*, which "by coincidence" came out just as I was writing this book. In many ways it is a classic example of what happens to too many couples. Lovers, wanting to be understood by each other, lose their way to each other, destroying their relationship step by step.

Brooke (played by Jennifer Aniston) and Gary (Vince Vaughn) are in love. They are not married, but are living together in a beautiful condo in Chicago. They have just had their two families over for dinner for the first time. The dinner was strained and not much fun, and they are both relieved to have the evening over. The last guest finally leaves, and as soon as the door closes behind them, Gary plops onto the sofa and flips the remote control.

From this moment on, things begin to deteriorate fast. Brooke wants him to help wash the dishes. He wants to relax and do it tomorrow. Yes, we are back to who will wash the dishes again.

"We'll clean up in the morning."

"I don't want to wake up to dirty dishes!"

"Who cares?" says Gary. (Meaning: who cares about the dishes?)

"I care!!!" shouts Brooke.

Sound familiar? Oh, yes, only too familiar and to too many. But read on.

Things get out of hand. Suddenly Brooke remembers all the uncaring and selfish things Gary has done, and how he has been taking for granted everything she has been contributing to their life together. She has been picking up after him, cleaning, cooking, buying groceries, and he has never appreciated any of this.

"You *never*..." cries Brooke, angry, indignant... knowing she is right!!!

"Not true!" Gary fights back, defending himself, wanting to be left alone to relax and to play his video game.

Brooke is furious. She *must* make her point.

And Gary is losing his temper. He has worked hard all day! He has busted his ass working hard all week!!! He wants to come home and relax, God damn it! But, of course, he can't!!! So fine. He'll help wash the dishes! He clicks the TV off and tosses the remote control. Let's wash the dishes!

But that's not good enough, of course, because that's not how Brooke wants it. Understandably, she wants him to *want* to wash the dishes.

And now the fight escalates. Accusations fly. Suddenly Brooke has had enough. She remembers all the other times Gary has not been there to help her, how he chose to be "selfish" and she had to do everything alone. He never supported her! He never did anything she had asked him!! He was never there for her!

"I am done!" she throws her hands in the air and turns to walk out of the room. And right there and then, consumed by all these emotions — Brooke ends the relationship.

But Brooke was right, wasn't she? She was so absolutely sure of it. She was fed up. She'd had enough of all of this — the fighting, the trying to get through, his "uncaring and selfish attitude." All the evidence was right there. He didn't give a damn about her, and she was crazy to be putting up with it for so long. She *knew* she was right and his reclining comfortably on the sofa while she was so upset trying to get him *to see* was proof of that. And so the only logical thing to do was to end it right there and then.

Wasn't it?

The words were said and there was no taking them back. Behind the closed doors now, they are both in shock. All life drained from his face, Gary slowly puts his clothes on and stumbles out of the apartment.

In the bedroom, she hears the front door close and tightens her jaw. She's gone too far and she knows it. But he will be back. He'll come to her and apologize, and she will reluctantly forgive him, and they will make up. He'll make it all go away. They will laugh about how impatient they are with each other and try to do better next time.

Gary goes to his friend for advice, or just to share his pain, but what he gets is what often happens when we solicit advice from people who are not qualified to give it. And to be fair — *there are few who really can give us good advice, when it comes to our relationships,* no matter how good their intentions may be. Here is a tip. If you feel compelled to seek advice, *turn to the person whose relationship works!* Isn't it simply common sense? And if you do not know such a person, which may only too often be the case, then seek your own counsel or look for professional guidance.

Gary's friend, while intending to help him, puts another nail in the coffin of the relationship. If she says it's over, he tells him, she must have a lover on the side. Solidifying the break up, even against Gary's protestations, bringing new suspicion and doubt where there had been none. Gary goes back home but doesn't try to talk to Brooke. Instead, he makes his bed on the fold out sofa in the living room, and by the time Brooke is back from work the next day, the war is on for real.

*   *   *

I WATCHED AND waited, and watched and waited, as did thousands of other viewers in theaters across the country. All of us waiting for the same thing. For somebody to wake up and stop this craziness. Who would it be — Brooke or Gary, that would remember their love and take the first step by starting to talk about what's real? Would he try to get her by herself and tell her how much she matters? Would Brooke stop her rollercoaster of new and inventive punishments and allow herself to actually *feel* the fear of losing the man she loves? Would either one of them put a stop to their adolescent behavior of trying to get back at each other and instead *have the courage to feel* anything at all?

So frightened are we at times to let ourselves feel the pain, that we will go to any extreme possible in order to pretend it is not there.

And that's exactly what we see Brooke and Gary do in *The Break Up*. They distract themselves from their emotions by punishing each other again and again. They get busy getting even, and it works for a while. It takes their mind away from what's happening and from the very real threat of losing each other for good. The anger, the rage, the need to punish and to win this fight takes over, shoving down the pain, blocking the memory of love and temporarily alleviating the fear of its loss. Hurt is replaced by self pity while pride gets in the driver's seat dictating each destructive move.

The Break Up was a popular movie, and the theatres were filled for weeks. I am sure it was clear to everyone there that Brooke and Gary love each other and do not want to break up. And yet they do everything possible to ensure just this, making things worse, broadening the rift between them and making it harder to turn things around. Stuck in their need to be understood, certain that they are right, stoically they refuse to feel their pain, refuse to fall apart and begin the process of healing.

Stop!!! We want to scream: It's enough!!! You've gone too far!

But the condo gets sold. All the bridges get burned. And when we are suddenly given a flicker of hope (to hell with the condo, they will buy a new one) and Brooke makes a shy attempt to patch things up by inviting Gary to come to a concert with her, and it appears that we are watching the beginning of a long awaited thaw, Gary accepts the peace offering, and then drops it, not trusting this sudden invitation in the midst a war and thus sealing the now inevitable end.

Reality sinks in, and suddenly there are no more reasons for Brooke's silly ploys to make Gary jealous, for yet another "I'll show you" attempt at punishing him, or for pretending she does not care. Alone in her bedroom she cries for the first time. And when Gary walks in and finds her, he finds the girl he loves that he hasn't seen in such a long while. He sees the crumpled Kleenex and Brooke's messed up hair, her swollen eyes and face smeared with tears. He drops his hands. Brooke?...crying over him? Could it be?! He can't take his eyes off her. He loves her more in this moment than he can ever remember loving her before. How could he have forgotten? Oh, Brooke...He wants to hold her, make it all go away, tell her how much he loves her...but he doesn't dare. How did it ever get that far? Can it be true that she actually still cares about him? Is it possible that she loves him still? What a fool he has been! What an idiot! Fighting her every step of the way. "I am sorry..." he begins, as his voice drops an octave. He reaches to touch her...but she pulls away.

"Don't!"

Talk! You want to shout at the screen. Talk to each other! Talk about your love, own your impact, feel the remorse, say you are sorry and mean it. Forgive each other. Forgive yourselves. Alas, this does not happen. Brooke is *resigned and has given up*. And though she is more honest and real with Vince than she has ever been since the fight, something has been broken and it is too late.

But is it?

The Difference between Resignation and Surrender

Resignation and *surrender* are two fundamentally different states.

Surrender is a gentle, humble place. There is no more fighting to get your way, no more trying to control anything. Only the pain and the truth of your situation. In surrender, *we accept what is.* We give up our control and by doing it, we *give in to something greater* than we are. And *we can be lifted* into the new light, and with it *into the new possibility.*

When we surrender our *insistence on having our way*, when we *stop demanding* it and *genuinely* let go — this very act creates *the space* for the Power of the Possible to bring new opportunities and outcomes that were not available to us before.

If you want to be full, let yourself be empty,
If you want to be reborn, let yourself die,
If you want to be given everything — give everything up.

Think about these words of Lao Tzu. Read them again. Allow their truth to fill you. Stay with them until a smile touches your face, as you glimpse the wisdom behind them.

Few people allow ourselves to experience true surrender, too scared of giving up the perceived power of staying in control. Even though, in truth, we can never control anyone or anything.

Resignation, on the other hand, is rooted in *feeling sorry for oneself.* We use self-pity as a balm, a numbing device to "protect" ourselves from feeling real feelings. It may be okay sometimes and in very small doses, for example, if it leads to feeling *genuine hurt and pain* and opens the door to remorse, but Brooke is not there yet, though, in the end, the process has begun.

Wiping away her tears, she tells Gary how much she has been hurt. She doesn't yet own her part in the break up, but it doesn't matter. Gary hears her for the first time.

"Why didn't you tell me that before?" he whispers.

"I did," Brooke says through tears.

"But not *like that...*"

No. Not like that.

She had never been honest with him or let herself be vulnerable. But instead spent all her energy trying to get him "to see," trying to get him to change, trying to get him to miss her, trying to "show him"...punishing him, trying to make him jealous by having falsified dates. All that for what? As Brooke herself tells her co-worker, "I don't want him to move out! I want him to change!!!" But what she is really saying is, I don't want to let go of control. I don't want to feel.

Stuck in her control, she wanted Gary to change, and he was

not changing. And instead of feeling the pain of this realization she decided *to manipulate him* into changing.

But it didn't work.

The more she tried to show him who was the boss, the harder he fought back. The more indifferent she acted, the more he believed her.

There is a difference between saying easily and without an agenda, "Honey, can you please help me with the dishes?" and saying the same thing with a built-in anticipation of a negative response — saying it with a charge because you know what he is going to say. And then, when the negative response does come, which proves that you were *right* in your expectation, and you hear something like "I really don't feel like it. I am tired, can we leave it for tomorrow?" getting all worked up and angry and righteous and interpreting this as "he doesn't love me, he doesn't care about me, he is selfish, what am I doing in this relationship?" Oh, our ego can have a field day with this one, given our permission.

I highly recommend *The Break Up* because that's exactly what Brooke did. She went on proving she won't be treated this way all the way till the relationship was really over.

*   *   *

HOUSEHOLD CHORES CAN be the bane of a relationship . . . or its saving grace. A middle-aged married couple I once knew well had been constantly fighting over the household chores. The more the wife complained and nagged her husband, the less he was interested in helping her with anything at all. In fact, he stayed away from the house as much as he could, while she grew more and more resentful, blaming him for her "ruined" life.

One evening, I overheard the conversation the wife was having with an old friend of theirs, a woman happily married to her husband for forty years. "I am so grateful to Solomon for helping me in the kitchen," the woman was saying. "I just want to hug him every time he does it. He works so hard and still he finds time to help me out at home."

"Grateful?!" came the indignant response from the other woman. "What on earth are you grateful for?? It is *his* house, it is *his* kitchen, they are *his* dishes... *the least* he can do is help you clean up! You slave all day long as it is, trying to maintain your home! And *you* are grateful!"

Need I say more? Is it any wonder one woman was getting all the help she needed without even asking for it, while the other one got nothing? Is it any wonder one couple was happy and the other one was not?

Brooke and Gary failed as a relationship, yet *they, as individuals,* did not fail.

Nothing is a failure, if we learn something from it.

They tried to deny their feelings and run away from their pain, but fortunately for them they did not succeed. *Running away from something is like running towards it.* You can't run away. And you can only run for so long.

And when they stopped, each in their own way, with Brooke realizing there was *nothing she could do to change Gary,* and Gary recognizing that he really loves Brooke and that *he has lost her,* it broke their elaborately built defense mechanisms, it broke their hearts, it stripped them of their bravados and fake personas and brought them face to face with the pain of their loss and the reality of their impact.

So often we run from heartache, terrified of feeling the pain, and yet it is in the depths of pain, in the heart of sorrow that we find *remorse* that can help us forgive ourselves and heal.

Remorse, feeling genuinely sorry for what we did, is so absolutely essential for the healing of Soul and yet so frightening to most people. Many would give their right arm just so they don't have to feel it, not realizing what a dangerous choice they are making. It is a fascinating phenomenon, and it is very important to understand it because it holds the key to all emotional healing.

Let us unravel it together.

Feeling Remorse, Forgiving Ourselves

No healing is possible without forgiveness of the self. And to forgive yourself, you must first feel *remorse*. You must first *own what you have done and genuinely regret it.*

Brooke couldn't yet feel remorse at the time Gary found her crying in the bedroom. All she could feel was how badly she had been treated and how "unappreciated" she had been. Self-pity by any other name is still self-pity. Had she been able to *own her part* in the break up there and then and feel sorry for *that,* she would have undoubtedly also seen her own *humanity,* and she would have seen Gary's. And it would have been easier for her to forgive both Gary and herself, allowing the Power of the Possible to fill the space *that forgiveness would have created* with healing, reconciliation and change. Unfortunately, it did not happen and the moment was lost.

Gary, on the other hand, experienced transformation. Moved by Brooke's tears, he was overcome by remorse and in the scenes that followed, a different Gary began to emerge. Losing the woman he loved had made him take a good hard look at himself. He didn't like what he discovered and resolved to change.

*   *   *

FORGIVING YOURSELF IS the most important thing you can do, if you want to be able to live your life free from pain. Even if, on the surface, it appears that you have nothing to forgive yourself for because you believe you were the victim and not the perpetrator. The truth is that one way or another and regardless of what actually happened, we always blame ourselves first. We always think about what we could have done differently, and we never stop replaying different scenarios in our heads. Years may pass, sometimes a life-time, yet peace doesn't come because blaming yourselves, abusing yourselves emotionally, feeling guilty and punishing yourselves has very little if anything to do with remorse. These things are, instead, simply techniques we use in order to avoid feeling remorse and our own forgiveness.

Remorse is different from feeling guilty.

Remorse is not the self effacement or self ridicule and self punishment that people use as its substitute.

Remorse is *genuinely feeling sorry for the things you did, deeply regretting them and regretting the impact you had.*

So often we won't let ourselves feel these things because we are afraid of seeing how "ugly" we are, choosing to beat ourselves up instead. And so self forgiveness remains unattainable, and peace never comes even if the people we've wronged have long ago forgiven us. This in itself can never be enough. We won't let it in because we don't believe we deserve the healing. Only genuine remorse opens the door to self forgiveness and makes it possible. Because if I say I am sorry, and don't really mean it, then when someone tells me "I forgive you," I won't *feel* forgiven. The best I'll feel is that I have succeeded in manipulating that person. And so my pain lives on and the healing can't come.

If you won't let yourself feel remorse for your actions, then no matter how successful you are, and regardless of how many wonderful things you have created in your life, you won't *feel* successful and happy, and you *won't* be able to *accept yourself.* You will always feel as if you are missing something. You will always wear a mask, afraid to be found out, and you will feel that you have somehow managed to successfully fool everyone else. Nothing will ever be enough because no external success will ever fill the empty hole that your refusal to feel remorse has left in your heart.

Inability to feel remorse is what's behind so many psychopathic disorders. Look into the cold eyes of serial killers—the dead, unseeing eyes that show no pain. Something is locked and broken in the psyche, and they will keep on killing, unable to feel sorry for what they've done, incapable of feeling remorse.

But what if what I've done is unforgivable? What if I don't want to forgive myself for it? What if I don't deserve forgiveness?

Yes, some things seem to be unforgivable, and yet *we must forgive if we are ever to be free from that pain.* "What's "unforgivable"?" you might ask. Nothing, in truth. But there are things we as society, and each one of us individually often believe to be beyond forgiveness and beyond self-forgiveness.

Those things are a betrayal of a trusted friend, the abuse of an innocent child, rape, murder, genocide and other crimes against humanity. There is no end to this list. And these are just some of the obvious examples. There are also the things you did that might not seem that horrible to anyone else, but to you are a source of endless shame and self-recrimination.

But how, you ask, how can I forgive myself for this? Maybe *you* can't. That's why the ultimate *forgiveness of yourself can only be received.* Forgiveness is a gift. It comes from beyond our realm. Forgiveness is not "deserved." It is always given, and given without condition. It is we, who put the conditions in place, blocking the forgiveness, refusing to forgive ourselves.

Without feeling remorse, without feeling deeply sorry for what we did, *we will keep blocking it forever.*

Feel your remorse. Feel the pain and the sadness and the deep and endless sorrow. Feel it, don't hide in self-recrimination, and don't deny it by beating yourself up. That's cowardly. That's your escape. And you can't escape from yourself and from what you did. Feel your remorse, cry your tears, drop to the depth of sorrow and keep falling. Have the guts, find the courage. Face what you did. Have the humility to accept that you may not know your Soul's path nor understand its ways. Feel the remorse, and — be surprised. No crime is so dark that it cannot be forgiven. God, Goddess, The

Greater Power, the Divine by any name you call it (even if you doubt or deny its presence) always forgives, always says yes.

Forgiven, you can bring compassion and forgiveness to the world. There is nothing our world needs more. Forgiven, you can bring understanding and healing to others like you, who don't believe they deserve forgiveness. Forgiven, you can bring goodness and truth and beauty and light into the darkest corners of human souls. You do not serve anyone by drowning in darkness and guilt. Feel the remorse, and allow the miracle of healing.

*   *   *

EVERY IMAGINABLE CRIME has been perpetrated upon people by other people throughout the history of humanity. The unforgivable crimes. Crimes that make our blood boil and in most cultures call for an eye for an eye. And yet they too must be forgiven, if we are to have a chance at ending this chain of pain.

Many will have a hard time with this statement. Many will fight it with their very lives. Only too many are doing so this very minute and every minute of their day. And so we have wars that seem to have no end and no beginning, we kill innocent people, we take lives, avenging, destroying, creating genocide and wondering what's happening to the world, asking when will it end, blaming, pointing fingers... refusing to feel remorse, refusing to forgive. Always having "reasons" for why not and insisting that others understand our reasons.

Always *needing to be understood* and *refusing to be understanding*.

Ensuring that nothing changes at all.

The things that are happening "out there" in the world at large are the reflections of the internal conflicts that are going on inside each one of us. The macrocosm reflecting the microcosm back to us.

There is nothing that is "out there" that is separate from what's "in here." But it is much easier to join the anti-war rally and to spend the day screaming in indignation, than to stay at home, quietly turning inward, feeling the pain and the remorse, feeling the anger, feeling the rage, feeling them and releasing them, so you can end the internal war with yourself and find your own peace. Then, if you choose to go to the same rally, you will stand in your dignity, filled with clarity and resolve, demanding the end of violence, but from a very different place. And your voice will be heard without you raising it by a single note. And you will make a difference, bringing the world that much closer to the peace we all seek.

Everything in our world begins and ends with us. And our re-action to what's happening out there shows us exactly where we are with own personal world. Do we feel compassion and sorrow and determination to create a better world, or do we feel righteously indignant and enraged one more time? Are we blaming and calling for revenge or are we filled with pain and sadness, reaching out to help and to serve? What drives us? Resolve and clarity of will, or hate and the need to destroy? The more indignant and enraged we feel at the events in the world, the more healing we need inside our own hearts.

To heal the world, we must first heal ourselves. To bring peace to the world, we must first find our own peace.

It begins with feeling the feelings that are difficult to feel. It begins with feeling the pain and then with feeling remorse. Remorse is the healing balm of magic. Remorse is the tears we shed that wash away our pain and sadness and remove the debris left by self judgment and self hate. Have the courage to feel it, and ask to receive forgiveness.

Just like forgiveness of another, *forgiveness of self can only be received*. Ours is to do our part. To feel the remorse, and to ask for self forgiveness.

Ask and it is always given. Ask and it is always granted. Allow for the miracle of remorse to lift you into the beauty of who you are. Receive the forgiveness, receive the change.

The unfortunate lovers in the movie *The Break Up* went to every length possible to avoid owning their impact and feeling remorse and the relationship was lost. But on a deeper level — they came out winners. Eventually both of them feel remorse for what they have done to each other and to themselves and are transformed by it. And out of the wreckage of their relationship they emerge changed, with more humility and more wisdom.

"There are a thousand things I would have done differently," says Brooke.

And Gary feels seen for the first time. There are a thousand things he would have done differently as well, and though they don't stay together, there is a healing, and with it a new possibility.

Communication: Why It Is Difficult and How to Make It Work

I am often asked to name the one most important thing to remember in order to make a relationship work. And, of course, there isn't just one thing. But if I were to isolate something specific, it would probably be *communication*. Without communication, *honest, direct and with no agendas,* a relationship doesn't have a chance. However, without feeling your feelings so you are not run by them or clogged by them, and can let them go, a clear, responsible communication is not possible.

The Break Up is a perfect example of what I am talking about. Not once since Brooke, in the heat of the fight, announced that "she was done" with the relationship, did the lovers make even the slightest effort to talk to each other. Nor did they let themselves *feel the pain* of their break up and *their fear of losing each other* for good. They woke up *only after* the relationship had been destroyed.

How could they possibly not feel their pain and fear? you wonder.

Very easily. Never underestimate the power of denial and our ability to shut off our feelings. Most people have been practicing it their entire lives. Amazingly, self deception, while impossible to keep up forever, can be maintained for quite a while, especially if one is pumped up by the adrenaline of rage and *the need to be right.*

The movie shows this very well. Focused on getting back at each other, Brooke and Gary managed to deny their feelings just long enough to actually kill their relationship. The only things they allowed themselves to feel were anger, rage, indignation and the desire for revenge with occasional bouts of self-pity mixed in, which isn't even a feeling, but an anesthetic against it.

Did they speak to each other at all during all this mess? Yes, they did, if you can call it that. They snapped, they were sarcastic, they taunted, they threatened but mostly they stone-walled each other. Instead of seeing the person they loved, they saw "an enemy" to be crushed and "triumphed" over. Even towards the end, when Brooke's resolve is broken and Gary finds her crying alone late at night, the real communication doesn't happen. *The possibility* is there, and we watch with bated breath, hoping for a different outcome... but Brooke cuts off the communication, the walls go up, Gary retreats... and it is over.

Talking from the heart can only be possible if the heart is open. So if you've closed your heart to the one you love because you are hurt or filled with anger, do not attempt to talk to him or her until you are open once more or you will end up making the situation worse.

Feel your feelings first, then get yourself, as much as you can, to a neutral place. Otherwise, how can you expect to be heard if you haven't dealt with your anger and hurt and are either whining and complaining or attacking instead of talking? How do you react to someone's whining? You want to get away from that person as quickly as you can, don't you? And what do you do when you feel attacked? You usually fight back, whether you are right or wrong. An attack calls for self defense. Unfortunately, this is still an instinctive human reaction.

Few people know how to talk from their hearts without throwing accusations at the other person and without *needing* to be understood. And if your goal is to make him or her see that you are

right, the *best you'll get is submission and resignation* which will soon
putrefy into *resentment.* You won't get closer and more intimate,
which is the purpose of the communication. You will, instead,
have successfully fortified yet another wall between the two of
you. No wonder relationships are difficult. No wonder some
people give up on them all together, while others just keep getting
married and divorced, married and divorced, married and divorced... hoping that one of these times, perhaps with the "right"
person they will finally get it right.

*   *   *

THE MOVIE *The Break Up* is a good example of how fire can slash
and burn in the absence of water. The fire inside Brooke, when in
the grips of that last fight, burns and escalates, unable to stop until
it is burning out of control, destroying everything in its way.

Only water can stop the fire and put an end to destruction. *Water, the love we feel* in our hearts, *pours over the fire,* surrounds it, *con-
tains it and calms it down.* When it comes to fighting a fight, most
people bring out their fire and turn it on full blast. We attack, we
crash, we destroy. On a bigger scale, we go to war, we drop bombs,
we kill. Consumed by fire, we dismiss the water as less important,
pushing the love away so that it does not interfere, dropping it,
drying it out.

Yet both elements are equally important and equally necessary, and they need to be balanced inside each one of us if we are
to find a way to relate to each other and to create a better world.

Again I turn to love. Again, I speak of feeling our feelings. Our
rivers run deep but never too deep to drown us, though that is our
fear. *Water is feeling your feelings,* knowing them, being responsible
for them and not being at their mercy.

Remember the love you feel, and you will not crash and burn. You
may *want* to destroy in the heat of the moment, filled with righteous
anger and rage but you won't. Your love will not let you. If Brooke
remembered the love, she would have stopped in time. Sadly, that's

not what happened. The urge to destroy was not contained, and before she knew it, she pulled the big guns and played the card that should never be played. Not unless you *really* mean it. And she ended the relationship in the midst of a fight to her own dismay, shock and disbelief. It was not something she planned, thought about or wanted to do at all. And the damage was permanent.

Two Things We Must Never Do

There are two things *we must never do or say,* unless we really mean them. Make them rules. Stick to them. No matter what. Don't break them. Have the character not to succumb to the "unbearable urge" to punish this one most important person in your life while in the midst of a fight and in the grips of being right.

These two things are as follows:

1. Regardless of how bad the fight or the circumstances get, *never threaten to leave.* (No ifs, no buts about it. Period.)

    You don't say it in anger and you don't use it in order to get your own way or as an ultimatum. Ultimatums don't work. This can't be news to anyone.

    Certain behaviors are unacceptable, such as physical abuse, aggravated assault. Certain other behaviors, while unacceptable to one couple, may be completely acceptable to another. This is personal and subjective and must be made clear in the beginning of the relationship. There has to be an understanding about them, an agreement made by both people. When it comes to everything else — you talk, you fight, you ask directly, you observe, you decide what you can live with and what you can't, and you make up your mind. Threatening to leave breaks the trust and shakes the very foundation of the relationship. Don't threaten anything.

2. *Never end the relationship in the spur of the moment. Never end
    it when emotionally charged.*

You end it only if you are ending it for real, having thought about
it and having made up your mind. *Say it only if you really mean it.* Say
it once.

It bears repeating: you never threaten to leave, and you only end
the relationship when you know it is over for you. If both people
agree on these two things, the relationship will feel more secure
and will have a stronger chance of surviving. Then we can talk to
each other from much safer ground and without the fear of our
lover walking out on us for good because of what we have just said.

Three Fears that Come with Relationship

I want to talk about particular *fears* that are *specific to being in a relationship* and that need to be dealt with, so they don't become debilitating.

When we are in love, most, if not all, of the fears we have dissipate and seem not to matter. Yet other fears come forth, the ones
we didn't have before — *fear of loss, fear of humiliation, and fear of rejection.* These very real fears stand in the way of our happiness and
need to be addressed if we are serious about creating a relationship and keeping it.

Love itself may be frightening at times, but, in truth, it is not
love that scares us. We can cope with love. We have done it for
eternity. It is the *intimacy* that inevitably follows love and that can't
be kept at bay, try as we might, and the *fear of humiliation* that
comes with it, that is the scariest thing of all.

I am talking about *emotional intimacy* between people, where all
the walls we've put up to protect ourselves from being seen will be
broken, threatening exposure, threatening vulnerability, threatening loss of control.

When we are in love, intimacy becomes inevitable, and before we know it, we *care* more than we ever intended to or knew we could. And suddenly things we never used to think about become frightening, making us lose our sleep, bringing anxiety, worry, stress. There is *fear of loss:* What if he leaves me? What if she falls ill and dies? Or gets hit by a car? What if something goes wrong in some unimaginable way and I will be alone again? There is *fear of humiliation:* What if I expose myself and show how much she really matters and she just laughs at me instead, or gets embarrassed and does not know what to say? It would be too much. I don't know if I could cope with that. I was alone before. I could go on like that forever... but now that I have tasted happiness...

When we are in love, the fear of losing the love we now have can be overwhelming. It is the fear we didn't have before, and as our love deepens, so does the fear. Born of love, it can become its dark companion. Yes, *the fear of loss* can be debilitating, and in extreme cases may lead to paranoid thinking, anxiety, fits of jealousy. It is unbearable to imagine that we may lose our love, now that we have finally found it.

If you suddenly, and seemingly out of the blue, feel terrified that something may happen to the one you love or find yourself frightened for no reason at all that she might stop loving you, all *it probably means is that you love her more* today than you did yesterday. Your love has grown, deepened, expanded, and *your fear is here to show you that.*

If you find yourself agonizing about *being humiliated,* it means the two of you have become much *more intimate.*

If you just can't get past the terrible *fear of being rejected,* it is simply showing you how *much you care,* and that the one you love *matters* more to you than you even knew.

Caring and loving are not the same, though often they can go hand in hand. You can *care* very deeply about people or a particular person or about certain things, issues and situations in the world... but not *love* them necessarily. Nevertheless, you can be deeply concerned about them and act in a helpful, giving and loving way. Certain professions presuppose caring (even if, sadly, it is not always the case). Doctors, nurses, teachers, nannies, journalists and political correspondents who selflessly put themselves in harm's ways in order to report the truth of what they see represent *caring* in action, but it may or may not be love as well.

When you are in love, however, it goes without saying that you also begin to care about the one you love, and that your intimacy with each other increases. And so you can expect each one of the three fears to alternately show up in your life as your relationship goes through its various phases.

Let's learn how to respond to these fears.

Love brings with it the *fear of loss.*
Intimacy brings *the fear of humiliation.*
Caring gives birth to *the fear of rejection.*

These fears seldom show up all together. Usually one of them stands out, showing us what's going on with us internally. We each have *our own personal ratio* between love, intimacy and caring: a different balance of how much of each, in proportion to the other two, is comfortable. This ratio is part of our psychological make up. It is how we are "put together." It is simply — what is.

Some people are very caring, but will have more difficulty with love. To others loving comes naturally, like flight to an eagle, and it is intimacy that feels most unsafe and makes them nervous. Yet others risk humiliation easily, not worrying about being exposed. Intimacy and love don't scare them that much, and it is caring that comes with difficulty. These people just don't know how to care, and so it is the most frightening.

*   *   *

WE LIKE TO maintain these three things — *love, intimacy and caring* — in the same proportion to each other *as we are used to.* This is our comfort zone. And as long as our life maintains its status quo, keeping this ratio undisturbed, the fears will not show up.

But then we fall in love, and everything is up for grabs. Love leaves nothing undisturbed and the status quo is gone forever. Love cannot and will not be controlled by our ratio of what's comfortable. It will bring chaos, transformation, healing, change. How did I live before meeting you? How could I exist without you? How did I wake up in the morning? How did I go about my day? I have never been so alive, so passionate, so filled with hope...and I have never crashed so badly, I have never known such pain...Flying one moment, drowning in the next one. A rollercoaster that must eventually subside, so that the flames can become embers, tempering the passion with intimacy and with caring.

Relationship is our shortcut to growth. It is the fastest way to all healing because of its guarantee to bring everything that we have kept hidden (even from ourselves) up for review.

And so the fears come. The possible loss of love is now unimaginable. The possibility of humiliation — unbearable, and we are paralyzed by fear of being rejected.

Which one of these fears stands out for you? Which one has become debilitating, creating all kinds of havoc in your life?

Identify it. Know what's going on with you, and then go about remedying your condition. It is a temporary state, a madness of the mind often not based on anything real, but simply caused by our loss of control and by stepping our of our comfort zone.

The fear is simply pointing out one of three things: either you have begun to care more than you ever did, or that you love more intensely, or that the two of you have become much more intimate.

Once you know what it is, *increase the other two, so that your disrupted ratio of comfort can find its balance again.*

Let me clarify this. Our ratio *does not consist of three equal parts* of love, intimacy and caring. These "amounts" (for lack of a better word) are *never equal.* How much of each one is comfortable for us to feel in relation to the other two differs for each of us. But it is not something you can adjust or change.

Understand that *our ratio will always remain what it is* for each of us. It must. It is just a fact. Return it to the balance that's right for you by increasing the two feelings that have not yet increased, and the fear that the imbalance has produced will be gone.

For example, if you've realized that it is *your increased love* that has disrupted the balance because you are suddenly so scared of losing it, *start caring more* as well. How do you do it? By *making a choice* to do so. Teach yourself *to pay attention*. Notice the things you never noticed before. Gently and carefully, start giving more of yourself. See the needs of the one you love and respond. Make them matter to you, and you will become a more caring person. And also, *become more intimate*, risk being vulnerable, share more of yourself and then reap the rich rewards. *See your fear of loss fade away,* and laugh with joy at how silly you've been. Embrace the new and deeper caring, rejoice in the new depth of intimacy with the one you so love.

Or if *the fear of being rejected* is showing you that *you must be caring more* than you cared before — *increase your love and your intimacy*. Become more loving, give more of yourself, rejoice in the presence of the one you love, celebrate their freedom, listen to them with your heart and with your eyes. And *step into deeper intimacy*. Be tender, be gentle, open your heart and risk being seen. Embrace the closeness and the vulnerability and *see the fear of rejection leave* without a trace as your love and your intimacy have been brought into balance with your new level of caring.

Similarly, if you are suddenly *terrified of being humiliated,* all it means is the two of you have gotten *more intimate. Increase your love and your caring* and the fear of humiliation will slip away.

It sounds like too much work (whispers the ego). Ignore its voice. It has never ever told us the truth. Besides it is really not that much work at all. All it takes is paying attention, understanding the reason behind the fear, and instead of fighting it, or running away from it, or letting it do its destructive work—consciously doing something to take care of it and as a result, maturing and growing yourself and your relationship.

*   *   *

IT TAKES COURAGE to love and to be real with the one you love. It takes risking looking like a fool and risking being rejected. For some people the temptation to run away as soon as intimacy shows up becomes too strong, and so they drop the love and they keep on running.

"You will be laughed at," whispers the ego. "It's time to pull the plug." And we listen, we get busy checking for holes in our walls, patching them quickly, putting on our fake personas—anything, just so we don't have to show who we are and what we are feeling. And the relationships get harder and harder because we are trying to do the impossible. *You can't stay together and continue to avoid getting closer,* unless the concept of living parallel lives is what's appealing. It is for many. It answers the fear of being alone and keeps the safety net in place, and you never have to share who you really are and never have to learn who it is that sleeps next to you in bed every night. And with time, sex becomes boring and unfulfilling as well.

Sex alone cannot sustain itself long term. Intimacy is the glue that keeps the relationship alive in all its forms of expression. Without emotional intimacy, the sexual intimacy cannot be enough, and we look for new partners, new husbands and wives, chasing passion, running from our pain, plagued by our fears and our addictions.

Have you noticed the ever growing addiction to pain killers? The pain killers that are killing people instead of their pain? How many pain killers does it take until the pain kills *you?* How many before we can't run away anymore? Is feeling pain so terrifying that we are willing to lose our life for it?

Antidepressants have their place. They make the "unbearable" temporarily more bearable, but they can't bring us real healing.

The sad fact is that most trained therapists and psychiatrists don't really believe that people can have emotional healing, and so their job becomes helping their clients to best get through life with the limp they already have.

They don't believe that *forgiveness is* truly *a possibility,* (and without forgiveness there can be no healing) and just like the people they are trying to help, in spite of all the years spent in therapy and analysis, they have not found their own peace. And so they treat their patients the way they treat themselves. It doesn't come from lack of caring or from indifference. It comes from their own pain that they have been unable to heal. It is the result of the upbringing that insists we must be strong, endure and never complain, never show our weaknesses, never be vulnerable, *love others,* but *not ourselves.* It is the result of the culture where men don't cry and women aren't supposed to get angry, and where we make no distinction between the importance of *feeling our feelings* so that we can let them go and not be run by them, *and ignoring our feelings* because they don't matter, pushing them inside and turning them into time bombs, thus letting them indeed run our lives, often covertly.

In a culture where intellect is glorified and intuition is ignored or dismissed, we reach for pain killers, hopelessly trying to kill the pain, and we drop bombs, responding to war with war. We hurt the ones we love most, sometimes losing them forever, and never forgiving ourselves for what we've done.

We have been doing this for centuries.

*   *   *

ALL THE STORIES I've told in the previous chapters of this book are the stories of people who couldn't run from pain any longer. Often it happened when they were backed against the wall. Often, they had hit bottom. That's what human beings do. We will avoid lancing the boil as long as we can. And if it doesn't kill us (emotionally if not physically), it is because it finally bursts. And we don't drown in it, as we feared. We are released from our pain and healed.

I am certain that many people watching the movie *The Break Up* were reliving their own experiences. Conversations about what had happened there no doubt continued for days, so relevant and close to home was the subject. Who was right, who was more right, who had to be punished, who had had enough, who had a point or who had succeeded in making a point?

Which point was it exactly?

I thought the point was to carry your love and to be responsible for your relationship, not to determine *who was right*. They were both "right" at different times. So what? Trying to determine who is right pretty much guarantees that the relationship will be damaged, and may be destroyed even if the couple manages to stay together for many years or even for a life time. Little by little and step by step the walls between them will grow higher and higher until they will not even remember why they got together in the first place. And the passion will die, and then the love as well.

It takes a lot to kill love. Love survives all kinds of abuse and still keeps on living. It will get bruised, it will get injured, but it will go on until something snaps in its very heart and the wound is fatal. The last straw. That last one that breaks the love's back.

Wouldn't it be great to know in advance which one of the wounds will be the last one? Wouldn't it be great if it came with a warning? Red lights flashing "do not proceed beyond this point"? Except I am not sure that people would stop even then, red lights or not. Too much fire and not enough water. Plus the voice of the ego is too seductive, and pride is too strong. You can't be the one to capitulate first. You *have* to get the other one to see that you are right!!!!! And no one stops until it is too late.

*   *   *

It's sad. And it's tragic. It's adolescent and immature, regardless of our chronological age. And yet it's an every day occurrence.

Two people destroying each other and their relationship in the name of pride, convinced they are right and blinded by it.

"But don't you see," whispers the ego as we give it voice, "don't you understand???"

"All I wanted is for you to appreciate what I did," complains Brooke through tears.

Oh, how seductive it is to sympathize with what she is saying. How many times we have all said the exact same words, looking to be understood, needing it desperately.

What's wrong with that? Nothing on the surface. But in truth — everything.

The Destructive Power of Self-Pity

The entire premise is wrong.

Needing to be understood comes from self pity. It comes from feeling sorry for yourself and therefore feeling that you *have a right to punish* others, those who don't understand how much you are "sacrificing" for them. How do we punish them? By becoming distant and cold, by withdrawing into silences, by shutting them out of our lives, by refusing to be intimate. By not sharing, not telling them what's going on with us, while expecting them to psychically figure it out on their own.

Something happens that makes us angry or upset, and instead of feeling the anger and hurt, and then either honestly talking about it or simply letting go, we become resentful. We sulk, we pout, we snap at people, we become nasty. Never telling what's wrong with us, never telling the truth and *withdrawing our love* from them. We can't be in this state and be loving at the same time. In this state, we can't *feel* the love. We can't really feel anything. Self-pity is a pill we take to block out all real feelings. It leaves us numb. Filled with hostility, we withdraw into this self-designed prison and can't be reached.

It is a lonely place, and everyone has been there. The only difference is that some visit it and leave, while others have made it their home — *a home where they suffer silently and stoically, and from which they punish other people and especially those who are the closest.*

Make it your home for a long enough time and see your life unravel in front of your very eyes. All Brooke wanted was for Gary to "appreciate" how much she was doing for him. All Gary wanted was for Brooke to "understand" how hard he was working.

It is nice to be appreciated for the good things we do. *Wanting* to be appreciated for them, *needing* that appreciation is another matter.

Do we look over our shoulder to see if anyone noticed that we have just helped an elderly person across the street? Or do we simply help her and be on our way? How did you feel when your mother told you over and over again that she had given up everything, sacrificed the career of her dreams in order to raise you? Warm and fuzzy? Filled with love and gratitude? Or do you cringe even now, remembering the time? And what about your father "breaking his back so you can have food on your table"? Why did you hate hearing it instead of being grateful? All they wanted was to be appreciated for what they did.

And they weren't. Not when they expected it and asked for it in this way. They were resented instead. And if they got you to appreciate them, it was only because their guilt-tripping worked. Yes, manipulation does "work." At home and then at school. That's when we first learn to guilt trip and to manipulate. We learn it early on, and we learn it well — so much so that for many it becomes automatic.

Thus the need to be "understood" and "appreciated" became ingrained, while in reality it is but a masked variation of feeling sorry for yourself. And people don't respond to it kindly. The energy of self pity is so unpleasant, they are repulsed by it. They want to get away from it as fast as they can. The world does not like victims and victim behavior. That's why when we *need* to be understood and appreciated, no one wants to understand us. We may get others to do something for us, but they will do it so they can get away from us.

It is a very low resonance, and everyone instinctively knows to stay away from it, so as to not get sucked into its low vibration. Victims suffer continuously and struggle all the time. Some complain, some suffer stoically, but the results are the same. Nothing comes easily, and if it does, it never *feels* that way anyway.

When we cloak ourselves in self-pity, we are making a choice to suffer and to struggle as a way of life. *Suffering and struggling are not feelings,* but rather attitudes, or moods, or conditions. They all have but one job description: to keep us stuck and to lock us in place. And from that place, we punish other people and sometimes ourselves as well.

This is made worse by the fact that in our culture, just like in so many others, stoic suffering is considered noble and good. Just think of the archetypal overworked, underpaid and unappreciated school teacher that "sacrificed" his or her life for us never complaining, yet sighing all the time because "no one cared."

If we learned anything about self-empowerment and creating success, we certainly did not learn it from that teacher. The teacher taught us something else instead — something we would have been better off without.

Pain as an Avenue of Growth

Suffering is different from *feeling pain,* even though in our language they are often used synonymously. If you think about it and let yourself feel the words and their energy, you can't help but notice the difference. *Suffering* is a choice to *carry your pain,* rather than to feel it.

Being with pain, ours or someone else's, breaks open our hearts and strips us of everything that's false. It is an encounter with one's soul, an intimate and sacred rite of passage. When we turn away from it, we are in essence closing the door to one of the most powerful avenues of growth. Until humanity as a whole, and each of us individually, learns how to grow through love only, the

Soul will use and continue to use the avenue of pain in order to reach us.

Few children in our culture are being taught and encouraged to feel their feelings. Is it any wonder, feelings remains so difficult for adults? So afraid are we of how much it would hurt to feel the pain, so well have we learned to avoid it, that many have convinced themselves that they actually have no pain at all.

It is there, right where we hid it, often dormant but awaiting its time. A time bomb ticking away, ready to go off without warning. We stumble upon it in the living of our lives, when a memory or a circumstance or an event suddenly triggers us and wakes it up. These are the times when once again we are given a choice — to have the courage to feel it, or to dismiss it and lose the opportunity for healing yet again.

I believe that intuitively and in the depths of our hearts everyone knows or senses the terribly high price we pay for refusing to feel our pain. And yet we do it anyway, and life becomes a continuous struggle, and hope is lost, replaced by cynicism and by what Thoreau called — *"quiet desperation."*

*   *   *

I REMEMBER A passage from a story I read when I was still a teenager. It moved me and I never forgot it, though, unfortunately, I have no memory of the book itself. I remember the main character visiting a friend whose woman had left him for another man. The door was unlocked, and he entered, finding the apartment to be a disaster and his friend gone. The apartment smelled rancid, filled with the stale smell of tobacco and unwashed clothes. Fighting the urge to open the windows, the man made his way past the overturned chairs and dirty dishes, walking first into the kitchen and then into the bedroom where the scene was even worse. Pizza boxes with old pieces of crust by the bedside table and on the bed, dirty plates with remnants of food on the floor, half finished beer bottles with missing lids, a bottle of red wine on its side with wine spilled onto the carpet. There were cigarette butts everywhere—in the overflowing ashtrays, in the kitchen sink, on the floor by the unmade bed. The sour air made the man nauseous, and he wanted to open the windows, draw back the curtains and let in the light, but he did not dare. He was trespassing, an uninvited guest, an intruder exposed to someone's dark secret. He had no right to be there and should probably leave before being discovered.

He heard the front door open and shut. Then his friend walked in, and it was too late to walk away. The guest was not ready for the devastation he saw—the empty eyes with no expression, the unshaved face covered with grey stubble, as if he'd aged ten years in two weeks. "I should have called first," started the man, but his friend smiled and shrugged, silencing him, waving his hand helplessly towards the mess in the apartment. The dark circles under his eyes betrayed many a sleepless night. The visitor took his friend's hand tentatively and felt it go limp in his strong grip.

They spent an evening talking and drinking. His friend had not slept in weeks. He had stopped taking showers and had lost at least twenty pounds.

"Everything fits me now," he tried to joke, but it was not funny, and he stopped, not knowing what to say next.

He was a mess. A half burned cigarette stuck between his index and middle finger, he was letting the smoke out his nostrils, and dropping the ash all over his clothes. The man looked away. Reaching for his own cigarette, he found a lighter amidst the heap of garbage on the coffee table, lit up and inhaled. He had given up smoking some time ago, but he needed it now, and he didn't care. What intense pleasure—to feel the nicotine in his head again, what forbidden delight in this sea of disaster. He was calming down now, inhaling slowly and deliberately, tapping on the floor with his foot. He had stopped listening to the man's story and just kept nodding from time to time, careful not to give himself away. It was more than he could handle. It was all too real, too naked and raw. He had never been with someone else's pain quite in this

way before, never saw anyone be so exposed, so...uncovered...
and he wanted to hide, to run away and never come back again.
But he did not dare. He just sat there pretending to pay attention.

From the moment he had entered the apartment and throughout the rest of the evening, one thought kept playing in his mind
surprising him with its intensity. He couldn't shake it off, though he
desperately tried. It was both a feeling and a thought, all pervasive,
insistent, pushing on his throbbing temples and robbing him of his
peace. It started soon after he walked through the door and grew
stronger and stronger during the evening, intensifying with each
passing hour, making him feel like a damn failure. From the minute
he had walked into the living room and had been accosted by the
horrendous mess, up to the current moment, a certain feeling was
spreading through his body until he couldn't think about anything
else. It wasn't pity, or compassion, or sympathy he felt for his friend,
it was — *envy*. When was the last time *he* had allowed himself to fall
apart like this? When was it last that he had just let himself go, let go
of appearances, allowed himself to be this vulnerable, feel this much
pain? He remembered well. It was the second year in college after
his girlfriend, Anne, had been killed in a car accident. That was the
last time. The last time he felt anything. That's when he decided.
Thirty years ago. Walking through his life like a zombie. All the success, all the money, all the women that came and went — all of it
that meant nothing, nothing at all. Never again, he decided then.
Never again to feel that much. And never again it was.

And here was his friend, the man he pitied and felt obliged to
go visit falling to pieces like a woman and making no excuses, lost
in his pain...and yet...somehow...so alive?

Again the thought came, pulled on him, and he swallowed the
smoke.

What wouldn't he do to trade places! What wouldn't he give to
be able to feel so deeply?! How richly he envied the poor bastard!
How much smaller he felt sitting there in his clean clothes and
superior attitude! *Son of a bitch,* he thought again, clenching his

fists and closing his eyes. *Damn you, you poor son of a bitch! What wouldn't I give to be in your place?! What wouldn't I pay!*

> *I want to know if you can sit with pain, mine or your own, without moving to hide it, or fade it, or fix it. I want to know if you have touched the center of your own sorrow, if you have been opened by life's betrayals, or have become shriveled and closed from fear of further pain . . .*

So writes Oriah Mountain Dreamer, and people copy her words and send them to friends, and read them to themselves before falling asleep. Finally — a permission to be real, to take off the false persona and just be who you are.

We are all tired of pretending, tired of wearing masks and hiding behind them. Perhaps it is time. Perhaps it is time to take them off. To begin to tread gently and tentatively over the iced lake of pain and at some point to dive into it.

In the heart of pain, no matter how dark it feels — there is always light, there is always healing. Your Soul steps in and brings you absolution. Your Soul, which waits patiently and never abandons you, steps in and lifts you into its light. We spend our lives running from pain, doing everything we can to avoid feeling it, yet only when we can run no longer, when we hit bottom, and the pain breaks us open, when we don't care if we live or die and often prefer to die, we let ourselves be touched by this light that has been there all along.

In Conclusion

All truth undergoes three stages. First it is ridiculed. Second, it is violently opposed. Third, it is accepted as self-evident.

— SCHOPENHAUER

We dance round in a ring and suppose, but the Secret sits in the middle and knows.

— ROBERT FROST

IT IS A WELL KNOWN FACT THAT the best way to hide something important is to hide it in plain sight.

As we've come to the end of this book, let me tell you a secret. This secret has been sitting in plain sight for a very long time, while you were looking the other way, focused on "the problems without solutions"—your personal problems, the problems of people you know, the problems of the world.

Things are not what they seem, dear reader. They seldom are. Even if on the surface it appears that everything is getting worse: more wars, more injustice, more genocide, more disease, more problems with the environment. Even if your heart breaks as you see the tragedies in the lives of people around you, or in your own life.

There is a light at the end of the tunnel. Times are changing. There is new freedom in the air. Freedom from pain, freedom from the past. And you are birthing it within yourself right now as you are reading this book.

Can you feel it? The stirring, the awakening, the magic?

Something different is in the air, and it is real. Not a promise — a Possibility, coming through, faster and faster. As fast as you can accept it. It doesn't matter if you don't understand it yet. It doesn't matter if you can't see *how*. Let go off your need to once again have everything fit into a neat and logical explanation. Let it be different this time. Some things are *a mystery*. Rejoice in it. Open your arms wide and embrace it. Embrace the Power of the Possible. *With humility and patience, look around you with different eyes.*

The signs of change are everywhere. In the way we experience time — it seems to be speeding up, doesn't it? Where does it go? No longer linear, try as we might... but then — it never really was. The old reliable "straight line" of cause and effect leading us from A to Z is no longer that reliable nor that straight... replaced by the understanding of quantum: the observer as *an integral part* of what's being observed *creating the observed reality according to his expectation*, different for each observer. Once ridiculed and dismissed, this truth is becoming self-evident.

There is no such thing as objective reality. There never was, even if most of us have collectively agreed to see and experience similar things in a similar way. In truth, everything is seen and experienced subjectively. *Everything is a choice.*

Adjust your sight, heal your senses, *change* "the observing and measuring devices" with which you view life and see the truth. See the Old dying (though not without a fight). See the New, here-to-unheard-of Future, rushing in, full force. Born out of the Power of the Possible, dreamt into reality by the dreamers, the incurable optimists, the romantics and the visionaries of our age — this future is taking over, one person at a time.

Join the dreamers. Believe that happiness is possible. Throw a grappling hook into the future of your dream and let it pull you towards it.

But dare I choose the Dream while so many people are suffering? How can *I* step into the joy and leave those less fortunate behind?

The Soul's choice for a lifetime is a mystery. Do not in arrogance and misguided zeal, presume *that you know what's best* for another and how another human being "should" live and grow. Be responsible for your own choice and not for someone else's. This does not mean you are indifferent and cold. It is the most *compassionate* thing you can do. You do not serve anyone by holding back your light. Reach out, give of yourself, give what you can — selflessly and in whichever way is right for you . . . and also know this:

One day spent in total joy, doing the things you love best — a day on the beach, for example, walking for miles on the wet sand, picking up shells, kicking the foamy waves with your toes . . . coming home to a good meal, a wonderful book . . . and falling asleep, exhausted and happy by nine o'clock in the evening . . . a day like this, spent without a worry in the world, has done more for the world at large than if you had spent all day writing letters of protest to your senator, focusing on all the wrongs that need to be righted.

I am not taking away from the importance of letters or from the importance of social activism. We already know how powerful and important these can be.

What I am saying is this: one person, spending an entire day filled with gratitude and joy — *becomes a homeopathic healing drop* — changing *the resonance* of the entire planet. I am not being grandiose. It is the truth.

Heal your pain — and there will be less pain in the world. Not *one less person* in pain. But *less pain.* It doesn't matter if it doesn't make sense to you right now. There is a part of you reading this that understands what I am saying perfectly.

The world is splitting. Two roads lie ahead of each and every one of us, but, as Robert Frost said, "we cannot travel both and be one traveler." We can choose joy, or we can choose pain. It is happening already, both in macrocosm and in microcosm. I am writing this in 2007. In another ten or twenty years from now this truth will be self-evident.

I once read on the park bench in Golden Gate Park in San Francisco an epitaph to a woman. This is what her husband wrote about her:

"She cried every day, but not from sadness, but because the world's so beautiful and life's so short." I am sure this woman had had her share of misfortune and pain. And yet she chose to live in gratitude and was moved by beauty.

Always, throughout times, there have been people who saw the Dream and who believed in it. They reached for it, dreamt it, hoped for it, imagined.

It wasn't time yet. The time is now.

Forgive your past. Let it go. Ask for it to be lifted and fill your heart with Hope.

Hope is one of our most powerful tools. This too is the secret that has been hidden right here, in plain sight.

Hope is a combination of the Power of the Future and the Power of Possibility. People who have no sense of the Future and no sense of possibility don't change and don't heal. But as soon as they get a sense of the Future, they start healing. Hope gives them the strength to do it.

Choose the Future of Dream. Hear its promise of joy and respond to it.

It calls for courage. It calls for trust.

With your eyes wide open, Step into The Possible. I will meet you there.

The Next Step

YOU'VE READ THE LAST CHAPTER AND finished the book, but our journey together may have just begun. I wrote this book to give you a taste of what's possible and of what has been standing in the way of your freedom. By now you may have noticed that this book is not a book only, but also a tool. To "zap" you and to awaken you to what you have known for eternity and are now beginning to remember. If, as I have hoped, you are left with more questions than answers, you may like to take further steps to explore the concepts and ideas expressed here in greater depth. I invite you to join me on this amazing journey as we heal and expand together.

I teach classes, teleclasses, workshops, and offer consulting and coaching services to people, groups, and organizations who want personal support.

You may want to get the audio programs that are available at bookstores and on my websites and listen to the material and the stories as you drive or relax at home.

There are always new things going on and new programs that I may be creating.

You can check my schedule and learn what's happening at the moment by going to my Web sites www.powerofthepossible.com and www.aurielamccarthy.com or by writing to me at author@ aurielamccarthy.com. I will do my best to answer your questions. You may also find the information you need by reading the material on the websites, for we will be continuously updating it.

If you'd like to join my mailing list and receive emails with updates and invitations, just sign up. You are very welcome there.